THE RACE WITHOUT
A FINISH LINE

Warren H. Schmidt
Jerome P. Finnigan

THE RACE WITHOUT
A FINISH LINE

AMERICA'S QUEST FOR TOTAL QUALITY

Jossey-Bass Publishers · San Francisco

For sales outside the United States, contact Maxwell Macmillan International Publishing Group, 866 Third Avenue, New York, New York 10022.

Manufactured in the United States of America

The paper used in this book is acid-free and meets the State of California requirements for recycled paper (50 percent recycled waste, including 10 percent postconsumer waste), which are the strictest guidelines for recycled paper currently in use in the United States.

Credits are on page 401.

Library of Congress Cataloging-in-Publication Data

Schmidt, Warren H.
    The race without a finish line : America's quest for total quality / Warren H. Schmidt, Jerome P. Finnigan.
       p. cm. — (The Jossey-Bass management series)
    Includes bibliographical references and index.
    ISBN 1-55542-462-7
    1. Total quality management—United States. I. Finnigan, Jerome P., [date]. II. Title. III. Series.
HD62.15.S36 1992
658.5'62—dc20   92-16530
                                                          CIP

FIRST EDITION
HB Printing   10 9 8 7 6 5 4 3   *Code 9281*

The Jossey-Bass
Management Series

Contents

90118

Preface

Quality is a race without a finish line. A focus on quality has made Xerox a stronger company, but we know we'll never be as good as we can be, because we'll always try to be better. We are on a mission of continuous quality improvement.
— David T. Kearns, 1991

This book is about a revolution. It's a revolution in the way Americans manage and work in organizations. Deming has called it the "Third Industrial Revolution." We're still in the early stages of this revolution, so we're all at different places in our understanding and assessment of its chances for success. Some are in the advance guard, convinced that this new way of managing organizations is clearly the wave of the future. Others are hesitant, watching and waiting to see whether this is just the latest in a long list of passing management fads. Some are critical, pointing out inconsistencies, failures, and weaknesses. And a large number of managers and students of management are just beginning to sense that a new movement is afoot. One thing is certain: this revolution has grown to the point where it cannot be ignored!

Our View of the Quality Revolution

The revolutionaries march under the banner of *quality*. In large
and small companies across the country, as well as in governmental agencies and voluntary organizations, the rallying cry is
"Quality!"—Total Quality. The idea of "customer first" is not
foreign to Americans, but until recently it has not been the
primary driver of management process, style, and behavior. For
some, quality is still just a buzzword, but for others it is a call for
action. For most people, it is still a puzzling array of seemingly
divergent objectives, statistical jargon, and management actions
that sound familiar but feel uncomfortable. Despite this confusion, some organizations have embraced the new management
process, mastered its tools, and begun to reap impressive benefits. At the top of this list are the twelve winners of the Malcolm
Baldrige National Quality Award and the two recipients of the
President's Award for Quality and Productivity Improvement for
federal agencies. They form the core of the case examples for
this book.

Total Quality can best be described as the art of continuous improvement with customer satisfaction as the goal. It is a
new way of doing things—a revolution in the way organizations
plan, develop products, manufacture them, deliver products or
services, and deal with their employees. Meeting the customer's
requirements is the measurement standard, and constant improvement of work processes is the method of besting the competition. It is called Total Quality Management (TQM), or
TQManagement. David Kearns, Xerox's former CEO and now
Deputy Secretary of Education, called it "a race without a finish
line."

For 300 years the primary measure of the economy was
productivity. This is no longer true. Productivity is still a competitive necessity, but speed and flexibility have emerged as new
demands—and these extensions require new standards. As
Anthony Carnevale (1990) noted in *Train America's Workforce*,
today's organizations must provide *variety, customization, convenience*, and *timeliness*. Each of these reflects quality—meeting the
customer's requirements. Quality is not just an output, but a

mind-set and work process that ensures the speed and flexibility consumers now expect. Organizations must run faster to deliver what the customer wants, but they must also run longer, because the competition keeps moving the "finish line" farther away—"a race without a finish line."

Carnevale points out that providing variety, customization, convenience, and timeliness requires organizations to change the way they structure tasks and utilize their human resources. The new global economy demands adaptive organizations that use the flexibility of teams, task forces, partnerships, and informal structures rather than inflexible pyramids of bureaucracy. In today's environment, power moves with knowledge, transcending traditional limits because it accompanies the people who work directly with suppliers, customers, and competitors.

Attempts to label this new economic phenomenon have not quite captured what is happening. Such labels as the "post-industrial economy" and the "service economy" or Alvin Toffler's "information powershift" (1990) don't fully explain what we're experiencing. It is clear, however, that the globalization of the economy, technical advances, and the increasing importance of time are affecting our nation and our lives and that our organizations must find new ways of operating.

America's productivity rate is still the world's standard. From 1981 to 1990, manufacturing productivity grew an average of 3.5 percent a year, compared to 2.3 percent a year in the 1970s ("U.S. Competitiveness Stages a Comeback," 1991). According to the Federal Reserve Board, at the close of the decade, productivity in United States factories remained 30 percent higher than the average productivity of eight other industrialized nations, including West Germany and Japan. However, the rate of productivity improvement among our world competitors is increasing much faster. According to Grayson and O'Dell (1988), if present trends continue, Japan will surpass America's productivity performance in 2003.

Historically, Americans are often first with new ideas, but recently we have had trouble staying in the race to commercialize, improve, and multiply the products of our inventions.

The need for speed and flexibility in the marketplace has put additional strains on management, calling for innovative methods and strategies. As new complexities sweep through the boardrooms and manufacturing floors of America, management is looking for new ways to meet the challenge. The most promising management process is TQM. TQM appears to be the best means of managing productivity, variety, customization, and timeliness because it recognizes that quality depends on understanding and meeting the customer's needs and wants.

It is now clear that the revolution in management is well under way. One key question, of course, is whether America will succeed. Will most managers view TQM as a temporary phenomenon that will fade, or will it be seen as a new way of life for building world-class organizations? We set out to find the answers by studying the experience of organizations in the vanguard of the Quality Revolution. We focused our primary (but not exclusive) attention on winners of the Malcolm Baldrige National Quality Award and the President's Quality and Productivity Award.

Our Backgrounds

We approached this task from two different perspectives—practical and academic. Finnigan was an early participant in the Quality Revolution, playing a front-line role at Xerox when that company, led by CEO David Kearns, turned around from a steadily losing market position to being the world's leading company in its field. Burt Meerow, president of Buyer's Laboratory, Inc., recently said, "Xerox is one of the few American companies that has looked the Japanese tiger in the eye, come close to being gobbled up, and come back to a position of prominence" ("Xerox Breaks into the Japanese Market," 1992).

Schmidt came to the Quality Revolution more recently, and with a more skeptical attitude. As a psychologist and academician, he has taught and consulted in the field of management and organizational behavior for many years. He has seen the management community get excited—and then lose interest—in a whole array of alphabetized management approaches, from

MBO and PERT to OD and TA. As a junior colleague of the early human relations gurus — Douglas McGregor, Abraham Maslow, Carl Rogers, Leland Bradford, and Ronald and Gordon Lippitt — he was part of the early group dynamics movement, which also promised a new approach to the way people should work together. As he witnessed the excitement of TQM enthusiasts, he kept asking, "What's really new here?" and "Is this likely to last?"

The Race Without a Finish Line is the result of these two approaches — Finnigan's experience in a Total Quality organization and Schmidt's research, primarily of Baldrige and President's Award winners. We try to combine perspective, analysis, and practical how-to-do-it principles in this book. We have included examples from both business and government, because the quality movement is surging ahead in both sectors.

Intended Audience

Throughout our writing we have tried to "practice what we preach," viewing our readers as customers and asking, "What are their needs and how can we meet them?" Who are our customers? They are the CEOs, administrators, managers, and students of management who are both intrigued and puzzled by the Quality Revolution. They have heard about TQM, Deming, and Baldrige, but they haven't quite decided what the Quality Revolution might entail for them and their organizations. They want to be more certain about (1) whether this is a new organizational paradigm to be taken seriously or just a passing fad, (2) how to explain the basic concepts to colleagues, and (3) how to launch a Total Quality effort in their own organization.

Purpose of This Book

One purpose of *The Race Without a Finish Line* is to bring into focus some of the learnings from the Baldrige Award–winning companies as they entered the corporate marathon conditioning program called Total Quality Management. A dozen companies were recognized as winners by well-trained, critical examiners for the Baldrige Award. Many others, however, improved just by using the Baldrige criteria as guides for self-examination and improvement.

Throughout this book we focus on questions like these: How did the Baldrige Award winners go about trying to become Total Quality organizations? What risks did they face? What problems had to be overcome? What experiences and stresses did they encounter? What was the payoff (besides an elegant trophy)? And—perhaps most important—what are these companies doing to keep the effort going?

Although many of our examples come from the Baldrige winners, we must keep in mind that for every winning company there are hundreds of other large and small companies that are embracing the TQM philosophy. Many of them are systematically gathering better data about their customers, encouraging everyone in the organization to suggest better ways of doing things (and listening to those suggestions!), and measuring progress in their performance. Some (3M, Ford, and Corning, for example) have decided not to apply for the Baldrige Award but have used its guidelines to assess their own effectiveness as quality organizations.

Our goal in this book is to give you, the reader (our customer!), a clear idea of what TQM is all about, to help you think about how it might fit in your organization (or division or department), and to help you understand the specific steps you might take to experience this new way of organizational life.

Overview of the Contents

Part One provides an overview of Total Quality Management, attempts to put the Quality Revolution into perspective, and suggests diagnostic questions to determine whether TQM is appropriate for the reader's organization. Chapter One examines the roots of the TQM movement and discusses the ten management theories and practices that have contributed to TQM. Chapter Two looks at the basics of TQM and the eight key principles it embraces. Chapter Three examines what public agencies are doing to advance or retard the Quality Revolution and looks at the special problems faced by public agencies in implementing TQM. Chapter Four discusses where TQM will work and where it won't and provides assistance in assessing an organization's probable success in implementing TQM.

In Part Two we offer a strategic implementation plan based on the key success factors we identified as common to all the Baldrige Award winners. Chapter Five looks at the planning required for successful organizational change and delineates the six key elements on which the TQM organization is built. Chapter Six discusses the first essential step toward TQM: solid, consistent leadership that must accept several basic premises about managing. Assuming that the leadership is committed to change, the next step is to put into place the organizational structure to ensure that the transition proceeds smoothly and effectively. In Chapter Seven we discuss three steps that need to be taken as quickly as possible to establish supportive organizational roles and structures.

Chapter Eight discusses data collection tools and problem-solving processes. We argue that since most problems require a team solution, everyone in the TQM organization is a problem solver and should receive training in a systematic problem-solving process. Chapter Nine focuses on the development and implementation of long-term educational programs since training has a very high priority in the TQM organization. Chapter Ten argues for the creation of meaningful recognition and reward systems. Reward and recognition both play an important part in stimulating and sustaining the Total Quality process. In Chapter Eleven, we argue that success in TQM depends on all members of the organization receiving clear, consistent, and credible messages about what is planned and what is going on. We offer nine guidelines for managers striving for an effective communication program.

Part Three looks at the Baldrige and President's Awards and their winners. We examine why and how these large and small organizations competed for these awards, how the competition affected them, what they learned in the process, and how they are maintaining an improvement process since winning their award. Chapter Twelve provides background on both the Baldrige and President's Awards. Chapter Thirteen highlights the twelve companies that have won the Baldrige Award since its inception. In Chapter Fourteen we argue for the importance of TQM in producing quality organizations with a commitment to continuous improvement.

The resources at the end of the book provide a glossary of TQM terms, a directory of TQM organizations and centers, and an annotated bibliography of TQM publications.

We believe that TQM deserves careful consideration. After examining some exceptionally successful companies that have applied this approach to their operation, we are convinced that TQM is *not* just a repackaging of old ideas or the latest "flavor of the month" in management technology. We believe it is a style of organizational operation that has demonstrated its value in our highly competitive Information Age.

Managing in the 1990s is more like steering a sailboat than a motorboat. With a motorboat you identify your goal, start up the engine, point the boat, and go. With a sailboat you identify your goal, but then you use the talents of your crew to make the best use of the winds and currents to move toward your goal. It takes more skill, more sophistication, and more teamwork—but it's also more fun. Many managers would say the same for Total Quality Management.

In our wide-ranging interviews, readings, and site visits, we have been amazed at the amount of creativity and fresh thinking that is going on among American managers today. We undertook this venture at a time when the American economy was shaky and American management and workers were being examined with a skeptical eye. We have learned a great deal from the organizations that have found a way to be successful in an increasingly competitive marketplace and have been exhilarated by the learning and excitement in many organizations. We hope that some of this enthusiasm comes through in this book and that *The Race Without a Finish Line* makes some small contribution to the creativity and learning that will make the Quality Revolution succeed.

Acknowledgments

The research and writing of this book has been an exhilarating experience for us for one principal reason—it gave us the opportunity to meet and talk with people who are exceptionally upbeat, purposeful, and competent. During the months following the Gulf War, when newspapers were full of stories about America's drift into a recession and its second-class status in the world, we were visiting vibrant American organizations where people worked together to achieve impressive goals—and enjoyed themselves. We found that those involved in the quality movement are generous people, willing to give time and share ideas. We are grateful to them for what they are doing to build this nation—and for taking time out to tell us about their experiences and learnings.

We think first of the Baldrige Award winners. They have demonstrated that exceptional quality is an achievable goal and that they're willing to help others—even competitors—learn how to do it. From their number we are particularly indebted to Paul Noakes of Motorola; Lou Carinola of Cadillac; Roy Bauer of IBM Rochester; Terry Hart and Michele DeWitt of Westinghouse; Nancy Chaffin and John West of Federal Express; Joe Cahalan, Sam Malone, and Norm Rickard of Xerox; Newt Hardie of Milliken; and Richard Allen and Ann Louise Shaeffer of Solectron. If there are useful insights in this book about how TQM really works in successful organizations, they are largely due to the candor of these colleagues.

Among the quality specialists in the public sector, we are especially indebted to Nina Sung and Ruth Haines at the Federal Quality Institute, John Watson and Thomas Hopp at the General Accounting Office, Rudy Garrity at the National Security Agency, Curt Reimann and his colleagues at the Baldrige National Quality Award Office, Hal Rosen from Naval Personnel Research and Development, Ron Walker from the Naval Post Graduate School, Thomas Walker of the Air Force, and Jay Gould III of the Defense Systems Management College. Much of our understanding about TQM at the local level came from Tom Mosgaller of Madison, Wisconsin; Jan Partain and Shelby McCook of Little Rock, Arkansas; Barry Crook of Austin, Texas; and Myron Tribus of Exergy, Inc., and the Community Quality Coalition. We appreciate the advice on education of David Langford of Mt. Edgecumbe High School, Sitka, Alaska, and Norm Deets and John Foley of the National Center on Education and the Economy.

Marty Russell was encouraging and helpful throughout this project, sharing her extensive knowledge and assisting us in getting connected with key people in the quality movement. She and Frank Collins supplied their firsthand information about the events leading to the creation of the Baldrige Award, which are reported in Chapter Twelve.

Along the way a number of consultants and experts have unselfishly shared with us their expertise and encouragement. Most notably we appreciate the guidance and assistance of David Nadler, president of the Delta Consulting Group (his work is the basis for most of our thinking on change management and transition strategy). Toru Iura and his associates at the Aero-space Corporation and the University of California, Los Angeles, and Dan Clausing at the Massachusetts Institute of Technology helped us to better understand the technical side of quality. Bill Petak of the University of Southern California helped us to see more clearly the importance of the industry-government-education relationship.

Encouragement is a key requirement for this kind of venture. At the beginning it came from Peter Jordan and Kirby Timmons of CRM Films, where the idea for a book and film on TQM first emerged. Bill Hicks, our editor at Jossey-Bass, showed a marvelous mix of encouragement, good humor, and toughness that kept us on track (and schedule). Without the professional guidance and attention of Mary Garrett, who managed the production of the book, and Helen Hyams, who copyedited the manuscript, this book would still be a dream. We thank them both. Throughout the past year, a steady stream of support came from our wives, Reggie Schmidt and Jo Finnigan, who handled cluttered rooms, our preoccupation, and neglect with grace and love. For their quiet support we are especially grateful.

Los Angeles, California   Warren H. Schmidt
August 1992   Jerome P. Finnigan

The Authors

Warren H. Schmidt is professor emeritus of public administration at the University of Southern California. He received his A.B. degree (1942) in journalism from Wayne State University, his M.Div. degree (1945) from Concordia Theological Seminary in St. Louis, and his Ph.D. degree (1949) in psychology from Washington University. He served on the faculties of the University of Missouri, Union College, and Springfield College before joining the faculty at the University of California, Los Angeles (UCLA) in 1955, where he held a number of administrative and faculty positions, including director of the Unified MBA Program and dean of executive education in the Graduate School of Management. He was granted emeritus status when he left UCLA in 1976 to join the faculty of the School of Public Administration at the University of Southern California.

Schmidt's writings and teaching in leadership, group dynamics, and organization development have been directed toward making organizations more productive and satisfying places to work. He is the author of several books and more than a hundred articles. His article "How to Choose a Leadership Pattern" (coauthored with Robert Tannenbaum for the *Harvard Business Review*) was designated an HBR Classic and has sold more than a million reprints. He has also been the writer or adviser for more than seventy management and educational films. One of his animated films, *Is It Always Right to Be Right?* won an Academy Award in 1971 and was honored as Training Film of the Decade by the Industrial Film Board in 1980.

In addition to his academic work, Schmidt has served as chairman of the Los Angeles County Economy and Efficiency Commission and currently is a member of the Los Angeles City Quality and Productivity Commission. He is a past board member of the NTL Institute and the board of governors of the American Society for Training and Development. He is a certified psychologist in California and a diplomate of the American Board of Professional Psychology. He has conducted executive and management seminars throughout the United States and abroad. Schmidt lives with his wife, Reggie, in Sepulveda, California.

Jerome P. Finnigan is human resources manager, Systems Competency Unit, Corporate Research and Technology for Xerox. He earned his A.B. degree (1959) in English from the University of San Francisco and was an intern in public affairs (1960) with the Coro Foundation. He taught high school English and coached football before entering industry with Pan American Airways at Cape Canaveral, Florida. He joined Xerox in 1966 and has held a variety of human resource positions in Los Angeles and Rochester, New York.

Finnigan's assignments have largely been in human resource development and organization development. He was an early advocate of quality circles in the late 1970s and was acting quality officer for the printing systems division during Xerox's implementation of Total Quality. He is a frequent lecturer at UCLA on Total Quality Management.

Finnigan is affiliated with the American Society for Training and Development and the National Alliance of Business. He is past chairman of the California Business Consortium for Management in Education and was a member of the state committee that wrote California's *Strategic Plan for Educational Options in the Twenty-First Century: Roads to the Future*. He is currently a member of California's Adult Education Steering Committee and the National Center for Research in Vocational Education's committee to draft new designs for the comprehensive high school. He lives with his wife, Jo Ann, in Rancho Palos Verdes, California.

To Reggie and Jo,
to whom quality comes naturally

THE RACE WITHOUT
A FINISH LINE

PART ONE

THE RACE FOR QUALITY: STARTING POINTS AND PARTICIPANTS

In this section we hope to give the reader an overall understanding of the background and basic concepts of Total Quality Management. We try to answer questions like these: What is really new or different about TQM? How does it fit with management theories and practices of the past? How is it working out in the places where it has been tried? What are the basic assumptions and principles on which it is based? Is this something every organization should consider adopting, or does it only apply to certain types of organizations? Perhaps most important of all: How do I decide whether this is a style of management that I should consider for my own organization?

In Chapter One we put this new approach to management into historical perspective by tracing the events that caused American executives to consider this seemingly non-American approach to management. We then uncover the extensive American management scholarship and practice that is pervasive in TQM.

In Chapter Two we identify the eight basic principles embedded in TQM and describe the changes in management behavior required to make this system work.

We add to the perspective in Chapter Three by reporting how TQM principles are being put to use in nonbusiness organizations—federal, state, and local government; school systems;

1

and institutions of higher education. Here we report on federal agencies that have won the coveted President's Award for Quality and Productivity Improvement.

In Chapter Four we pose some diagnostic questions to try to help readers decide for themselves whether TQM is something to consider seriously in their own organizations.

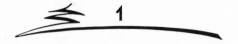

1

The Roots
of the TQM Movement

It is a wretched taste to be gratified with mediocrity when the excellent lies before us.
— Isaac D'Israeli

Thoughtful executives and managers tend to examine new organizational theories and practices with both hope and skepticism. They are eager to find new approaches to puzzling and persistent problems, but they are also wary of innovations that all too often promise much and deliver only frustration and disappointment. They have learned to ask questions:

- Is this really a new concept or just a new label for something we already know about?
- What is the evidence for its usefulness?
- Is this something that will fit my organization?
- How can I explain it to my colleagues (and especially my boss or board)?
- What are the risks and what are the potential payoffs if we try it?

These questions are particularly sensible when exploring the concept of Total Quality Management. Although most of the

elements of TQM are familiar to American managers, in combination they provide a new way of thinking about managing an
enterprise. This is a case where the whole is indeed greater than
the sum of its parts! The differences between traditional management and Total Quality Management are highlighted in
Table 1.1 (Coopers and Lybrand, 1989).

   Achieving a consistently higher quality of products and
services for customers requires a significant difference in the
way managers and workers view their roles, responsibilities, and
relationships. TQM involves a change of organizational culture,
with greater emphasis on collaboration and teamwork. The
focus is on discovering root causes (usually across functional
lines) and improving the process of creating services or products. In Part Two of this book we describe the six key factors we
have found in the Baldrige and President's Award–winning
TQM companies we have studied: (1) a very high level of man-

Table 1.1. Comparison of Traditional and Quality Management.

	Traditional Management	*Total Quality Management*
Quality defined	Products meet specifications Focus on postproduction inspection	Products fit for consumer use Focus on building quality into work processes
Customers	Ambiguous understanding of customer requirements	Systematic approach to seek, understand, and sat- isfy internal and external customer requirements
Errors	A certain margin of error, waste, and rework is tolerable	No tolerance for errors; do it right the first time
Improvement emphasis	Technological break- throughs such as automation	Gradual but continuous im- provement of every function
Problem solving	Unstructured problem solv- ing and decision making by individual managers or specialists	Participative and disci- plined problem solving and decision making based on hard data

Source: Coopers and Lybrand, 1989. Used by permission.

agement leadership and commitment, (2) supportive organizational structures and roles, (3) quality-oriented tools and processes, (4) tailored educational programs, (5) innovative reward strategies, and (6) full and continuing communication. Our studies and experience have convinced us that TQM is not just another technique; it is a new way of organizational life. It is not just an approach to be tested in a limited way; it is a new paradigm of management. W. Edwards Deming called it "The Third Industrial Revolution."

Although we treat the "Total" in Total Quality Management as applying to *both* quality *and* management, the starting point for management thinking begins with a focus on the product or service the organization is delivering to its customers. Following are definitions of quality developed by four of the key leaders of the Quality Revolution (see Resource A for biographical information):

> "...a predictable degree of uniformity and dependability at a low cost, suited to the market."
> W. Edwards Deming (1986)

> "...fitness for use, as judged by the user." Joseph M. Juran (1989)

> "...conformance to requirements." Philip B. Crosby (1979)

> "...full customer satisfaction." Armand V. Feigenbaum (1956)

At the outset we would like you, the reader (*our* "customer"), to know that our study of the theory and practice of TQM by some of America's leading companies and governmental agencies has led us to three conclusions:

1. The current world competitive situation makes the examination of TQM a "must" for any enlightened executive or manager.

2. TQM is deeply rooted in American organizational theory and management practice.
3. The accomplishments of the Baldrige Award winners (and the "also-ran" applicants as well) dramatize the power of the TQM process and American companies' competence to implement it.

The growing momentum of the Quality Revolution creates some urgency for executives and managers to understand clearly the implications of TQM and to assess its appropriateness for their organization. In our studies we have been impressed with the many creative ways in which executives and managers in both the private and public sectors have undertaken to improve the quality and productivity of their products or services. The examples reported in this book are only the "tip of the iceberg" of the innovation that is going on in the United States today.

TQM and the World Competitive Situation

America's position in the international marketplace is eroding at an ever-increasing pace. C. Jackson Grayson and Carla O'Dell emphasize the urgency that many others have expressed in the title of their 1988 book, *American Business: A Two-Minute Warning*. American business does not have long to make the changes necessary to survive into the twenty-first century. The changes that Grayson, O'Dell, and many others recommend have quality as a central focus and a new way of conceptualizing the management process as a key requirement. Assumptions and habits that worked well in the 1950s and 1960s, when a war-torn world clamored for vast quantities of goods, no longer work in a world that demands quality. The "let well enough alone" or "if it ain't broke, don't fix it" approach may have been tolerable once, but it has become a formula for disaster in the 1990s. In a market with no limits, management's flaws are concealed; under competitive conditions those flaws become fatal. The governmental arena experiences similar pressure from citizens to get more for their tax dollars. The result has been a growing number of private and public executives attending seminars and examining the feasibility of applying a TQM approach to their own organizations' struggle for survival and growth.

In the years following World War II, American industry was unchallenged. American products were respected throughout the world, and its management methods were eagerly learned and copied by foreign companies. American management consultants and educators were in great demand. It was a "golden age" of expansion and prosperity for America while the rest of the world played catch-up.

By the 1990s, the industrialized world had not only caught up, but in some cases passed the United States. In 1985 we shifted from being a creditor nation to debtor status for the first time in this century. (The U.S. Department of Commerce made the announcement on September 16, 1985.) It has been a hard pill to swallow! Many explanations have been given for this shift. Some argue that America's workers (especially those who are unionized) are overpaid and not conscientious. Others contend that America's factories are aging. Still others blame investors who are only interested in short-term profits and who are unwilling to build for the future. A rash of company takeovers, leveraged buyouts, and a variety of Wall Street manipulations have kept top executives occupied with developing defensive, short-term strategies. Some critics have even suggested that perhaps our management skills aren't as great as we had thought—that any management looks good in an expanding market where the competition has had to recover from a devastating war. The most shocking statement of all came from Deming (1986), who stated that 85 percent of the quality problems in American industry are the fault of *management*.

Regardless of the cause, some American companies have been shocked to find that their cost of manufacturing products was actually greater than their foreign competitors' selling price. For example, in 1979 Xerox discovered that their Japanese competitors priced their copiers at almost half of what it cost Xerox to manufacture the same product, and the Japanese got their products to the market in half the time (Xerox Corporation, 1990a)! Most embarrassing of all, people in the United

States began to prefer products made abroad, not just because they were cheaper, but because they were *better*. Playing catch-up has not been easy because customers' expectations continue to rise — the finish line keeps moving farther out.

One of the most careful studies of this change was undertaken by a commission convened by the Massachusetts Institute of Technology in 1986. The MIT Commission on Industrial Productivity Report (Dertouzos, Lester, and Solow, 1989) cited five reasons for America's competitive advantage following World War II:

1. The American market was eight times larger than the next largest market.
2. Americans were superior in technology.
3. American workers were more skilled on the average than those in other countries.
4. The United States was far richer than other nations.
5. American managers were the best in the world. (The "best and brightest" were attracted to business in the United States; abroad they were attracted to colonial management or the military.)

These conditions are dramatically different in the 1990s. The competitive "playing field" has leveled off and perhaps has even begun to tilt in favor of America's competitors. Some argue that the major handicaps American managers have to deal with are assumptions and attitudes developed during the years when markets seemed almost limitless and the quality of a product was not critical to its acceptance by eager customers. (One is reminded of Henry Ford's dictum that customers could have any color Ford they wanted as long as they chose black.) Here are some basic beliefs that American managers still find hard to accept:

- It actually costs less to make a high-quality product than a product of poor quality.
- Increasing the reliability of a process reduces its cost.

- The relationship between boss and subordinate is not inherently adversarial.
- Lack of education does not mean lack of intelligence (workers can offer more than hired hands).

In the late 1970s, many American companies began to reexamine their operating assumptions and to experiment with various ways of involving employees in improving their work processes. "Quality circles" were the most common vehicles for eliciting suggestions on how to improve operations. The results were mixed but positive enough to demonstrate that employees *did* care about improving their work life and that they had ideas on how to bring about improvements. Managers also began to look more closely at how their most effective competitors were doing things and started to learn from them. "Benchmarking" entered the managerial vocabulary to describe the process of learning from the best in your field. For many these were eye-opening experiences, and improvements resulted. However, in most cases they were not enough to halt the decline of market share. All too often quality circles and other employee involvement activities occurred only at lower levels in the organization and competitive benchmarking focused only on costs. It became clear to a few that something more fundamental was needed—a clearly defined vision and strategy, initiated and energized from the top, in which all employees could participate. Reinforcement for these conclusions came from at least three sources (Xerox Corporation, 1983):

- Japanese companies had become extraordinarily successful in world markets due largely to the business discipline and management process embedded in Total Quality Control. Using a marketing strategy based on understanding and meeting customer needs with quality products and services, they penetrated one market after another with amazing ease.
- Leading European and Scandinavian (and some American) companies began to focus on quality (rather than the bottom line) as the primary objective with some success.

- Phil Crosby's book *Quality Is Free* (1979) demonstrated that ignoring quality was costing American companies 15 to 20 percent of their sales dollars.

A few American firms began to try a new approach in their organizations known as Total Quality Management. These companies decided to direct the energies and talents of their people to the pursuit of a single, common goal — *quality*. Quality was no longer a vague notion of intrinsic worth, but a measurable standard of functionality and reliability. *Total Quality* was defined as "satisfying the external and internal customers' requirements." Bill Ginnodo (1991), of the Quality & Productivity Management Association, sees this trend as beginning in the mid 1970s, when organization development practitioners began to emphasize "the quality of work life" as an important dimension of worker satisfaction (Figure 1.1). This focus on worker motivation and potential has systematically led to the empowerment principles that are such a key ingredient in TQM.

The Roots of TQM in American Management Theory and Practice

TQM was not made in Japan, but it was tested and enriched in that country. American theorists, executives, and managers have a long and impressive history of addressing the following key problems of organizations:

- How to coordinate and motivate human talent for maximum effectiveness
- How to make decisions
- How to improve production processes
- How to control for the quality of the results

Japanese experience with these concepts sheds light on the potential power of practicing more consistently what American scholars and managers had learned through many years of experimentation and practice. It is not surprising that it was Americans who introduced quality in Japan. In his desire to

Figure 1.1. The Quality Evolution.

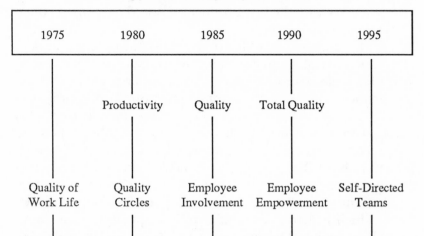

Source: Ginnodo, 1991. Used by permission.

ensure that the Japanese would have reliable radios (to improve occupation communications), General Douglas MacArthur engaged American engineers Homer M. Sarasohn and Charles W. Protzman, employees of his Civil Communications Section, to teach the Japanese how to manage modern manufacturing plants (Dobyns and Crawford-Mason, 1991). As part of their efforts they offered an eight-week seminar for Japanese executives, including a course on statistical quality control (Sarasohn wrote a text in Japanese titled *The Industrial Application of Statistical Quality Control*). The Japanese Union of Scientists and Engineers (JUSE) was intrigued by Sarasohn's book and prevailed upon the Economic and Scientific Section of MacArthur's staff to bring Deming to lecture in Japan. A former statistician with the U.S. Census Bureau, Deming had helped MacArthur's staff with a census of the Japanese population. Deming's first lecture, "Elementary Principles of the Statistical Control of Quality," was given in July 1950 to 230 Japanese engineers and scientists.

Deming taught a new philosophy of quality that had evolved from his work with the War Production Board to improve American war materiel.

The Japanese readily embraced Deming's theories and techniques. By 1979 quality management had propelled Japan into a leadership position in the world marketplace; it continues to enhance that nation's economic position in the world. The result has been that management theories and practices that once seemed idealistic and theoretical have now been shown to be practical and realistic. And most of them bear a "Made in America" label! The name Total Quality Management was first suggested by Nancy Warren, a behavioral scientist in the U.S. Navy, in the summer of 1985, according to Mary Walton (1990).

Much is made of the notion that "quality will not work here" because it is "Oriental." Although there are cultural differences between East and West, the experience of many American firms demonstrates that this is not a key barrier to TQM. A greater difference often exists in the minds of executives in the two countries. Japanese executives seem to take a more orderly, less pressured, approach to achieving long-term goals than appears to be the case in many U.S. companies. As one Japanese associate said, "We try to manage as though we or our children will be in the company 30 years from now" (Tragash, 1989). There is nothing inherently alien to Western cultures in the Japanese methods of implementing Total Quality, nor is there anything "magic" or esoteric about their tools and techniques. The Japanese approach is intensely logical and depends more on the use of facts than on hope and exhortations.

Two major streams of theory and experimentation have influenced management practices in the United States: (1) technology-oriented theories that have focused on how to do things with greater precision and efficiency and (2) socially oriented theories that have focused on how to get people in an organization to work together in ways that are more productive and satisfying. Some managers have been guided more by the first stream, believing that a rigorously controlled approach to running an organization is more realistic than any approach that depends too heavily on the interest, commitment, and judgment of people (especially lower-level workers). Other managers have followed the preachments of the "humanistic" approach—trusting, developing, and involving people as their strategy for producing organizational health. In TQM these two approaches come together in ways that reinforce each other.

At the same time, however, some beliefs and principles that have guided American managers in the past have been found to be dysfunctional in an organization devoted to quality. These beliefs and theories seemed to make sense in an era of nonstop expansion but prevent the development of an organization that can compete in the quality-conscious marketplace of the 1990s.

As you examine TQM to decide whether it is a promising way of life for your organization, it is useful to understand (1) the beliefs, concepts, theories, and practices that contribute to TQM and (2) those that are dysfunctional.

Management Theories and Practices Contributing to TQM

We find that insights from eleven areas of management study and practice are centrally involved in TQM (Figure 1.2).

1. Scientific Management: Finding the Best Way to Do a Job. Frederick Taylor (1911) is usually regarded as the father of "scientific management." An engineer with a deep interest in productivity, he believed that the major responsibility of management was to find the best way to do a job and then train the worker to do it that way. When this occurred, the company's costs would be minimized and the worker could be rewarded more generously. Time-and-motion studies became the order of the day, and assembly lines produced everything from automobiles to dishwashers in record time and at remarkably low cost. American industry became the leader of the industrialized world.

The concept of using measurement to make steady progress took hold and found later expression in such management concepts as zero defects and management by objectives. Usually these efforts were conceived of as periodic, rather than daily, events and as the responsibility of specialists within the organi-

Figure 1.2. Management Theories and Practices Contributing to TQM.

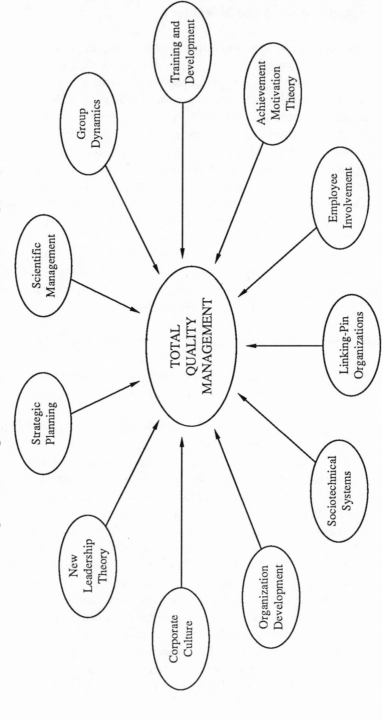

zation, rather than the daily responsibility of the average worker. The engineering specialists experimented until they found the best way to accomplish some task. The supervisor or trainer then instructed the worker, and the worker carried out the instructions until the engineer developed a better way to do things. The process would then be repeated. The worker was "motivated" to do the job according to instructions by a combination of rewards and threats of punishment.

TQM extends this concept of finding the best way to do a job to the entire system. Like the efficiency experts of the scientific management era and the industrial engineers who followed them, TQM places a heavy emphasis on gathering data to measure results with precision. TQM operates on one significantly different assumption, however—that the person performing a given job, rather than some manager or outside expert, is often the best qualified to discover the most efficient way to implement and improve the process. (This TQM assumption elevates the worker to the position of problem solver.)

2. Group Dynamics: Enlisting and Organizing the Power of Group Experience. Some of the earliest controlled experiments involving groups occurred in the late 1920s in the Hawthorne, Illinois, plant of the Western Electric Company (Roethlisberger, 1941). These experiments demonstrated, among other things, that groups of workers had a powerful influence on their individual members' performance on the job. But the major investigation of group behavior began nearly twenty years later with the creation of the National Training Laboratory in Group Development in Washington, D.C. Under the leadership of Kurt Lewin, Kenneth Benne, Leland Bradford, Ronald Lippitt, and others, groups were formed and their processes studied (Cummings and Huse, 1989). The results included new insights into the processes that facilitate or block group decision making, and an array of techniques was developed to make groups more creative and productive.

TQM places a heavy emphasis on group planning and problem solving. Interdepartmental teams develop plans for integrating their efforts. Task forces examine organizational processes to prevent errors and increase productivity. Producer-customer meetings are held to better identify customer needs and concerns. To increase the usefulness of these sessions, TQM organizations train their managers and employees in ways to plan and conduct different kinds of group meetings. In organizations where this is done, meetings are not regarded as unnecessary interruptions of work, but as key arenas in which ideas for continuous improvement are developed and commitments are made.

3. Training and Development: Investing in Human Capital. Some kinds of training investment in human capital have always occurred in industrial organizations. During the Industrial Age, the unskilled were trained by experienced workers or managers to operate machines in factories. Supervisors and managers, however, often had to develop their own knowledge, insights, and skills by informal observation and trial and error. The development of nontechnical competence was usually treated as an individual, rather than a corporate, responsibility. The perceived value of training for an organization's success happened gradually. In 1944 a small group who had the responsibility for training supervisors and employees in their organizations formed the National Association of Training Directors (NATD). Many of the leaders of the group dynamics movement were active in this association, which has become an increasingly forceful voice for the importance of investing in the "humanware" of an organization. Although most industrial firms still pay lip service to training ("People are our most important assets" appears in almost every annual report), budgets for training are often the first casualties in cutbacks. However, the NATD, now the American Society for Training and Development (ASTD), speaks with an ever more powerful and persuasive voice, insisting that the fast-moving information society requires an ongoing learning program to keep personnel at all levels up-to-date and increasingly skillful to remain competitive. Over the years the training directors, consultants, and behavioral scientists in ASTD have developed a wide range of learning theories, strategies, techniques, and materials to increase many kinds of human intellectual, social, and mechanical competence.

TQM places a high priority on training employees at all levels. Top executives have to learn how to better articulate their vision, listen, delegate, and train. Managers and supervisors have to learn how to more effectively involve and empower subordinates. Employees who are at the bottom of the traditional organizational chart have to learn how to listen to customers, keep records, and solve problems. Fortunately, organizations have an impressive array of literature, professional personnel, and sophisticated materials to draw on in their efforts to transform their organizations into learning communities that continually seek to improve their ability to provide quality products and services. What is required, however, is a solid commitment of executive attention and resources. Xerox, for example, spends $257 million on training, which is 4 percent of its annual payroll. At IBM the number is $750 million (5 percent of payroll), and at Motorola it is $42 million (2.6 percent of payroll) (Carnevale, 1990).

4. Achievement Motivation: People Get Satisfaction from Accomplishment. Despite the persistent myth that workers are primarily interested in an easy job with high pay, solid research evidence shows that human beings get satisfaction from accomplishment. In fact, under the right conditions they enjoy reaching ever more challenging goals. Abraham Maslow (1943) wrote brilliantly about the need for "self-actualization." Douglas McGregor (1960), building on Maslow's work, wrote: "The motivation, potential for development, the capacity for assuming responsibility, the readiness to direct behavior toward organizational goals are all present in people. Management does not put them there. It is the responsibility of management to make it possible for people to recognize and develop these human characteristics themselves." He called this view of management "Theory Y," in contrast to a "Theory X" view that regarded people as basically lazy, irresponsible, self-centered, resistant to change, and gullible. David McClelland (1966) identified the "need for achievement" as one of three important psychological needs (and one that could be strengthened by training).

TQM is based on Theory Y assumptions about people. Managers must trust their subordinates before they can comfortably empower them to take responsibility. They can give their full attention to improving the organizational arrangements in which their subordinates do their job only if they have confidence that those subordinates want to do quality work. Since a TQM organization is built on a bottom-up information system, confidence in the whole work force's interest in achieving the organization's goals is implicit. Developing managers' confidence in their subordinates sometimes requires training. Some have highly developed skills in "carrot-and-stick" approaches for motivating subordinates. Others have perfected techniques for manipulating subordinates to do what they want them to do while concealing their real purpose. These skills and techniques are both irrelevant and dysfunctional in a TQM organization. This relearning on the part of some managers is one of the biggest challenges in developing an effective TQM organization.

5. Employee Involvement: Workers Should Have Some Influence in the Organization. The concept of quality circles, or worker-management team meetings, was born in the United States in the late 1940s as a means of improving labor-management communication and solving problems on the factory floor. Although quality circles had some success, they didn't enjoy wide popularity in this country. The primary cause for their failure was managers' resistance to workers' suggestions, violating the principle that "you shouldn't ask for data unless you're prepared to act on it." The concept of quality circles had a rebirth in Japan in 1962 on the recommendation of JUSE (Japanese Union of Scientists and Engineers, 1980), with dramatic results. (Joseph Juran reported on Japan's success with quality circles in a 1967 article titled "The Quality Circle Phenomenon.") Ten years later quality circles migrated back to the United States when Lockheed Missiles and Space Division launched a quality circle program at its facility in Sunnyvale, California. Seven years later the International Association of Quality Circles (IAQC) was formed in San Francisco. By the mid 1980s, hundreds of American companies had initiated quality circles and the IAQC was renamed the Association for Quality and Participation (AQP).

TQM organizations draw on the quality circle experience. The original model of quality circles consisted of eight to ten workers meeting with their supervisor once a week on company time to identify problems and make recommendations for solutions. That concept has been expanded to a broader definition of teamwork with small groups of workers at all levels. These work groups or cross-functional teams meet regularly to examine their ongoing operation and the quality of their products and to identify areas for improvement. In the TQM organization, such teams are considered to be an essential part of the management system, providing on-site diagnostics, data, and process recommendations. Federal Express (1991) calls them Quality Action Teams. More than a thousand of them involve people at all corporate levels around the world.

6. Sociotechnical Systems: Organizations Operate as Open Systems. Over the years, organizations have been defined in many ways — as "the lengthened shadow of one person," as legal entities, as bureaucracies, and as complex social machines. Since the 1960s, however, the growing tendency has been to think of them as *open systems* (Katz and Kahn, 1966). This refers to an input-throughput-output model in which organizations take resources from their environment, modify them and add value, then put the products back into the environment. An organization's success depends upon its ability to add value to whatever it requires from its environment. A key characteristic of any system is the interdependency among all the elements, so that a change in one element results in a change elsewhere. The introduction of a new machine or management system in one department may change the scheduling in several other departments.

TQM has made the *system* dimension of an organization more explicit and precise. It focuses attention on the interface between elements that affect one another. This interface is treated as a "supplier-customer" relationship. Beginning with the part of the external environment that provides the input, the responsibility of the "supplier" is to learn, understand, and then meet the customer's requirements as fully as possible. The customer's responsibility is to make certain that the supplier knows her needs and expectations and is kept up-to-date as they change. The customer also wants to be certain that the supplier has the capacity to meet the requirements and a work plan to deliver them. Within the organization the same process goes on. Each department—and indeed, each person—is viewed as being the customer to whoever provides the necessary materials or ideas and a supplier to whoever uses its output until a final product or service is delivered to a paying customer.

7. Organization Development (OD): Helping Organizations to Learn and Change. Organization development was a natural offspring of the group dynamics movement. If you could train a group to be more productive, why not train the whole organization? Although some executives at large companies still call on outside experts to examine their organizations and recommend changes, others learned that changes were more likely to occur if the people in the organization were involved in the data collection, analysis, and decision making. One widely used definition describes organization development as "an effort (1) planned, (2) organization-wide, and (3) managed from the top, to (4) increase organization effectiveness and health through (5) planned interventions in the organization's 'processes,' using behavioral-science knowledge" (Beckhard, 1969, p. 9). Central to the effort is the systematic gathering of data from people throughout the organization (rather than from just the top managers) and their involvement in shaping the change.

TQM includes almost all of the values, assumptions, and processes of organization development. It presses for the use of solid data for analysis and decision making. However, it adds two important elements: emphasis on quality and insistence on measurable results. Most OD interventions are helpful in initiating changes and building organizational teams, but give less attention to measurable, systematic improvements of the product.

8. Corporate Culture: Beliefs, Myths, and Values That Guide the Behavior of People Throughout the Organization. Stanley Davis (1984) described corporate culture as consisting of two kinds of beliefs: *guiding beliefs* and *daily beliefs*. Guiding beliefs define the organization's vision—its mission and its fundamental values. Daily beliefs describe how things get done in the organization—how decisions are made, communication flows, and control is exercised. Guiding beliefs are formulated at the top; daily beliefs emerge from observation and experience. The literature of corporate culture has added important theories and insights into the behavior of people in organizations.

TQM applies these theories and insights. It recognizes the absolute necessity of developing a vision of a continually improving organization committed to excellence in what it does and how it does it. The guiding belief of quality is central to everything the organization undertakes. This commitment is reinforced through carefully crafted communication and training. For example, Xerox's CEO, David Kearns, would not permit anyone to trivialize his vision by using "LTQ" to refer to his goal of creating "Leadership Through Quality." In the same way, Motorola capitalizes "Customer" to remind everyone that this is the target of all that they do.

9. The New Leadership Theory: Inspiring and Empowering Others to Act. Leadership has always been a key topic in the study of organizational life. It's been a phenomenon that's hard to define but that is easily recognized. Early efforts to find common qualities in leaders proved to be inconclusive (Stodgill, 1974). As the focus shifted to "What do effective leaders *do*?" the roles of leaders and managers were often interchanged. For example, the *Harvard Business Review* classic on leadership, "How to Choose a Leadership Pattern" (Tannenbaum and Schmidt, 1973), actually deals with various ways in which a *manager* makes decisions with or for his group. The distinction between managing and leading has become clearer with the research and writings of James MacGregor Burns (1978), Warren Bennis and Burt Nanus (1985), and Jim Kouzes and Barry Posner (1987). All of these scholars emphasize the importance of the leader's ability to create and communicate a vision that inspires followers. Bennis argues that while managers give their attention to doing things right, leaders focus on doing the right things. Kouzes and Posner underscore the importance of strengthening others by sharing power and information to "get extraordinary things done in organizations."

TQM is based on this concept of leadership. There was a time when the principal concern of top management was to control the behavior of the workers. The planning and decision making was done by managers, the competence was in the machinery, and the workers could rightly be thought of as "hired hands." But when the success of an organization depends on the ability of its employees to gather data, solve problems, take responsibility, and change, the picture also changes. The motivation, commitment, and creativity of "hired brains" cannot be controlled—they must be elicited and nourished. We like Ross Perot's statement that "inventories can be managed, but people must be led." We have found that this is the spirit that permeates TQM organizations.

10. The Linking-Pin Concept of Organizations: Creating Cross-Functional Teams. In his research, Rensis Likert (1967) noticed that high-producing managers appeared to be using the principle of supportive relationships. He proposed that a typical organization would operate more effectively if it was thought of as a cluster of groups linked together, with managers functioning as "linking pins." Each manager in Likert's model would be a leader of one group (of subordinates) and a member of a second group (consisting of the manager's peers and boss). In such a scheme, communication would flow more easily and decisions across departmental lines would be made more realistically than in a straight bureaucratic system. It would also make fuller use of the subordinates' experience in each group.

TQM incorporates this same philosophy. Hierarchical relationships are minimized and team relationships are fostered. Cross-functional teams examine and diagnose problems in order to identify ways to improve systems and processes. At Cadillac (1991), they attribute much of their effectiveness to their Simultaneous Engineering Teams, which bring together people from different disciplines (marketing, design, engineering, and manufacturing) to develop plans for new models.

11. Strategic Planning. Major American organizations have given an increasing amount of attention and effort to strategic planning, which is the process through which key executives and managers determine where they want to go, and how and when they are going to get there. It involves an examination of such fundamental questions as: What business are we in? Who are the important stakeholders in our organization? What are our strengths and weaknesses? What is happening in the marketplace that might affect our business? Where do we want to be five to ten years from now? What is our mission? What are our long- and short-term goals?

In the past, much of this planning was left to the planning staff—the experts who could analyze trends and economic conditions. Increasingly, however, planning has become a team effort as executives have discovered that the planning process is valuable for building the management team and developing commitment to achieving the plan's goals. Executives also discovered that lower-level managers have valuable inputs for shaping the plan.

This same rationale dominates the TQM approach to shaping the organization's future. TQM recognizes that some of the most valuable data for planning comes from those who are closest to the customers, and this data must be taken into consideration in making any customer-oriented plans. In some respects, then, TQM takes the strategic planning process to its logical conclusion—involving almost everyone in the organization in some way. When this is done effectively, the entire culture of the organization supports the efforts to carry out the mission and achieve the organization's goals.

Incompatible Management Theories and Practices

While TQM embraces many familiar management approaches, it clearly rejects others, or uses them only in a greatly modified form. It is worth noting what these are and why they won't work in the Total Quality organization. Seven such approaches are portrayed in Figure 1.3.

1. Bureaucratic Management: Direction from the Boss; Compliance from the Subordinate. In a bureaucratic organization direction and power flow from top to bottom. The people at the bottom of the organizational chart (those who actually produce the goods or services for the customer) carry out the instructions of the boss who supervises their work. Direction from the boss, compliance from the subordinate, and the "chain of command" define how communication is expected to flow in a bureaucratic system. Once a system is established, it is intended to operate without change. Each department and each individual has a clearly defined responsibility and each is held accountable for carrying it out. The consequence for the employees, as Argyris (1957, pp. 20–21) pointed out, is too often "an environment where (1) they are provided minimum control over their work-a-day world, (2) they are expected to be passive, dependent and subordinate, (3) they are expected to have a short-time perspective, (4) they are induced to perfect and value the frequent use of a few superficial abilities, and (5) they are expected to produce under conditions leading to psychological failure."

In the new economy, knowledge is power and those who serve customers and their requirements must be empowered to use their knowledge quickly and effectively. Rigid management systems that limit worker action will not long survive in today's competitive world. It is interesting to note that more than twenty-five years ago Warren Bennis (1956, p. 31) was predicting the death of bureaucracy, contending that this form of organization "is becoming less and less effective; that it is hopelessly out of joint with contemporary realities." The collapse of totalitarian regimes in the political world and the spread of TQM in the organizational world represent a fulfillment of this prophecy.

The TQM organization is conceived of as a string of internal suppliers and customers. Departments and individuals get materials, process them, and pass them on to their internal

Figure 1.3. Management Theories and Practices Not Compatible with TQM.

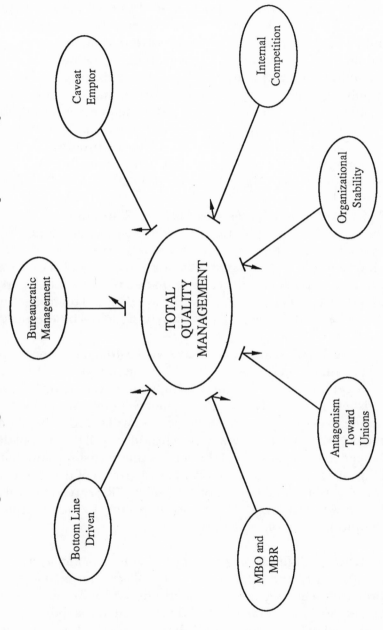

customer, until at the end the final producer delivers the organization's product or service to the external customer. In this model the organizational pyramid is inverted. At the top are the employees who make the final product. Those below them — including managers and supervisors — have the responsibility of supplying them with the time, resources, and conditions that enable them to deliver the product the customer wants. People and departments — as customers — have the responsibility to tell their internal suppliers what they need to produce for their customers. The chain of *command* is transformed into a chain of *communication*, which flows in both directions.

2. Caveat Emptor: Let the Buyer Beware. This phrase, coined in the early years of capitalism, limited the producer's responsibility for delivering the best product. It was the customer's responsibility to examine the merchandise for flaws, the goal of the smart producer was to deliver as cheaply made a product as the market would accept. The producer's effort was directed toward getting the highest margin of profit on everything sold — if necessary, at the buyer's expense.

A TQM organization places the customer's interests first. As Peter Drucker (1977, p. 89) put it: "The purpose of a business is to get and keep customers." The goal is to develop not just satisfied customers, but *loyal* customers — people who will stand in line to get a dependable product and will bring a friend with them. No need here to beware; the producer will provide all that is needed — and more! TQM operates on the assumption that if customers are satisfied, the profits and growth of the supplying organization will take care of themselves. (Research at Cadillac has shown that it costs five times more to get a new customer than to keep an old one.)

3. MBO and MBR: Management by Objectives and Management by Results. MBO and MBR have been well-accepted management practices. They seem sensible and fair. Objectives are set and agreed to by boss and subordinate, and the subordinate is evaluated and rewarded on the basis of how well the objectives are met. In some organizations the subordinates have a very large voice in setting the objectives; in other organizations they are set by the boss.

Although TQM organizations set goals and measure results, their focus of attention is outward, rather than inward (in fact there is an increasing use of policy deployment and quality-function deployment—methods of assuring goal setting from the customer's needs through the organization—which we'll discuss in Chapters Eight and Fourteen). MBO and MBR place the emphasis on individual or departmental control and achievement; TQM places the attention on how well the customer is being served. In an article titled "Total Quality Leadership vs. Management by Results," Brian L. Joiner (1987) notes some of the limitations of management by results:

- Managers negotiate goals that they can exceed (some of which may already have been secretly accomplished and stored).
- Last-minute crises occur regularly to meet some monthly quota.
- Problems are hidden from management if quotas are met.

Joiner (1987) reports a typical problem caused by management by results in the now defunct Soviet Union: "Several years ago there was a surplus of large nails and a shortage of small nails. Why? Managers were held accountable for the *tons* of nails produced. Later the control was changed to the *numbers* of nails produced. This led to a shortage of large nails, since smaller nails gave higher counts." David Packard, of Hewlett-Packard, has said, "Show me how I'm rewarded and I'll show you how I work."

4. Internal Competition: Encouraging Each Department to Be Number 1. Competition can energize and stimulate people to do their best. Most records are broken in a competitive situation. This fact has led some organizations to encourage competition among individuals, departments, and divisions with contests and rewards. The downside to competition, of course, is that winning can become so important to some people that they begin to view their fellow workers as rivals to be beaten, rather than as colleagues to be helped.

TQM emphasizes the achievement of the total organization. It emphasizes teamwork and team accomplishment in every way possible, using problem solving and planning teams across departmental and divisional boundaries. The concept of every department being both a customer and a supplier underscores the interdependence of every individual and unit. The goals are organizational goals, rather than individual unit goals—and reward systems are tailored to communicate and reinforce this concept. The focus is not just on what one person or one department has done, but on how that has contributed to the organization's ability to meet customer requirements.

5. The Strategy of Organizational Stability: "If It Ain't Broke, Don't Fix It." Many organizations strive for stability and predictability. The ideal situation for some executives is to create an organizational system, staff it with good people, and maintain it with as little change as possible. The burden of proof is always on the person who suggests a new way to do something. The emphasis is on control and stability, rather than on innovation. Only when the need becomes clear does the organization respond. TQM organizations, on the other hand, are committed to continual improvement. Change is the norm, not the unwanted exception. Managers focus their attention on the process, continually asking, "Why are we doing it this way?" and "Is there a better way?" The continual use of feedback from customers, changes in the marketplace, and ideas from workers and managers demand that change be the norm, rather than the exception.

6. Antagonism Toward Unions: Workers' Interests Are Basically Different from Managers' Interests. For most executives unions are at best a nuisance and at worst an enemy. Unions are always making demands and trying to keep workers from being too productive. They restrict management's freedom to manage the way they want. Each year American companies spend large amounts of effort and money to maintain open shops and resist organizers' efforts to enlist workers' support for more benefits and controlled productivity. Workers' interests are assumed to be different from management's. In addition to ever-higher wages, workers are assumed to want job security, which is usually translated as stability and limited output. Management, on the other hand, wants to keep costs down and increase productivity. Managers are trained to "motivate" workers, who, it is assumed, would otherwise do as little work as possible (as in McGregor's Theory X).

Conversely, TQM organizations operate on the assumption that workers, like owners and managers, have a stake in creating a market of satisfied and loyal customers. Their job security is directly linked to their organization's success in a competitive marketplace. Their perspective is unique and valuable, and their loyalty and commitment are essential. If they are represented by a union, the union leaders become partners in formulating TQM strategy and implementing quality improvement. For example, the United Auto Workers (UAW)–General Motors Quality Network, established in 1987, recognized that a consistent joint quality-improvement process was needed to improve competitiveness (Cadillac, 1991). Xerox (1990a) and the Amalgamated Clothing and Textile Workers Union (ACTWU) agreed to sponsor joint study teams to examine uncompetitive and excessively costly operations.

7. Bottom-Line Driven: The First Test for Every Decision and Action. Business exists to make a profit. Given this fact, the bottom line comes to represent the organization's ultimate measure of success or failure. In some companies this is the only goal that really counts. Every proposal is accepted or rejected on the basis of how it will affect the bottom line. This is considered by some to be the ultimate sign of realistic planning. In companies where this kind of thinking is dominant, the goal is that of producing at the lowest cost and selling at the highest price that can be attained. Success is measured by the size of the difference.

TQM companies know that they need to be profitable, but they focus their attention on satisfying their customers. They operate on the assumption that if their customers are satisfied, the bottom line will take care of itself. In practice, this point of view has a more long-range feel than does bottom-line thinking. More effort and resources are committed to planning, training, and team building on the assumption that this investment is essential for creating a quality product or service and an organization committed to continual improvement. In some non-TQM organizations these activities are often considered needless expenses, since their contribution to the bottom line is not absolutely clear and measurable. There is a growing body of evidence and experience in American organizations, however, that demonstrates the value of investing in human resources.

Demonstrations of TQM Effectiveness: The Baldrige Award Winners

The creation of the Malcolm Baldrige Quality Award in 1988 has helped to demonstrate what a quality organization looks like. This award — to some extent modeled after the Deming Prize in Japan (see Resource A) — has provided many American companies with guidelines for examining their products and processes in a systematic way, success models from which to learn, and the incentive of world recognition. A study of twenty of the highest-scoring applicants for the 1988 and 1989 Baldrige Awards, conducted by the U.S. General Accounting Office (1991, pp. 2-3), arrived at these conclusions:

- Companies that adopted quality-management practices experienced an overall improvement in corporate performance. In nearly all cases, companies that used total quality management practices achieved better employee relations, higher productivity, greater customer satisfaction, increased market share, and improved profitability.
- Each of the companies studied developed its practices in a unique environment with its own opportunities and problems. However, there were common features in their quality management systems that were major contributing factors to improved performance.
- Many different kinds of companies benefited from putting

specific TQM practices in place. However, none of these companies reaped those benefits immediately. Allowing sufficient time for results to be achieved was as important as initiating a quality-management program.

Let us discuss in more detail each of the major factors that we believe are contributing to the Quality Revolution in the United States.

The creators of the Malcolm Baldrige Award sought to reinforce America's new interest in Total Quality. They hoped that this award might do for American industry what the Deming Prize has done for Japanese industry. The Deming Prize—named after W. Edwards Deming—is given annually by the government of Japan to the companies that have done the most outstanding job of improving the quality of their products and organization. It has become a kind of "Academy Award" for Japanese industry—a most coveted symbol of recognition. It was hoped that the Baldrige Award might provide the same kind of stimulation for American companies.

Congress enacted the Malcolm Baldrige National Quality Improvement Act in August 1987. Twelve thousand companies requested applications in 1988. By 1991 that number grew to 167,000 (U.S. Department of Commerce, 1991). Three companies received the Award in 1988, two in 1989, four in 1990, and three in 1991. These twelve companies passed a rigorous inspection of their ability to achieve "the highest levels of overall competitiveness." All of the winners report that the effort to meet the Baldrige criteria required major changes in the way they planned and managed their companies. This effort required fundamental changes in the behavior of everyone in the organization. These are the companies that can testify to the power of TQM:

- 1988 Westinghouse Electric Corporation, Commercial
        Nuclear Fuel Division
        Globe Metallurgical, Inc.
        Motorola, Inc.

- 1989 Milliken & Company, Inc.
       Xerox Corporation Business Products and Systems
- 1990 Cadillac Motor Car Division, General Motors
           Corporation
       Federal Express Corporation
       IBM Rochester
       Wallace Company, Inc.
- 1991 Marlow Industries
       Solectron Corporation
       Zytec Corporation

These winners of the Baldrige Award are just a small sample of the American companies that have adopted Total Quality Management as their basic style of operation. Many excellent TQM companies have not applied for the Baldrige Award because they view the application as a time-consuming process that does not yield sufficient return on their investment. Some use the Baldrige guidelines for privately assessing their operations. Most have found that the basic tenets and practices of TQM make sense and that they are consistent with American beliefs, values, and culture.

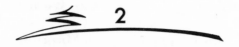

The Basics of TQM

*Quality is never an accident, it is always the result of
intelligent effort.*
                                                —John Ruskin

Total Quality Management (TQM) goes by many names, but it
has a single goal: customer satisfaction. TQM draws its appeal
and power from many theories, but it has a single focus: a
process that produces consistent quality. It is not a program, but
a way of organizational life. The basics of TQM philosophy and
process can be stated simply: to design and manage a process
that satisfies the customer in an increasingly effective way. In
some organizations this way of life is called Total Quality Control. In others it is labeled Company Wide Quality Control or
Total Quality Improvement. In the Department of Defense,
where the TQM designation was coined, this approach to management has been renamed Total Quality Leadership (TQL),
since leadership outranks management in military thinking.

Regardless of the label, however, the process we call TQM
throughout this book has three characteristics that distinguish it
from other management theories or quality control programs:

- It is company-wide in purpose and process. It is the way in which an organization carries on *all* of its activities, not just product delivery functions.
- It emphasizes steady, continuous improvements through the use of facts and the reduction of variability.
- Its focus is on improving performance by turning the organization into an efficient engine for satisfying customer requirements.

TQM has evolved from simple work production systems guided by principles of statistical quality control to a complete management process by the addition of employee involvement strategies, statistical control training for employees, and the adoption of *Kaizen* (a Japanese word meaning "good change"). *Kaizen* is the philosophy that defines management's value-added role in continuously encouraging and implementing small improvements. TQM managers have four key responsibilities:

1. To provide vision and leadership
2. To document and standardize the processes and empower the workers to carry them out efficiently
3. To continuously improve the processes
4. To innovate, introducing substantial changes when necessary and feasible

Management's role can be described as threefold: *prioritize, standardize,* and *improve.* They set operating policies and priorities and standardize work processes, instruct and coach workers on how to use the tools of Total Quality, and strive to improve performance by identifying opportunities to innovate and diagnosing problems in the work process through feedback and dialogue. Although the *Total* in TQM modifies both *Quality* and *Management,* it is management that provides the true impetus for making Total Quality the guiding process of the organization. For that reason we prefer to label the findings of TQM as *TQManagement.*

We have found that successful Total Quality organizations stress the importance of managing the total process. We think

TQManagement captures the essence of this thinking. In this chapter we will (1) review some of the definitions of TQManagement that American organizations have adopted, (2) focus on some of the underlying principles, and (3) describe what TQManagers do that's different.

In many ways TQManagement gets back to the basics of good business and good management: Know your customer and your customer's needs. Find the best way to create and deliver your product or service. Keep trying to do it better, and the bottom line will take care of itself. In the confusion of a "permanent white water society" (Vaill, 1989) it's hard, but more important than ever, to keep focused on the basics.

TQManagement is a disciplined approach to keeping everyone's attention directed to the actions they can take to keep the organization on course toward providing greater customer satisfaction. This begins with knowing what TQManagement means within your organization and with having a definition of the process that is uniquely suited to your situation. Federal Express (1991, p. 14) put it this way: "Quality means doing the right thing the first time. . . everytime. End result: 100 percent customer satisfaction, 100 percent on-time deliveries and 100 percent accurate information available on every shipment to every location in the world."

In the Department of Defense, TQL is defined as "both a philosophy and a set of guiding principles that represent the foundation of a continuously improving organization. TQL is the application of quantitative methods and human resources to improve the material and services supplied to the organization, and the degree to which the needs of the customer are met, now and in the future. TQL integrates fundamental management techniques, existing improvement efforts and technical tools under a disciplined approach focused on continuous improvement" (U.S. Department of Defense, 1989).

At Lockheed Corporation they define TQM this way: "Continuous quality improvement is a philosophy and an attitude for analyzing capabilities and processes and improving them repeatedly to achieve one objective: customer satisfaction" (Lockheed, 1989, p. 4).

Probably the most widely used specifications for the TQM process are the fourteen points developed by Deming (1986, revised 1990) as guidelines for management (Exhibit 2.1).

Eight Principles Underlying TQManagement

In our review of the literature and our interviews with executives in many TQManaged companies, we consistently see eight principles at work. We see them in public and private organizations, in service and manufacturing industries.

1. The Principle of Customer Satisfaction

For many years business leaders have proclaimed that "the customer is always right" until it has become a cliché. TQManagement organizations make this the guiding principle for

Exhibit 2.1. Deming's Fourteen Points for Management.

1. Create and publish to all employees a statement of the aims and purposes of the company or other organization. The management must demonstrate constantly their commitment to this statement.
2. Learn the new philosophy, top management and everybody.
3. Understand the purpose of inspection, for improvement of processes and reduction of cost.
4. End the practice of awarding business on the basis of price tag alone.
5. Improve constantly and forever the system of production and service.
6. Institute training.
7. Teach and institute leadership.
8. Drive out fear. Create trust. Create a climate for innovation.
9. Optimize toward the aims and purposes of the company the efforts of teams, groups, staff areas.
10. Eliminate exhortations for the work force.
11. a. Eliminate numerical quotas for production. Instead, learn and institute methods for improvement.
    b. Eliminate M. B. O. Instead, learn the capabilities of processes, and how to improve them.
12. Remove barriers that rob people of pride of workmanship.
13. Encourage education and self-improvement for everyone.
14. Take action to accomplish the transformation.

Source: Deming, 1986 (revised 1990). Used by permission.

everyone in the organization. Quality is, in fact, defined in terms of how fully the customer's needs are met. Jack Germain, senior vice president and director of quality when Motorola won the Baldrige Award, reported: "I cannot emphasize too strongly how important it was for those of us at Motorola to formulate Total Customer Satisfaction as our fundamental objective. By formally articulating and publicizing this objective, we are able to place Customer needs at the very heart of everything we do. TOTAL CUSTOM ER SATISFACTION drives all our business planning, both long-range and near-term" (Germain, 1989). Xerox (1983) tells its employees: "We will understand our customer's existing and latent requirements. We will provide all our external and internal customers products and services which meet their requirements."

The customer need not be the consumer of the organization's product. One important new concept of TQManagement is that *every* part of the organization has a customer whose needs must be understood and met. The marketing division is the customer of the manufacturing department, which in turn is a customer of the engineering department. In each case it is the responsibility of the producer to determine what the customer department needs in order to do its job in an optimal way. The other side of the coin is that customers need to take responsibility for letting their suppliers know their needs. The net result, of course, is a kind of teamwork that is lacking in many organizations. For example, when engineers design products without getting good input from the sales and service people who understand the customer's needs, they risk creating a good product that has no market. When they design products without being aware of manufacturing's limitations, precious time is lost getting the new product into production. The key concept is *interdependence*. Internal customers are not stand-alone departments, but rather are mutually dependent on each other to (1) design for reliability, (2) design for manufacturability, (3) design for supportability and repairability, and (4) design to meet the imaginative understanding of the external customers' needs. As one executive put it, "No more 'heroes fixing problems,' but 'teams improving processes.'"

Motorola provides all its engineers with training in Design for Manufacturability and Design for Assembly (Wiggenhorn, 1989). In Design for Manufacturability they are taught specific skills that help them introduce new products at significantly lower defect rates. In Design for Assembly they learn how to apply fourteen simple but highly effective design rules, such as minimizing the number of assembly surfaces, eliminating flexible parts and parts that tangle, and using components that are either symmetrical or distinctly asymmetrical.

2. The Principle of Challenge

TQManagement is clearly built on McGregor's Theory Y beliefs about people in the workplace — that they *want* to take initiative and do a good job. David McClelland's (1966) research on human needs also supports this concept. Most of us get satisfaction from having a clear, challenging (but achievable) goal, making progress toward that goal, and celebrating when we reach it. This is particularly true if this challenge is pervasive throughout the organization and if there is a supporting recognition and reward system.

Globe Metallurgical (Leach, n.d.) uses departmental teams composed of hourly employees who meet weekly to discuss improvements that are unique to their department. The employees meet either before or after their regular shift and are paid overtime for the meeting. The meetings are chaired by an hourly employee who is the team leader. The purpose of the meeting is to generate ideas; improve quality, efficiency, or cost; and weed out extraneous ideas. Ideas from each team member are recorded on a form that is reviewed by a Quality-Efficiency-Cost (QEC) Committee. The disposition of each item is written on the form and posted in a designated area in the plant. When the employees return for the next shift following a meeting, they can immediately see the disposition of their ideas. It should be noted that there are no time clocks and all employees participate in profit sharing, which on the average is over $5,000 per year, paid in quarterly installments based upon each quarter's results.

3. The Principle of Process

Having set the goals, the manager's full attention is given to developing ways to reach them. Just as a healthy diet and exercise produce a healthy body, a well-designed process will produce the desired results. There is a management formula that is worth remembering:

$$Qp/d \times (E + C) = R$$

The Quality of the plan or decision
× (multiplied by)
the Effort and Competence to implement it
= (determines) the Results

We know of many excellent plans that produced meager results because there was little effort or competence to carry them out. On the other hand, even mediocre plans that are implemented with commitment and competence sometimes produce impressive results.

IBM Rochester (1991) recently strengthened its strategic initiatives by formulating improvement plans based on six critical success factors. Each senior manager "owns" one of the six factors and assumes responsibility for plans and implementation related to it. Progress toward achieving improvement is closely monitored. Support processes are part of this network. The quality process is a continuous loop that begins, ends, and begins again with each customer. (This is described more fully in Chapter Thirteen.)

In the TQManagement organization, managers keep their eye on the *process* — the ordered sequence designed to produce a given result. If there is an error, its analysis becomes a learning event with the goal of spotting the flaw in the process that caused it. Improving the dependability of the process is the major focus of attention.

4. The Principle of Continuous Improvement

This is where we have learned most from the Japanese, sometimes at a high cost. Americans usually feel more comfortable with short, intensive bursts of activity. We like to search for inventions that are breakthroughs, that represent a whole new approach to a problem. We enjoy investing ourselves in projects that have a clear beginning and end. Then we like to pause and enjoy our success before tackling the next challenge. "Desert Storm" represented a "perfect" American-style war: a clear objective—to free an invaded country—a detailed plan for using massive power, and a decisive battle that lasted only 100 hours. In contrast, the Japanese have demonstrated the power of *Kaizen*—the process of continual improvement—the day-by-day, week-by-week discovery of small steps that make the process increasingly more efficient, more economical, and more dependable. The fable of the tortoise and the hare comes to mind, often with the same results at the end of the race! Products invented in the United States, from microchips and TV sets to automobiles and motorcycles, are examples of American inventions that are now produced more elegantly and economically by Japanese committed to the process of *Kaizen*. American companies have demonstrated, however, that this commitment to continual improvement can also become a characteristic of U.S. enterprise.

Every Baldrige Award winner we interviewed commented on their systematic efforts to improve the quality of their service or product. At Federal Express (1991) they broadcast a daily Service Quality Indicator score over their TV network to monitors in every Federal Express center. Key managers meet every day and look at those numbers to understand what problems have arisen. Quality Action Teams study and develop plans for eliminating errors. According to CEO Fred Smith, the march toward improvement will not stop until 100 percent perfection is achieved.

5. The Principle of Collaboration

In our more philosophical moments, most of us would agree that "no man is an island" and no part of an organization is self-sufficient and independent. But in practice it is easy to strive for independence, which becomes associated with freedom and the

power to control our environment. We don't like to be told how
to do our job by people who don't really understand our specialty. TQManagement says that the easy days of comfortable
isolation are over for organizations that want to survive. Interdependence is the new cornerstone of the customer-driven organization. Each part of the organization is privy to data that the
others need to do their job in the most effective and efficient
manner. Sales knows about emerging customer needs that designers should be aware of. Engineers know about new technology that makes possible changes in manufacturing processes. Managers in the manufacturing division can sometimes
suggest small changes in designs that will increase the efficiency
of production. One of Deming's (1986) original fourteen points
was: "Break down barriers between departments." Rummler and
Brache (1990) describe it as managing the white spaces in the
organization horizontally, not just vertically.

The M.I.T. Commission on Industrial Productivity, in its
report *Made in America* (Dertouzos, Lester, and Solow, 1989),
states that American product development and production are
hampered by technological weaknesses in development and
production, and by failures of cooperation. Technological weaknesses stem from American engineers' preference for research
and original design work and an undervaluing of such "essential
downstream engineering functions as verification and testing of
design, manufacturing, and product and process improvements" (p. 79).

6. The Principle of Change

The three building blocks of an organization are hardware,
software, and *humanware*. Change begins with the humanware.
Many companies have found that expensive machinery won't
function if the people operating it have decided that they don't
like it. Projects launched with a great flourish soon get bogged
down if they don't make sense to workers far down the organizational ladder. Even the most powerful executives discover that
there is a high degree of volunteerism in every organization.
Fortunately, the extensive social science literature on change

and resistance to change provides important concepts and procedures for bringing about needed changes.

M.I.T.'s Ed Schein (1985) has identified three levels of organizational culture: *artifacts, values,* and *basic assumptions. Artifacts* consist of observable activities, behaviors, events, and rituals. *Values* are statements about what is good or bad (often used to explain an artifact). *Basic assumptions* are commonly held views of the world that are taken for granted and usually drive much of the organization's behavior.

We have observed that many organizations wishing to change their cultures find it relatively easy to make changes in artifacts and values, but fail to challenge their deeply held beliefs about customers, the organization's mission, the means of achieving performance goals, people, motivations, and what level of quality is achievable. These beliefs are the most critical elements of any organization. They determine what executives and managers pay attention to, what options they consider, and what problems get their priority attention.

7. The Principle of Measurements

Some would argue that drawing attention to the principle of measurements was one of Deming's most important contributions. It is at the heart of managing by fact and *Kaizen.* Goals that cannot be measured are merely slogans. Progress cannot be determined by guesswork or impressions. Particularly when groups of people are involved, checkpoints and numbers are the only certain way of assessing progress. Numbers and charts are more likely to mean the same thing to different people than are words. Motorola (Norling, 1989) provides a prime example. They stated at the outset that they would measure progress by the reduced number of defects per unit of work. They counted the defects in every 100 orders to establish a baseline. Then they set their company goal: to achieve a level of only 3.4 defective parts out of every million produced—virtual perfection. The goal would be achieved in six steps—one step in each of six years with the final step occurring in 1992. Measurable goals not only serve to keep people accurate in their assessment of success but also serve to energize people through feelings of accomplishment and challenge. (A fuller description of Motorola's "Six Sigma" target is presented in Chapter Thirteen.)

8. The Principle of Persistence

TQManagement is a process that does not visualize an end. It is far from being a "program," "project," or "experiment." It has the characteristics of a marathon, rather than a sprint. The up-front thinking, planning, and effort necessary to get Total Quality under way will not pay dividends in the short run. Like any change of organizational culture, the effort must be undertaken seriously with enough faith in the outcome so that people will persist through the unexpected frustrations and the rough spots. We like the image of the marathon, not only because it suggests a long-lasting effort, but because the preparation for the race is itself a healthy process. Runners condition themselves to the point where the actual winning of the competitive race is no longer as important as their increased health, vitality, and stamina. Even the "losers" are better off!

Americans do not have a reputation for patience and persistence. We pride ourselves on our quickness to respond to problems and our creativity in finding solutions. As investors we are impatient for results. We tend to applaud problem solvers rather than problem preventers. Although TQManagement does not by any means discourage creativity, it constantly reminds an organization that it is playing for the long-term achievement of almost perfect service to customers. Those who want to be realistic about launching a TQM effort must therefore assess their own comfort with this longer view.

What TQManagers Do That's Different

Principles are only words until they are translated into operating strategies and management behavior. Most executives and managers would probably subscribe to the principles we have discussed. Some would express reservations about implementing them in their own organizations, however, for a variety of reasons. The time, the money, or the people may not be available to set the organization on a whole new course of operation. If they could stop and start over again, perhaps a better course could be set, but the need to survive precludes any kind of idealism right now.

This is where it might be helpful to look closely at what successful TQManagers do and the strategies they employ to move forward in a steady, planned way. In some cases a shift in emphasis is required; in others it's a whole new kind of behavior. There are a dozen critical behaviors of TQManagers:

1.   They give priority attention to customers and their needs.
2.   They empower, rather than control, subordinates.
3.   They emphasize improvement, rather than maintenance.
4.   They emphasize prevention by inspection of the process.
5.   They encourage collaboration, rather than competition.
6.   They train and coach, rather than direct and supervise.
7.   They learn from problems, rather than minimizing them.
8.   They continually try to improve communication.
9.   They continually demonstrate their commitment to quality.
10. They choose suppliers on the basis of quality, not cost.
11. They establish organizational systems to support the quality effort.
12. They encourage and recognize team effort.

In this section we discuss and illustrate how management behavior changes in a TQManaged organization.

1. TQManagers Give Priority Attention to Customers and Their Needs

This is basic. Salespersons do this as a matter of course. Their survival depends on this kind of knowledge. Their primary task is to help the customers see how the company's product can meet their needs. Their focus, however, is often more on persuading the customer to buy, rather than on learning from the customer. All too often the customer is viewed only as a target, rather than a resource. When this happens, the customer's changing requirements may go unnoticed, and colleagues in the organization who design and manufacture the company's products are deprived of critical data. Quality companies have discovered that salespersons, customer service representatives, telesales representatives, and others with direct customer contact can be a valuable source of customer feedback *if* they are trained to ask rather than tell, *and* if the organization is prepared to accept and act on the feedback.

In an organization where quality is defined as meeting the customer's needs, this is less likely to happen. Everyone in the organization becomes more customer-conscious. Baldrige winner Wallace Company (1991) has a Total Customer Involvement program that requires all Wallace associates (their name for employees) to visit at least one customer at least one full day a year. They are asked to "walk a mile in the customer's shoes" so they can gain a better appreciation of the customer's needs. Not surprisingly, many customers have asked to make reciprocal visits to Wallace.

This is true for internal customers as well as for those who buy the company's products. Each department — and indeed, each person — begins to ask, "Who are my customers?" — that is, who makes use of whatever my department produces? The imagery begins to take hold that every part of the organization is both a customer and a supplier. The goal then becomes that of knowing what the customers need to do their job and of delivering the product to them in the time and condition that they require.

2. TQManagers Empower, Rather Than Control, Subordinates

This is the "leap of faith" that many managers find hard to make. One of the reasons they have risen to a managerial position is because they have been willing and able to take responsibility. With success also comes a certain amount of anxiety, because that success is now dependent upon what other people — their subordinates — decide and do. It is not surprising that many new managers feel anxious and want to keep control firmly in their own hands. It is easy for them to assume that their subordinates do not feel the same level of commitment to the job that they have. TQManagers start with a different assumption: that subordinates *want* to do a good job and will get a sense of satisfaction from achieving clearly defined goals. Sterling Livingston's research on the "Pygmalion Effect" makes it clear that when managers communicate this kind of trust and confidence, they increase the probability that subordinates will do their best (Livingston, 1969). Deming (1986) puts it crisply: "Remove barriers that stand between the hourly worker and his right to pride of workmanship." (We would change this to "any worker.")

Managers who are freed from the anxiety of constantly checking on subordinates are able to focus on a different set of issues: How can I help my subordinates get the resources they need to do their job? How can I make the work environment more conducive to healthy work? How can I improve the process by which we add value to the material we receive from our supplier? What can I learn from the problems that occur? What kind of rewards and recognition will mean the most to the people I supervise? Another of Deming's fourteen points is: "Find the problems. It is management's job to work continually on the system."

What do TQManagers do with subordinates who can't handle responsibility? They confront them with the goals, their record, and the discrepancy. The issue then becomes: "What caused this—and what can *we* do about it?" It becomes a problem to be solved. If it becomes clear that a subordinate either cannot, or does not want to, change his behavior to achieve the required goal, he must be removed from that job. TQManagers trust people and try to provide optimal opportunity and support, but they also recognize that the decision to accept responsibility ultimately lies with each individual subordinate. At Milliken & Company (1990), any employee who detects a quality or safety problem has the power to halt the production process.

3. TQManagers Emphasize Improvement, Rather Than Maintenance

This is perhaps the hardest thing for some managers to do. There is a high drama in making major changes. It's fun to look for breakthroughs. It's satisfying to develop plans, set them in motion, and then watch them go. "Hanging in there" is less dramatic. Trying to improve something that is already working well lacks challenge for some and has led to the sayings: "If it ain't broke, don't fix it" and "Leave well enough alone." The TQManagement process has demonstrated the power of doing exactly the opposite. Here a different motto is in force: "There's always room for improvement" or "If it isn't perfect, improve it." It is the steady day-to-day changes that have been responsible for the emergence of Japanese success in the marketplace.

In their award-winning book, *The Leadership Challenge*, Jim Kouzes and Barry Posner (1987) emphasize the importance of "small wins." They cite the example of Seattle businessman Donald H. Bennett, the first amputee to reach the summit of Mount Rainier. When asked to explain how he managed to do it, he responded, "One hop at a time." Solid progress is made that way by people who have a clear goal. Wallace's Paul Vita ("Baldrige-Winner Wallace...," 1991, p. 4) says, "You have to have continuous improvement. If you stand still, no matter how good you are today, you'll get run over by the crowd that once was behind you but is doing better."

4. TQManagers Emphasize Prevention by Inspection of the Process

This is a somewhat controversial idea, and one that needs to be carefully considered. It certainly is true that "an ounce of prevention is worth a pound of cure." It is also true, however, that if you wait to try something new until all the bugs have been worked out, you may never get started. Perfection can be the enemy of creativity. Tom Peters and Bob Waterman (1982), in their attention-getting *In Search of Excellence*, found that the successful companies they studied followed a policy of "Do it, fix it, try it." This strategy has its place in an innovative company. Finding the balance between preventing problems and developing better processes is a continual challenge for creative managers.

When errors are detected by the customer, the cost can be very high. Errors detected by the final inspector are also costly.

TQManagers, therefore, try to head off problems earlier in the
process. Deming (1986, p. 29) makes the point that inspection is
too late, ineffective, and costly. He states: "Inspection does not
improve quality, nor guarantee it." He argues that if the make-
inspect system that has been traditional in most American
companies were applied to making toast, it would be expressed,
"You burn, I'll scrape." In a company where everyone feels responsible for quality, the cost of error declines markedly.

    Some of the Baldrige Award winners, including Cadillac,
IBM, and Xerox, make an annual "Holes Report," identifying all
of the defects they can find in their present way of operating.
Task groups are then assigned to plug these "holes" with procedures that work better. At Milliken (1990), most manufacturing processes are under the scrutiny of real-time monitoring
systems that detect errors and help pinpoint causes. The resultant data, some of which is analyzed with the aid of computerized expert systems, supports process improvement efforts to
predict and prevent the causes of errors. To speed progress in
this area, process improvement specialists—often reassigned
production managers—analyze and improve processes, including those in such nonmanufacturing areas as billing and customer service. Since 1981, a 60 percent reduction has been
effected in costs, including less rework, discounts for off-quality,
payment of freight on customer returns, and other cost items.

5. TQManagers Encourage Collaboration,
Rather Than Competition

Competition sometimes prods people to do their best. Track
records are usually broken in competitive settings. Competition
energizes and adds drama to many human endeavors. It's quite
natural, then, to see it in the workplace when a department or
division tries to become recognized as the best. Sometimes top
management encourages this type of rivalry, assuming that
everyone will try harder to win. This strategy may work, but it
also has a downside. If I am in competition with you, it may make
it more difficult for me to view you as a colleague. I may begin to
view you as a rival, an opponent—someone to defeat. When that

happens, as we have seen in many organizations, people may find many subtle ways of working against each other, withholding information that might help others or trying to undermine their reputation with the boss. And, of course, where there are winners, there are also losers!

Organizations committed to Total Quality cannot afford this kind of rivalry. Instead, the emphasis is on teamwork— collaboration between departments, collaboration with customers and suppliers, collaboration between union and management. Cadillac (1991) found that by creating interdepartmental teams in their Simultaneous Engineering process, they could significantly reduce the time required for making styling changes in their automobiles. Coordinated efforts trimmed 50 to 85 weeks from what had typically been a 175-week process.

6. TQManagers Train and Coach, Rather Than Direct and Supervise

Traditionally American organizations have given low priority to training. Training budgets in business and government are usually the first to be cut when there is a budget crunch. Many executives give lip service to developing the competence of their employees—and then move on to more "important" issues. TQManagers, on the other hand, know that a training investment in themselves and their employees is central to the accomplishment of their organizational goals. Quality experts Philip Crosby, Joseph Juran, and W. Edwards Deming all include it in their lists of "musts." Deming (1986) notes it twice in his list of fourteen points: "Institute training" and "Encourage education and self-improvement for everyone." Particularly noteworthy is the fact that training in Total Quality companies usually starts with the top executives, who thus convey the message that learning is to be the norm in the organization. Robert Reich (1989), the Harvard social economist, predicted in a recent speech that "every successful organization will have to become a learning community."

The Baldrige winners would all agree with the maxim: "Quality control starts with training and ends in training." They have all invested heavily in building the competence of their people. In 1990 Cadillac (1991) provided their skilled hourly workers eighty hours of formal instruction in such areas as quality improvement, leadership skills, process modeling, statistical methods, and health and safety. Every Total Quality company we talked with regards quality training as an investment, not a cost. Since 1987 Wallace (1991) has invested about $2 million in formal training of its 280 people. Xerox (1990a) provided its 120,000 employees six days of basic quality training and has followed that up with myriad courses as part of its post-Baldrige "quality intensification effort."

7. TQManagers Learn from Problems, Rather Than Minimizing Them

How an organization deals with problems—and especially failures—tells much about that organization's culture. In many companies a great deal of effort goes into covering up or minimizing mistakes. "CYA" is a technical expression commonly used to describe how one avoids taking responsibility for something that goes wrong. There is a marked contrast in TQManagement organizations. One of Deming's (1986) key rules is: "Improve constantly and forever the system of production and service." There is something healthy and inspiring about people who feel strong enough to take a steady look at a problem and begin to ask, "What caused it?" and "How can we avoid it in the future?"

Wallace Company (1991) has an interesting policy for handling customer complaints. Any problem referred to a trained associate manning the Total Customer Response Network must be answered within sixty minutes. If it must go to a higher authority, the standing rule is that anyone needed to resolve the problem, including the president, may be interrupted to deal with it. If it cannot be solved within the deadline, the associate can settle the matter on her own, as she deems best, with the full backing of the company.

Dealing with complaints and solving problems are only part of the task, however. The more important strategy is to use problems as learning experiences. The key questions become: What happened? What caused it to happen? How can the process be improved so that this doesn't happen again? Sometimes a chain of events can be traced, resulting in new insights that then lead to new approaches.

Many companies have adopted a form of "product postmortem" called a Presidential Review. At Xerox such reviews can last as long as a day and are attended by the CEO and his staff. The product development team (usually a cross-functional team) presents the history of their work against the original plan (supported by documentation), highlighting the deviations—both better and worse—from the plan and identifying the cause for any deviation. This process can be thought of as the Check and Act steps from Deming's (1986) Plan-Do-Check-Act (PDCA) circle (Figure 2.1) applied to product development. The purpose of a Presidential Review is to isolate the causes for deviation and assure that these results are communicated to other product development teams, thus providing a focus for improving development practices in order to assure predictability in future programs.

8. TQ Managers Continually Try to Improve Communication

Anytime you ask a group of managers to identify major problems in their organizations, you can be certain that communica-

Figure 2.1. Deming's PDCA Circle.

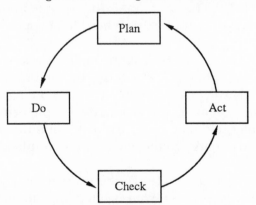

Source: Deming, 1986. Used by permission.

tion will rank high on the list. If Total Quality is to be the
responsibility of everyone in the organization, they all have to
understand the goals and the strategy for reaching them, the
progress that is being made, the successes, and the remaining
challenges. They have to know about top management's commitment to quality and believe that it is not just a slogan or a
program, but an expected way of life. It is perhaps even more
important that everyone in the organization feels free to express
their views and their ideas. The majority of good ideas for
improving operations come from the people who are doing
those operations—from the bottom, rather than the top of the
organization. At Federal Express (1991), employees are encouraged to be innovative and to make decisions that advance quality goals. They have installed the Digitally Assisted Dispatch
System, which communicates to some 30,000 couriers through
video screens in their vans. The system permits a quick response
to pickup and delivery dispatches and allows couriers to manage
their time and routes with high efficiency.

People must know they are listened to and that their ideas
are considered and have some impact, or they will soon keep
their ideas to themselves. Quality circles work when management implements suggestions; they quickly die or become a
waste of time when nobody seems to take suggestions seriously.
Wallace Company (1991) has one rule that is strictly adhered to:
suggestions put into the suggestion system must be responded
to within one day. The key point is that people must know that
they are listened to and heard. When this happens, a flood of
new ideas emerges.

What goes for the boss-subordinate relationship also applies to interdepartmental relationships. Communication is the
glue that holds a TQManagement organization together. This is
where the concept of teamwork and the supplier-customer relationship comes into play. A department that is the consumer of
another department's product must let the supplier know about
its needs.

At IBM Rochester (1991), the transformation of the engineering change process from printed copy to an on-line system was successfully completed by a quality-improvement team.

The process owner, a line manager, was also a member of the team, which worked closely with customers from across the site. The team began by modeling the process to identify bottlenecks and process inhibitors and by performing root cause analysis to determine process problems. The team restructured the process flow and unnecessary steps were removed. To implement the new process, education and support were provided to customers across the Rochester site. The result has been realized in improved product cycle time, efficiency, and communication.

9. TQManagers Continually Demonstrate Their Commitment to Quality

In some organizations, senior executives may be put in the position of endorsing projects that someone else then manages. This is not true in Total Quality companies. Here the CEO and the top executives must "walk their talk" every day. Their actions, rather than their words, will communicate their level of commitment. In some cases this may mean taking significant risks as the organization changes course. Goals that would get immediate results may take a back seat to longer-term objectives. Without this kind of commitment, however, TQManagement will never become the centerpiece of the corporate culture. Feigenbaum (1956) put it succinctly: "A quality-control program must have the complete support of top management. With lukewarm management support, no amount of selling to the rest of the organization can be genuinely effective."

At Westinghouse's Nuclear Fuel Division (Westinghouse Corporation, 1989b), senior staff also comprise the Quality Council, which establishes the division's quality policy and goals. The Quality Council reexamines its goals and measurements each year. These measures serve as the reference points for department and work group quality-improvement efforts. Progress on more than sixty measures is reported in monthly division operations meetings of the council plus other key managers.

10. *TQManagers Choose Suppliers on the Basis of Quality, Not Cost*

Most organizations try to reduce their cost of doing business by seeking out the most inexpensive suppliers of services or material. TQManagers look first for quality, however. They know that quality begins with the use of the best materials. It may be apocryphal, but the story is told that when Scott Carpenter was strapping into his Mercury space capsule before being launched down the Atlantic Test Range, he was asked by a reporter what he would like to say to the American people before the hatch was closed. Carpenter is reported to have replied, "I would just like everyone to know how consoling it is to know that everything in this capsule was built by the lowest bidder."

One of Deming's (1986) rules is: "End the practice of awarding business on the basis of price tag alone." He argues that the policy of trying to drive down the price of anything purchased, with no regard for quality and service, can drive vendors and good service out of business, and says, "The ways of doing business with vendors and customers that were good enough in the past must now be revised to meet new requirements of quality and productivity." Feigenbaum (1991) puts it this way: "Incoming material control involves the receiving and stocking at the most economical levels of quality, of only those parts, materials, and components whose quality conforms to the specification requirements." It is interesting to note that Baldrige winner Wallace (1991) began its move toward Total Quality because one of its largest customers, Celanese, said in 1985 that it would be certifying major suppliers by radically new standards of "quality" service and would be reducing sources to those who met those standards. At Xerox, (1990a), the number of suppliers was reduced from approximately 3,500 to about 500 "quality-certified" suppliers.

The concept of teamwork in some Total Quality companies extends to suppliers. Planning teams of suppliers and customers are formed to review the total job to be done and determine the quality and timing of supplies. The time-saving "Just-In-Time" delivery of materials can only be accomplished and maintained with this kind of close collaboration, which changes the emphasis in the relationship from bargaining for the best price to planning for the best product.

Genichi Taguchi and Don Clausing (1990, p. 75) wrote in a *Harvard Business Review* article: "In Japan it is said that a manager who trades away quality to save a little manufacturing expense is 'worse than a thief'—a little harsh perhaps, but plausible. When a thief steals $200 from your company there is no net loss in wealth between the two of you, just an exchange of assets. Decisions that create huge quality losses throw away social productivity—the wealth of society."

11. TQManagers Establish Organizational Systems to Support the Quality Effort

Many organizations have launched new campaigns with much fanfare and enthusiasm, only to see that enthusiasm fade as time wears on. The routine soon is ignored. Commitments seem to be less important. Efforts sag as problems emerge and other things compete for attention. The commitment to continual improvement is no different. It must be supported in a systematic way. So TQManagement organizations establish monitoring groups. These groups are called by various names. In Wallace Company (1991) it's the Quality Management Steering Committee. In Cadillac (1991) it's a group of Joint Quality Councils, led by a general manager and a representative of the UAW.

At Milliken & Company (1990), commitment to quality and customer satisfaction begins with Roger Milliken, CEO, and Thomas J. Malone, COO, who devote more than half their time to Milliken's "Pursuit of Excellence" process. Through the company's Policy Committee and Quality Council, Milliken's senior managers establish the environment and provide the leadership for quality improvement; they also closely monitor the progress of each company unit toward quality goals.

12. TQManagers Encourage and Recognize Team Effort

Encouragement is a central requirement of TQManagement. Small wins must be recognized. Steady progress must be re-

warded or interest will fade. Kouzes and Posner (1987) discovered in their research of several hundred successful manager-
leaders that recognition is one of management's most powerful
tools. The most successful executives used dramatic means to
show their appreciation for work well done. In the words of
Renn Zaphiropoulos, founder of Versatec, "When you give someone a check, don't mail it, have a celebration" (Kouzes and
Posner, 1987, p. 257).

At IBM Rochester (1991), employee contributions are
recognized by luncheons and receptions, as well as monetary
rewards. At Wallace Company (1991), associates get company-
wide recognition for participating in training and project teams
and for the results achieved. "Quality wins" are cited in the
company newsletter. John Wallace, CEO, sends congratulatory
letters to quality winners. Teams get special dinners and picnics
as celebrations. At Xerox (1990a), management hosts a Teamwork Day in October at three Xerox U.S. locations, which provides quality-improvement teams a venue to present their results
and processes. In 1991 over 15,000 employees, suppliers, and
customers attended these events. Xerox teams may also compete for annual Teamwork Awards, which provide both recognition and monetary rewards.

TQManagement is a new style of organizational life. It
builds on several decades of management study, experimentation, and practice. Individual aspects of TQManagement have
been around for a long time. The difference in the 1990s,
however, is the linkage of these separately tried principles and
practices into a coherent new set of standards for operating a
modern organization. In a time of intense international competition, many organizations are feeling a new sense of urgency
to examine the relevance of TQManagement to their own
operations.

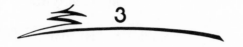

Using TQM
in a Public Sector Setting

For forms of government let fools contest;
Whate'er is best administer'd is best.
                                    — Alexander Pope

Although the most widely publicized TQManagement efforts
have occurred in business and industry, it is encouraging to note
that federal, state, and local governmental organizations have
also produced dramatic results by following the same principles. This is particularly important because a quality business
operates best when it is served by a quality government. It is hard
to imagine operating an elegant Total Quality business in a
corrupt or poorly managed country. In this chapter we describe
some of the efforts governmental agencies are making to apply TQManagement principles in serving *their* customers —
citizens — and in supporting the Total Quality movement in the
United States.

   The efforts and successes of TQManagement in the public sector are particularly impressive because government administrators are under special constraints. Their directives and
priorities may shift with changes in the elected political leadership, their power to provide rewards and promotions is often

restricted, and the cost of taking a risk that fails can be a highly publicized disaster. Despite these limitations, both appointed and career public officials have found that the principles of TQManagement can help to provide better service to the public, often at significantly reduced costs.

It should be noted, however, that some scholars and administrators question the appropriateness of TQManagement for a governmental agency. Radin and Coffee (forthcoming) point out that significant factors in the public sector constrain the use of this style of management. They cite, for example, the great uncertainty in an organization where programs are subjected to political influence, annual budget processes, and turnover in political leadership. They also point out the multiple sources of control and accountability, with the same agency having to respond to local, state, and federal "customers" who have differing needs and priorities. Their prediction is that TQM will join the other "failed efforts to change the way the federal government does its business. . . PPBS, ZBB, MBO, quality circles and many more." We discuss some of Radin and Coffee's criticisms in Chapter Fourteen, where we examine the future of the quality movement.

In this chapter we cite examples of the impressive ways in which administrators in government are enhancing the quality of the service they provide and supporting TQManagement efforts in the private sector. Readers who want additional information are encouraged to contact the Federal Quality Institute (FQI) or the Public Sector Quality Improvement Network (see Resource B for addresses).

TQManagement Efforts at the Federal Level

Government as a Stimulator and Monitor of Quality

In the United States, the federal government encourages and monitors quality for business and for its own agencies. Its role of encourager is demonstrated most clearly by the annual presentation of the Malcolm Baldrige National Quality Award by the president of the United States. This "Academy Award" for excellence in business enterprises has been dramatically successful in focusing attention on quality and providing a set of guidelines for helping business organizations to assess their level of excellence. The legislation creating the award was signed into law on August 20, 1987, and the first awards were presented in 1988. Each year the number of applicants has increased. In 1991 the Baldrige Office received requests for 220,000 application forms! Although only about 100 companies actually have applied each year, many more use the application guidelines for assessing and improving their organizations (U.S. Dept. of Commerce, 1991).

Perhaps the most powerful result of the Baldrige Award has been the stimulation of many executives and managers to learn about TQManagement and to see its results. This "managers learning from managers" process has been stimulated by the requirement that Baldrige winners must share their knowledge with others for at least a full year after winning the award. Most of the winners to date have done this, not just in speeches and written material, but by conducting day-long workshops with names like "Showcase Seminars" and "Quality Forums." Our studies show that more than 500,000 managers have attended these educational events in the past three years. We'll discuss the Baldrige Award in more detail in Chapter Twelve, but we'd like to note here that this one activity administered by the federal government, in close partnership with the private sector, has had a profound impact on the spread of Total Quality practice in the United States.

A second important contribution of the federal government was the General Accounting Office (GAO), study of quality organizations reported in Chapter One (U.S. General Accounting Office, 1991). This study was undertaken at the request of Congressman Donald Ritter and twenty-nine other members of Congress to "examine the impact of formal total quality management practices on the performance of selected U.S. companies." Because the GAO has a solid reputation for integrity and objectivity, its findings have been particularly salient. It is interesting to note that immediately after the conclusion of its study, the

GAO launched a Total Quality training program for its own top personnel!

The Department of Defense

The U.S. Department of Defense (DoD) has been in the forefront of the quality revolution. In 1988 this massive governmental agency published its *Total Quality Management Master Plan*, defining as its strategy the achievement of "one broad, unending objective: continuous improvement of products and services. . . . 'Product' means not only the weapons and systems fielded by military personnel but the result of all acquisition and logistics functions, including design, procurement, maintenance supply, and support activities. Everything that DoD does, every action that is taken, every system that exists, involves processes and products that can be improved or services that can be performed more efficiently" (p. 1). The long-range (seven-year) goals were four in number:

- Establishing TQM as a way of life
- Having all DoD personnel directly participate in continuous process improvement
- Widespread defense industry implementation of continuous process improvement
- Congressional understanding and support for TQM

Through the extensive training of its own personnel and its influence with its industrial suppliers, the DoD has been a major force in spreading the concept of TQM.

The Federal Quality Institute

A 1988 executive order (E.D. 12637) called for the establishment of "a government-wide program to improve the quality, timeliness, and efficiency of services provided by the federal government." This order grew out of the recognition that the federal government is the largest consumer and service provider in the country. The idea for a Federal Quality Institute was initiated in

1987 by the Office of Management and Budget and won the approval of the President's Council on Management. The Institute opened its doors in June 1988 with a staff of six senior executives, four of them borrowed from other federal agencies. The purpose of the institute is to familiarize government administrators with Total Quality concepts and to help them implement the process in their departments. The FQI provides three services for its colleagues in the government: (1) quality-awareness training courses, (2) a list of approved private sector quality experts, and (3) a Quality and Productivity Information Center.

The first director of the FQI, Paul Sweetland, stated that the "quality goal" of the federal government was to "provide high quality timely products and services to the American public, using service delivery systems that are responsive to customer needs and make the most effective use of taxpayer dollars" (Sweetland, 1991, p. 1). In a presentation on March 28, 1991, in Cocoa Beach, Florida, he proposed four key changes in management to carry out this goal:

1. *Not management by rules, but empowerment with guidelines.* Develop guidelines, but empower employees to make the decisions necessary to satisfy the customer—to deviate from the guidelines (within the bounds of the law) if the guidelines don't result in satisfying the customer. Develop guidelines and procedures taking the customer's point of view.

2. *Not organization by function but organization by process.* Organize into teams that carry out major processes or serve specific customer segments. If organizing by process is not possible, require that all units nest their individual missions within the larger mission and explicitly state how they focus on their customers.

3. *Not up-focused or in-focused, but customer-focused.* Get rid of subjective, top-down, in-focused, procedurally based evaluations of individuals. Redeploy people and resources to processes that have the greatest impact on customers. Make virtually all nonstrategic information widely available. Delegate authority to the lowest feasible levels and as near to the front line as possible. This will facilitate eliminating all layers of manage-

ment whose major purpose was communication, oversight, and assignment of work.

4. *Not purposely impersonal, but purposely caring.* Manifest caring and concern for employees and customers in balance with concern for quality in business aspects. Change the basic strategy to providing equal satisfaction, instead of equal treatment. Train and empower front-line people to be responsive to customers, friendly, and caring. Train employees in the fundamental of "recovery" (the art of handling mistakes). Extend hours of availability to customers. Make all forms user-friendly.

The FQI also administers both the President's Award for Quality and Productivity Improvement and the Quality Improvement Prototype Awards. (An agency must have at least one Prototype Award to be eligible for the President's Award.) The President's Award, which is given to the agency that demonstrated the most exemplary quality improvements, is discussed in Chapter Twelve. The first two President's Awards were given to the Naval Air Systems Command in 1990 and the Air Force Logistics Command in 1991. The Quality Improvement Prototype Award is given annually in recognition of excellence in implementing Total Quality and achieving quality-improvement results. Winners receive their awards at the Annual Conference on Federal Quality and Productivity Improvement. These selected agencies serve as models for the rest of government. Some examples follow of what agencies have done to be designated as a Quality Improvement Prototype.

Internal Revenue Service: Ogden, Utah, Service Center (1989 Quality Improvement Prototype Winner). During the 1988 filing season, 5,700 federal employees opened, extracted, sorted, batched, stamped, edited, checked, entered, double-checked, and triple-checked more than thirty million tax documents from fourteen states, in addition to correcting errors, answering taxpayer correspondence, and ensuring compliance with tax regulations. In 1986 this center began applying principles of Total Quality to its operations. Managers and employees worked in teams to improve their operations and make service to the customer a priority. Special post office boxes and telephone numbers were provided to taxpayers who had difficult cases. Union officials actively participated as full partners in improvement efforts. *Result:* New systems have provided taxpayers with faster, more efficient means of filing their returns—and saved the federal government over $3.5 million in a two-year period.

NASA Lewis Research Center, Cleveland, Ohio (1989 Quality Improvement Prototype Winner). This Center is the National Aeronautics and Space Administration's lead center for research-and-technology development in aircraft propulsion and space power. Its primary "products" are the research, technology, and hardware needed to keep NASA and the nation preeminent in air and space science. It has approximately 4,000 employees (2,700 civil servants and 1,300 service employees). In 1982 the Center changed its management practices to follow TQManagement principles. *Result:* By 1988, Lewis employees had increased the number of their technical publications by more than 30 percent and the number of their disclosures of inventions by nearly 50 percent. The quality of the Center's research also improved significantly on the basis of such measures as expert reviews, percentage of awards earned, and customer satisfaction surveys.

Navy: Naval Publications and Forms Center, Philadelphia, Pennsylvania (1989 Quality Improvement Prototype Winner). This Center processes over 200,000 customer requests per month and provides accounting services for thirty agencies. It began applying TQManagement principles to its operation in 1987. Quality and productivity improvement teams now operate throughout the Center. Processes have been improved through the use of internal quality measurements at key points within each process. Emphasis has been placed on customer satisfaction, customer-oriented conferences, enhancements to ordering procedures, and renovations to the warehouse facilities for optimum storage. *Result:* The Center is now able to exceed its goal of processing a receipt within seven calendar days over 85 percent of the time.

Veteran Affairs: Kansas City, Missouri, Medical Center (1989 Quality Improvement Prototype Winner). The Center has undertaken a comprehensive effort to improve the quality of its patient care since 1985. Central to the Center's initiative is a clinical Quality Management Program that scrutinizes all inpatient care, identifies problems, analyzes trends, provides for peer review, and ensures resolution of difficult professional issues. The Center also asks for continuous customer commentary on its services from veterans and their families, as well as staff involvement in developing new ways of increasing consumer health, comfort, and satisfaction. During the last two years the Center treated 17,000 patients. *Result:* The Center shows marked improvement in mortality rate, length of stay, and patient satisfaction.

Defense Industrial Supply Center (DISC), Philadelphia, Pennsylvania (1990 Quality Improvement Prototype Winner). This is one of six centers providing logistical support to a variety of worldwide customers. DISC introduced Total Quality in 1986. The center focuses on defining quality through customer expectations, eliminating rework, making program decisions based on hard data, and involving all employees. *Result:* In fiscal 1989, 98.4 percent of all orders were filled and shipped on time, compared to 97 percent in fiscal year 1987; back orders have decreased by 11 percent; and supply availability is 89 percent—the highest in five years.

Naval Aviation Depot, Cherry Point, North Carolina (1990 Quality Improvement Prototype Winner). This depot repairs, overhauls, and modifies military aircraft. It's the only one of six such depots run by the U.S. Marine Corps. The depot undertook a Total Quality program to improve management leadership, increase communication among managers and employees, add gainsharing incentives, involve employees, and provide intensive training in statistical process control and other analytical skills for assessing improvement in work processes. *Result:* The average cost for repair of an engine component dropped as much as $7,000 per unit from 1985 to 1987. Standard repair and maintenance on one type of aircraft dropped as much as $55,000 from

January 1985 to September 1987. Through a gainsharing incentive, employees received 46 percent of the more than $1.8 million saved in the first quarter of 1988.

Air Force: Sacramento Air Logistics Center (AFLC), Sacramento, California (1991 Quality Improvement Prototype Winner). The Center's basic mission is logistics support for assigned weapons systems, including the F-111, A-10, A-7, F117 stealth fighter, and advanced technical fighter. TQManagement was introduced in 1987. The AFLC vision, "Partners in Excellence," supports an active partnership between customers, suppliers, managers, labor unions, and the work force at large. *Result:* In fiscal 1987, 40 percent of F-111 fighter planes were "mission capable" at any given time, by the end of fiscal 1988 the mission capable rate had risen to 74 percent, and by the end of fiscal 1989 the rate had risen to more than 76 percent. One experimental project resulted in savings of $3.4 million and a gainsharing award of $1,361 to each of 1,311 employees.

1926th Communications-Computer Systems Group (CCSG), Warner Robins Air Logistics Command, Georgia (1991 Quality Improvement Prototype Winner). The CCSG plans, manages, and operates information systems; acquires and maintains computer resources; and employs computer technologies throughout the Air Force Logistics Command. Its communications mission encompasses all air traffic control, common-user, and specialized communications for the Center and all tenants located on Robins Air Force Base. The commitment of quality began in 1988. Among its communications tools is a "Quality Bill of Rights" (*Quality Improvement . . .*, 1991, p. 9):

- The right to challenge business as usual
- The right to be heard
- The right to expect commitment to quality
- The right to place quality before production
- The right to feel genuine pride in AFLC products and services

Result: On-time delivery of critical computer parts rose from 96.4 to 99.6 percent over three years. Computer on-line time also increased from 94.6 to 99.6 percent, representing an increase of hundreds of hours of computer use to twenty thousand customers. Savings in dollars amounted to more than $8 million.

TQManagement Efforts at the State and Local Levels

Arkansas

One of the most aggressive Total Quality programs for a state has been developed in Arkansas. It began with a community initiative in Batesville in July 1987. An all-day orientation for local leaders encouraged them to send teams to a training program on quality management in the fall. A diverse group of organizations enrolled teams and the training ended with a celebration in which teams presented the results of their improvement projects. At the first celebration, projects ranged from ConAgra's improved methods of frying chicken to city government's reduction in vehicle downtime.

When Governor Bill Clinton attended Batesville's celebration in February 1988, he became convinced that quality management was essential for state government. He was already a strong supporter of quality manufacturing, but at this celebration he came to understand how the principles of quality management can work in all types of settings. A team of hourly workers who presented a well-thought-out solution to a problem admitted that they had had a hard time getting started on the project because no one had ever asked them to think before. Recognizing that employees represent a wealth of untapped knowledge, Governor Clinton accepted an offer by Arkansas Eastman to loan an executive for a year to help state government establish a quality-management program.

After several months of planning, six pilot agencies and the governor's office started their quality journey in January 1990. By August 1990, the state government's Inter-Agency Training Program began conducting ongoing classes. During the summer and fall of 1991, more than ten thousand state employees received an orientation on quality management. A Quality Advisory Council advises the governor and ensures consistency in the spread of quality management throughout government. A state coordinator of quality provides professional support for the network of departmental quality coordinators.

The commitment of the state government to quality was further demonstrated by legislation that (1) assures that no state employee will lose employment due to efficiencies resulting from quality-management projects, (2) provides a mechanism to transfer or reallocate funds between agencies that are made necessary by quality-management implementation, (3) establishes a quality-management training fund, and (4) creates a quality-management board to oversee these activities.

Madison, Wisconsin

To understand the process by which TQManagement begins to transform local government, it is useful to examine the history of the city of Madison, Wisconsin. The beginning can be traced to a day in May 1983 when the mayor, Joseph Sensenbrenner, sat in on an hour of W. Edwards Deming's lecture at the University of Wisconsin before giving him an official welcome to the city. What he heard was sufficiently intriguing to make him want to learn more about this approach to management. He was facing difficult budget problems, with the citizens of Madison resisting both tax increases and cuts in services. He chose the city's motor equipment division as the first place to try out Deming's approach to problem solving. The problem was the slow servicing of city-owned vehicles. The result of his tracking the problems through several city departments was the discovery that although each department was doing its job right, the *system* was preventing a solution. The tendency of both workers and management was to focus on an easily identifiable problem, find a workable solution, fix the problem, and move on without studying the underlying causes or looking at the overall system that may have contributed to it. Mayor Sensenbrenner applied Deming's methods; the outcome of his effort was to cut vehicle turnaround time from nine days to three days and to save $7.15

for every dollar invested in improvements—an annual net savings of $700,000 (Sensenbrenner, 1991).

Mayor Sensenbrenner next attended a four-day seminar with Deming and began working with William Hunter and other members of the faculty of the University of Wisconsin, as well as other consultants. He helped to found the Madison Area Quality Improvement Network (MAQIN), which includes academic, professional, and corporate members and which is probably the most creative and powerful local Total Quality network in the country today. With the success of the motor equipment division behind him, the mayor decided to gradually introduce the Quality and Productivity (QP) philosophy throughout city government. From early 1984 to mid 1985, the city concentrated on presenting training and awareness sessions ranging from two hours to three days. Approximately 450 to 500 city employees, as well as managers of about 25 percent of the city work force, attended these early sessions, in addition to a number of the city's twenty-two Common Council members. They were joined by Wisconsin governor Anthony Earl and his cabinet, as well as by some key executives from the private sector. (See Chapter Fourteen for more on MAQIN.)

These sessions stimulated a variety of QP projects in many different city agencies, including the parks division, the personnel division, the engineering division, public health, and the police department. There was clearly an interest in QP concepts at all levels of city government. David Miller, an aide to Mayor Sensenbrenner, had been an informal leader and supporter of these efforts. When he left city government to join a consulting firm, the mayor established a QP Steering Committee. The role of this committee was to oversee QP activities and chart a direction that would ultimately lead to the complete organizational transformation of the government. The Steering Committee was chaired by the mayor and included the director of planning and development, the director of public works, the public health director, the personnel director, the labor relations director, the police and fire chiefs, and a mayoral aide. The Quality Improvement Mission Statement has been revised periodically. The current version is:

The mission of our Quality Improvement initiative is to introduce, cultivate, and sustain within all City agencies, the constant and widespread practice of involving employees from all levels of the organization in a meaningful and cooperative team effort which is based on a critical analysis of relevant data, including customer input, for the purpose of continually improving the efficiency and cost effectiveness of City Services.

The QP Steering Committee authorized a "first wave" of four projects and began to recruit and train QP facilitators from among interested city employees. Each of the fifteen selected were given fifteen days of intensive training from an external consulting group. The training familiarized them with the QP philosophy and taught them the analytical and meeting-facilitation techniques necessary to carry out a QP project and present the results.

The city of Madison's approach to TQManagement has been influenced not only by the pioneering giants in the field — Deming, Juran, and Kaoru Ishikawa — but by faculty members at the University of Wisconsin and Brian Joiner. The Joiner Triangle (Scholtes, 1988) has been used widely to focus attention on the three key ingredients of quality improvement (see Figure 3.1).

In Joiner's formulation, these are the key definitions:

- *Quality:* Meet and whenever possible exceed the needs and expectations of customers; develop an obsession with continuously improving every process involved in the creation of goods and services.
- *Scientific approach:* Adopt a scientific approach to problem solving, including data collection and analysis and the practical use of statistical tools.
- *All one team:* Manage using the input of all employees, especially across department lines, in order to blend the knowledge, skills, and needs of everyone into a better end result and a teamwork that extends beyond the organization

Figure 3.1. The Joiner Triangle.

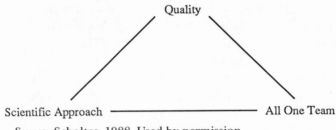

Source: Scholtes, 1988. Used by permission.

to vendors, the community, and other organizations. Effect teamwork with customers, suppliers, regulators, and, where legal and appropriate, competitors.

When it became clear that the QP program required full-time leadership, Mayor Sensenbrenner eliminated one of his mayoral aide positions from the 1987 budget and recruited and appointed the first city quality and productivity administrator in the United States. The person selected was Tom Mosgaller, a citizen of Madison with a rich background in organization development and consulting.

With a QP administrator aboard, the Steering Committee began developing a strategic plan with three-year goals and a driving philosophy, which became known as the city's QP Diamond (see Figure 3.2).

As he worked with department heads, Mosgaller found that their differing reactions to moving their organizations in the direction of Total Quality fell into four categories:

- *Explorers:* Intrigued persons ready to risk because their values and management style are compatible with Total Quality philosophy
- *Pioneers:* Persons who watch to see what happens to the Explorers, then move to join in expanding the movement
- *Settlers:* Persons who join the movement when it is clear that this is the way to go

Figure 3.2. Madison's Quality Diamond.

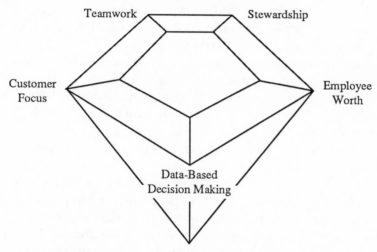

Source: City of Madison, Wisconsin. Used by permission.

- *"Missourians":* Persons who have lingering doubts and resist change as long as possible

This Total Quality effort went smoothly until a new mayor, Paul Soglin, was elected. Soglin had been a popular mayor in the early seventies, then dropped out of the political arena for several years. During his campaign he charged that QP had produced "too much talk and too few results." Two days after the new mayor took office, the QP administration was moved from the mayor's office. The QP Steering Committee stopped functioning. Mosgaller's title was changed to director of training and organization development. The mayor ordered an audit to assess the costs and benefits of the QP operation. The results were persuasive: an investment of $350,000 in training had produced a savings of $1.3 million from the first nine projects—and the payoff of the training was still going on!

Mayor Soglin's final reservations about the value of QP were swept away in 1988. The city faced a major crisis when a windstorm that stripped the leaves from Madison's trees was followed by a heavy snow and freeze. Storm drains were clogged and people feared that their grass was being killed. The newspapers hammered away at the mayor to do something to clean up the mess. He did. He ordered Mosgaller and the director of the street department to form a QP team to solve the problem. Sensing the significance of this opportunity, the director asked the mayor to appoint one of his aides to witness a disciplined problem-solving approach to this problem. Using the first-hand knowledge of the street workers (who knew, for example, that leaves don't fall the same in every section of city), the team made a proposal to the mayor that required no additional funds and solved the problem.

With Mayor Soglin's solid support, Madison's QP program has since moved forward with departmental project teams, an expanded training program, and a precedent-setting cooperative TQM training program involving state government employees, University of Wisconsin, Madison, employees, and local technical college support. Mosgaller's goal is to get everybody in the city thinking in terms of *process*—how each department contributes to the delivery of some service to the customer. When the mayor set five "Goals for the City," five interdepartmental teams were formed to plan how each department could make the goals a reality. The spirit of the Madison QP effort is captured in the title of a short video of its activities: "Making the Best Even Better."

Even the Madison police department has become a strong promoter of QP. In addition to introducing statistical analysis within the department to determine how to deploy their limited resources, the police have developed a questionnaire they give to every thirty-fifth person with whom they officially come in contact. To the Madison police department, both the citizen who asks for help and the criminal who must be detained are considered "customers" for whom the police are striving to improve service. Their approach illustrates the difference between *features* and *quality* in providing quality services. Features are what suppliers provide to serve a particular function, while quality describes *how well* a feature is delivered. For the Madison police, arresting someone is a feature, and the way it is done demonstrates quality. The officers know that the way they treat someone who is arrested has a great deal to do with how that person will regard the law in the future. In managing crowd control, the Madison police hand out a card with the following seven statements:

1. We facilitate citizens' right to assemble and protect their right of free speech.
2. We use restraint in the use of force. We protect people first and property second.
3. We dialogue with participants before, during, and after demonstrations.
4. We show leadership as peace-keepers in preparation and training for events and in area police strategies.
5. We focus on enabling citizens to exercise their constitutional right. The focus should not be on us.
6. We are open with citizens and the mass media and communicate constantly with them.
7. We pursue continuous improvement in our methods.

Austin, Texas

About a thousand miles southwest of Madison, the city of Austin, Texas, launched a program in 1991 titled "Building Austin's Standard in Customer Service" (BASICS). The program has three central goals:

1. To save money, while enhancing existing services
2. To win praise from citizens impressed with service quality
3. To add new services citizens want

The "Blueprint" book describing the program presents the rationale for TQManagement in government by suggesting how each key group of public servants would benefit (*Blueprint for the Way We Work*, 1991, pp. 3–4):

- *Elected officials* will gain increased confidence in public employees' ability to carry out their programs. Constituent complaints will drop and this will be reflected in the next election.
- *Top career administrators* will continuously improve how they accomplish their mission. A vision of excellence will help reduce turnover and increase morale. New means will be found for improving the quality of service and reducing costs.
- *Middle managers* will have greater control over their budgets, be able to concentrate on improving systems to prevent problems, and "reap the greatest reward of a manager: watching your people grow."
- *Employees* will be given the challenge, training, tools, and authority to self-manage their work. They will gain greater job security, leadership training, and higher pay.

One of the most intriguing concepts in the Austin workbook is "managing the moments of truth." A *moment of truth* is defined as "an episode in which the customer comes into contact with any aspect of the organization, and thereby has an opportunity to form an impression. These impressions layered one on top of the other, form the customer's opinion about an organization" (p. 2). Since these moments of truth occur when the supervisor or manager is not around, the front-line employee must have the training, the desire, and the feeling of empowerment to do what is necessary to deal with the customer's problem.

Los Angeles

Does the TQM approach work in larger metropolitan areas? It is safe to say that interest is growing at a rapid rate. In 1992 the Los Angeles City Productivity Commission requested, and received, a new charter from the city council renaming itself as the *Quality and Productivity Commission*. The new commission now has conducted seminars on quality for its own members, department heads, and deputies of city council members. The County of Los Angeles has recently engaged Marty Russell, a pioneer in shaping the Baldrige Award, to modify the Baldrige criteria to fit public agencies' requirements more comfortably.

Community Quality Coalition (CQC) and Transformation of America

The CQC is the cooperative venture of two separate efforts. In the early 1980s, Ford Motor Company, General Motors, Westinghouse, and the Nashua Corporation provided the impetus to launch the American Quality and Productivity Institute (AQPI) with the express purpose of establishing "community quality councils in every community in the USA." About the same time, the Transformation of America (TA) project got under way at Jackson Community College in Jackson, Michigan. TA's objective was to provide educational facilities and competence to teach Total Quality throughout America. Since AQPI was increasing the demand for Total Quality and TA provided educational opportunities, both organizations soon realized that they could help one another (Tribus, 1991).

In 1984, AQPI and TA met to plan an experimental joint project to be conducted in Kingsport, Tennessee. The object was to integrate their promotional and educational competencies into a single project that would touch all the elements of the community. The result was a Community Quality Coalition that was represented by large manufacturing organizations, small businesses, service companies, state and local government, and the schools (Lusk, Schwinn, Schwinn, and Tribus, 1990). In addition to Kingsport and Madison, CQCs have been effective in Erie, Pennsylvania, and Norfolk, Virginia. It was a CQC in Batesville, Arkansas, started in 1987, that provided the incentive for the governor and the state to launch their Total Quality effort. There are now a half-dozen CQCs throughout Arkansas.

Public Sector Quality Network (PSQN)

So much public sector activity has occurred that many state representatives have come together to form the PSQN. Among other things, PSQN is creating an electronic bulletin board through which the various state agencies are beginning to share information with one another. Both CQC and PSQN recognize the importance of transforming America's schools and the valuable assistance Total Quality can play in that transition, and both are working with the American Association of School Administrators (AASA) to determine ways to cooperate in improving the quality of America's educational systems (Tribus, 1991).

Total Quality in Education

Education certainly represents a significant opportunity for TQManagement. While it is generally agreed that TQManagement would benefit American schools, there is much less understanding of how to go about the process and what kind of support school administrators will require. For the last few years, W. Edwards Deming has held an annual seminar aimed at teachers. Attendance at these seminars has been steadily increasing and many educators have been inspired by his book *Out of Crisis* (Deming, 1986) to try Total Quality in their school operations. At their March 1991 annual convention in New Orleans, AASA for the first time had seven sessions devoted to Total Quality in education. All seven sessions were standing-room only and TQManagement will be the centerpiece of the 1992 conference (Tribus, 1991).

Implementing quality in the schools is not a simple task. School administrators, school board members, and students are not taught to view the schools as a "system." They are caught in the old paradigms of managing and as they struggle to make the necessary changes, they must rely on outside forces to teach them and support them in improving their system. This conviction most certainly was a factor in the decision of David Kearns, the Xerox CEO who led that company's quality effort, to accept the position of deputy secretary of the U.S. Department of Education.

Richard Cyert, president emeritus of Carnegie Mellon University, told a Los Angeles conference of educators and industrialists that "instead of leading business firms in this [quality] area, the academic institutions, and this includes most business and engineering schools, tend to follow practice, rather than lead it. There is a belief that the kinds of actions involved in TQM are not the proper business of the academic" (Cyert, 1991). Although higher education has been slow to embrace TQManagement, some significant experiments occurring around the country demonstrate how a quality approach to education can make a difference.

Sacramento County Schools

David Meaney, superintendent of the Sacramento (California) County Office of Education (SCOE), began the first public education, K–12, organization-wide application of Total Quality in the United States in 1986. SCOE provides educational-option programs at forty sites (including operation of a vocational high school) for 4,500 students. The district employs 600 teaching, administrative, and support employees. From its inception, the focus has been on three core values: (1) the client, (2) continuous improvement, and (3) involvement of everyone. Every employee receives a minimum of three hours of training (facilitators receive more). Department teams have identified their customers (other SCOE departments, students, county school districts, and parents), documented the requirements, and flow-charted their major work processes. SCOE's continuous improvement processes have resulted in a warehouse redesign, a new purchasing process, and a safety plan for the vocational high school (that team consisted of students, faculty, and police). Meaney believes that Total Quality "can offer schools a new and quality way to do business" (personal communication).

Gilbert High School, Gilbert, Arizona

In 1988, when Tricia Euen, the business curriculum chair at Gilbert High School (Gilbert is a Phoenix suburb), became concerned about the relevance of Gilbert's business classes, she surveyed local business leaders to learn their needs and what they wanted their employees to know. It was her first introduction to the terms Total Quality, statistical process control, and continuous improvement. With the help of Janet Gandy of the Arizona Department of Education, Euen solicited the aid of Finn Warraama and Jim Martin of McDonnell Douglas Helicopter in developing two classes—one called "Work" and another called "Leadership Management." Both classes were based on Total Quality concepts. The response by students and teachers was overwhelmingly positive. In 1989 Dolores Christensen joined the faculty when Euen moved on to Gateway Community College. With the continued support of McDonnell Douglas, Christensen and Gandy decided to drop the two "special" classes and incorporate TQM into all of Gilbert's business classes. Christensen, who uses TQM as a management tool in addition to teaching it to her students, says, "The kids love it. After the first two weeks they learn that the quality of their work depends on them and that is when they begin to take ownership for themselves" (personal communication). She adds enthusiastically, "Sometimes it seems like magic." In April 1990, Gilbert was recognized by the Arizona chapter of the American Society for Quality Control. Recently Gilbert completed Arizona's periodic accreditation review; on the basis of those results the transition team that guided the review process has decided to implement TQM throughout the school and all its programs.

Mt. Edgecumbe High School, Sitka, Alaska

More than a few miles north of Gilbert High School, in a climate and setting far different from that of Phoenix, a similar but more dramatic story has unfolded. Mt. Edgecumbe High School (MEHS) is a state-operated boarding school—the only such public school in the United States. It was once operated by the Bureau of Indian Affairs, but was closed in 1983. In 1986 it was reopened by the Alaska Department of Education with a focus on entrepreneurship rather than vocational skills alone. There are 200 students, mostly Native Americans, from all over the state. For 90 percent of the students English is not their native language, and many do not speak English well. Their long-term prospects were not bright: the dropout rate from school was high and Alaska has the highest suicide rate in the nation (Tribus, 1991).

In 1988 David Langford, an MEHS teacher, was working on a superintendency certificate at Arizona State University. Since ASU's program requires an internship at a local school district, Langford was assigned to work with Gilbert High School to share his experiences with hands-on projects and entrepreneurship. Through Tricia Euen he met Jim Martin, the continuous improvement director of McDonnell Douglas Helicopter. Martin explained what Total Quality was about and gave Langford and Euen several films to view and a bibliography. Langford's fire was lit. To quote him: "I went wild, bought every book on the list, contacted everyone I could find in industry who was into TQM, and drilled them on its application to education. My phone bill was $300–$400 per month that summer and my wife thought I had gone off my rocker" (personal communication).

Langford soon read everything Deming had written. He talked with Myron Tribus, one of the founders of CQC and a Deming disciple. He watched Juran's videotapes and read Kaoru Ishikawa's work to understand better what was happening in Japan. He became a Total Quality advocate, but because the administration and other faculty were uninterested, the most he could do with what he had learned was to introduce the Deming methods to his computer class. His students were enthusiastic about the concepts, in first one class and then another. He knew he was on to something.

Langford and Euen agreed to set up a sister-school arrangement and had a team of MEHS students join Gilbert students in a "Quality Education" conference in February 1989. The students from Sitka and Gilbert made joint visits to local businesses that used Total Quality (most notably Motorola). Langford was now a "zealot for quality" in education.

Upon his return to Sitka, Langford incorporated what he had seen in Phoenix into his classes and his students began using continuous improvement. During a student-faculty assembly in the spring of 1989, his students used an English project to argue for changes in dormitory rules, employing continuous-

improvement processes—in fact, their presentation was a tu-
torial on the Deming method of the use of facts. The English
teacher, Kathleen McCrossin, joined Langford as a quality advocate (Dobyns and Crawford-Mason, 1991).

Larrae Rocheleau (MEHS's superintendent) and Bill Denkinger (its principal) were cool to the idea of TQM, so Langford
forged ahead, never giving them the chance to say yes or no. But
the reaction of the students couldn't be ignored and Rocheleau
finally agreed to allow Langford to train the staff. A year later
Rocheleau and Denkinger attended a Deming seminar. They
came to understand Langford's enthusiasm when they saw the
enormous emphasis on continuous improvement and the depth
of what Deming was saying.

With no one to advise them, Langford and Rocheleau
began to apply Total Quality concepts to all aspects of MEHS.
They instituted a course called "Continuous Improvement" and
encouraged students to apply Total Quality processes to their
work in the school, their jobs, and especially their lives. Students
began to keep control charts on their study habits. They at-
tacked the design of the curriculum and, in collaboration with
the teachers and administrators, changed the schedule of instruction. The students studied Deming's fourteen points and
translated them into their educational environment, identifying
customers and suppliers in the school system. Their proposed
changes to the curriculum were adopted; they include a deployment flow chart of the educational process. The curriculum was
just a small part of the educational experience that was examined and developed at MEHS. The flow chart considers the
environment for learning, the way teachers and students inter-
act, the teachers' style of presentation, and the underlying assumptions about student and teacher behavior. The students
and Langford together have developed a Quality Evolution
Diagram to define the educational outcomes they wish to
achieve (see Table 3.1).

Each student, in consultation with a counselor, identifies
a realistic level to achieve. Students may wish to go more deeply
into some subjects than others. The school sets a minimum set
of competencies for which all students are required to attain

Table 3.1. Quality Evolution Diagram.

Level I	Knowledge	Remember, recall, recite
Level II	Comprehension	Explain, interpret, compare, summarize
Level III	Thinking	Put to use, apply in new situations, critique

Source: Tribus, 1991. Used by permission.

Level I, and some parts of Level II (such as arithmetic) are also required. Each student is expected to perform a Plan-Do-Check-Act cycle with a teacher to establish a learning plan, monitor progress, and develop corrective action when required.

It is too early to fully evaluate the outcome of the MEHS effort. The cost of instruction per pupil is the same as it is in other schools in Alaska, but the productivity is higher. (The operating cost of MEHS under the Bureau of Indian Affairs was $6 million—the current budget is $3 million.) Langford says, "New students that come into this system kind of go through a shock for a while—they can't quite believe that we could trust people that much" (Dobyns and Crawford-Mason, 1991). Here are a few of the changes and accomplishments (Tribus, 1991):

- The class schedule was changed to provide four 90-minute classes per day to allow time for lab work, hands-on projects, field trips, thorough discussions, varied teaching styles, and in-depth study.
- Teachers now ask students for input on classroom management, manage the class in a way that allows input, and facilitate decision making.
- Students are viewed as customers: management has provided better tools, such as computers, laser discs, science equipment, tutors, and expanded study times. Library training is accomplished on a need basis and is curriculum-driven, resulting in greater use of the library because its purpose is very clear.
- Increased emphasis on technology and training of faculty has resulted in a technology-based staff and a 2:1 student-computer ratio.

- Reorganization of the classroom schedule has allowed for an additional three hours of staff development and preparation time per week.
- Students have requested and received more technology (computers) and curricular additions (U.S. History, Russian, physics, calculus, and advanced quality training).
- The computer lab, library, and science facility are open at night to all students, at their request.
- Twenty-five student trainers have assumed responsibility for training other students in the quality sciences.
- With students and administration working on the problem of tardy students by statistically monitoring the process and removing special causes for variation, a school-wide focus on the need for improvement and changes in the system has resulted in reducing tardiness to fewer than ten students per week. Morning classes often start before the scheduled time because students are there and ready.
- Students help control and prevent discipline problems through positive peer pressure. Withdrawals reached a low of only 1 percent for the second semester of 1990.
- Managing the system instead of the teacher and increasing teacher participation in decision making has improved teacher morale. There was zero turnover in 1990–91.
- Rather than using standardized assessment tests, MEHS measures its success based on the success of students after graduation. A survey of graduates over five years showed that 46 percent were attending postsecondary school, 38 percent were working full-time, 5 percent were homemakers, and 3 percent were in the military. Only 11 percent were listed as "unknown or unemployed." Prior to the establishment of MEHS the dropout rate for this population was high. Now most students graduate and many go to college (although only 2 percent of native Alaskan students who enter the University of Alaska ever graduate).

Probably the best measure of MEHS's progress is provided by one of the students. Lisa Marie Polk told Lloyd Dobyns and Clare Crawford-Mason (1991), "Well, CIP (continuous-improvement process) has helped me to hit—as Mr. Langford calls it—the big 'M,' maturity. I mean, it used to be where I didn't really care much about anything. I came here, and I started to understand CIP and understanding quality and productivity. All of a sudden it just got kind of implanted in my mind. All of a sudden, I find myself adapting it to everything I do in school-work, and keeping my statistics, and my grade calcs, and everything. That's helped me grow up."

Universities and TQM

In August 1991, America's leading quality corporations (American Express, IBM, Motorola, Procter & Gamble, and Xerox) sponsored a Total Quality Forum, an annual gathering of academic and business leaders. The 200 participants heard Robert Kaplan, professor of business administration at the Harvard Business School, report on the state of quality in America's universities. It was not encouraging (Robinson and others, 1991). Kaplan surveyed twenty leading business schools in the United States and learned that only 20 percent of the introductory operations-management courses spend more than three sessions on quality. He also surveyed four operations-management journals and learned that in the 278 articles published in the last few years, there was virtually no direct coverage of TQM. The forum developed three objectives: (1) to identify the core knowledge generic to Total Quality, (2) to develop a Total Quality academic research agenda, and (3) to develop faculty understanding and commitment to TQM. As a result, the CEOs of the sponsoring companies published an open letter in the November–December issue of the *Harvard Business Review*. In their letter (Robinson and others, 1991), the CEOs made the following recommendations:

> *For Business*: (1) Open dialogue with the academic community. Invite academics and students to your facilities to study your TQM practices. If you do not already have them, set up formal relationships with local colleges and universities, encouraging re-

search of your TQM practices. (2) Identify TQM
leaders within your organization and make them
available to local colleges and universities for seminars and lectures. (3) Communicate your TQM
needs to the administrators and faculty where you
recruit. Establish formal guidelines for hiring that
include a minimum acceptable curriculum of
TQM training. Make TQM an integral part of on-
campus interviews.

For Universities and Colleges: (1) Learn what
leading TQM organizations here and abroad are
teaching their employees. Encourage company visits by your faculty and develop closer relationships
with local TQM companies. (2) Establish a research
agenda in total quality management. Deans and
faculty members should begin discussing the role
they want TQM to play in future research projects.
(3) Take an inventory of your curriculum, measuring the proportion of quality related course content in core courses as well as electives.

TQM University Challenge

One follow-up action to the forum occurred in January 1992,
when six corporations selected eight universities to participate
in a new joint educational effort called the TQM University
Challenge (Xerox Corporation, 1992). It was both popular and
competitive. Fifty-five universities applied for the eight slots and
twenty-seven were selected as finalists. In the spring of 1992 each
sponsoring company hosted up to 100 engineering and business faculty members and administrative personnel from their
"match" university. Each university completed a week of on-site
education about TQM in practice at their host company. The
universities were then encouraged to implement what they had
learned, including a focused customer survey and an internal
assessment of their implementation efforts. All of the participating companies are providing support to their partner universities during implementation. The matches are: Purdue with

Motorola, University of Wisconsin at Madison and Tuskegee University with Procter & Gamble, North Carolina State University and Georgia Institute of Technology with Milliken, Massachusetts Institute of Technology and Rochester Institute of Technology with IBM, and Carnegie Mellon University with Xerox.

Oregon State University

Oregon State University began a TQM effort in 1989, with the goal of implementing it throughout the university by 1994. They began by visiting TQM companies (Ford Motor Company, Hewlett-Packard Company, and Dow Chemical Company), having a visit by W. Edwards Deming, reading key books and articles, and sending the president and several key managers to a TQM class. The reaction of the faculty was mixed, with some faculty members being concerned that "quality control" might suggest uniformity, or bringing everyone to the same level. Partway through the process, L. Edwin Coate (1990, p. 100), the vice president for finance and administration, reported these learnings:

- You must have support from the top.
- "Just do it!" (Don't study it to death.)
- The teams are critically important—and they must be trained.
- You need a champion. (It takes a long-term commitment of time and money.)
- Breakthrough planning helps.
- Try the service side first! (Usually it pays to start with a unit that's having trouble, because they know they need help.)

Coate also did a telephone survey to twenty-five colleges and universities and found that seventeen of them were implementing a TQM focus in some part of their graduate or undergraduate curriculum, usually in business or industry-related courses. Of the twenty-five schools, fifteen had initiated significant efforts in the service area and ten had efforts under way in the academic area.

The task for the TQM University Challenge participants and schools like Oregon State is not easy, but it is important. Deming (Dobyns and Crawford-Mason, 1991, p. 91) is harsh in describing the need: speaking of business schools, he said, "What they do is teach students how business is carried on. That's how to perpetuate it, exactly what we do not need. Nothing could be worse." Myron Tribus (Dobyns and Crawford-Mason, 1991, p. 92), a former dean of engineering at M.I.T., says, "It is easier to move a graveyard than to change a curriculum." But he is optimistic, adding, "I forecast that within ten years the business schools will be solidly behind this [quality] movement" (Dobyns and Crawford-Mason, 1991). Tribus's forecast seems a good bet, considering the effort at Oregon State, the Quality Forum, and activities at other schools, including the University of Chicago, which announced its intention to include TQM in its Graduate School of Business.

Most people involved in the Total Quality movement agree that every sector of society must understand and utilize Total Quality methods if the United States is to remain a leading world-class nation. As the CEOs said in their open letter: "Our system of higher education is one of this country's most powerful competitive weapons. Working together, companies and institutions of higher education must accelerate the application of total quality management on our campuses if our education system and economy are to maintain and enhance their global positions" (Robinson and others, 1991, p. 94–95). Government's understanding and practice of TQManagement principles is a critical ingredient. As managers from business and government team together at quality workshops and myriad conferences, a variety of networks are developing and the TQManagement movement is gathering momentum.

Again we must note that installing TQManagement in governmental and educational organizations is often much more complicated than transforming a clearly focused private enterprise. There are multiple customers to be considered and many more restraints and complexities. It is, therefore, reassuring to witness the growing number of networks, newsletters, and other linkages being created to share ideas and strategies.

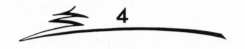

4

Where TQM Will Work (and Where It Won't)

Change can be a force to be feared, or an opportunity to be seized. The choice is in our hands.
— *The Winds of Change*

There is something compelling about Total Quality Management. It appeals to the idealistic side of most executives and managers: to strive for the best. . . to keep improving. . . to empower subordinates. . . to have everyone in the organization working as a team. It's the stuff of inspirational speeches. It would be great to be a Baldrige winner, or even to come close. But is TQManagement a realistic idea for *your* organization? Can you really trust your workers that much? What happens to the bottom line if you start investing heavily in training? Doesn't the goal of continual improvement get to be a drag at some point? And how will people stand up under the pressure of constantly trying to do better in a race that never ends?

Sensible CEOs will ask questions like these about their companies, and division managers will ask them about their divisions, before trying something as radical as TQManagement. We cannot emphasize too strongly that although TQM incorporates many familiar features, it is *not* simply a program you add on to what you are now doing. Instead, it represents a commitment to a new way of life for your organization. Some people will welcome it; others will resist. The payoff will be great, but so is the investment of energy, thought, and time. And there is always risk.

In many organizations bosses, colleagues, and subordinates have learned to be skeptical of new management approaches or slogans. They have learned from experience that many of them may be launched with great fanfare ("the flavor of the month"), but that they may gradually fade into the background as the organization grapples with day-to-day crises. The sensible reaction is therefore to pay lip service to top management's latest pronouncements—and then wait to see what *really* happens.

This chapter is intended to help you think about TQM in a very realistic way. It is designed to help you diagnose your own organizational situation whether you are a CEO, a department manager, or a staff person interested in making your organization more effective. All of the Baldrige winners did the kind of exploration we are suggesting before they "took the plunge." Some felt they had no choice (Xerox's market share was falling and Wallace Company was in danger of losing their best customer if they didn't make quality changes). Others (IBM Rochester and Motorola, for example) made their decisions without any particular outside pressure to change. The Zytec Corporation (1991), from its beginning in 1984, started out with a focus on quality, service, and value. In every case, however, the CEO and top executives went through a process of careful analysis before making a solid commitment to lead and manage their companies in a different way to become Total Quality organizations.

In his book *I Know It When I See It*, John Guaspari (1985, pp. 26–27) tells the fable of Punctuation, Inc. It begins with the boss's announcement: "Starting today Punctuation, Inc., will produce higher-quality products than anyone else!" He tells his excited workers how this lofty goal will be reached: "Try harder! Do better!" But the workers thought they were already trying their hardest and they wondered, "Do better at what?" Rather than improving quality, the boss's edict hurts morale, creates confusion, and leads to poorer quality. After much difficulty and frustration, Punctuation, Inc., finally finds the road to quality when the boss decides that "management has no other job but to fix the system." (Deming would concur.)

"Fixing the system" usually involves transforming values and expectations—a process much more complex than solving traditional organizational problems. Like the boss in *I Know It When I See It*, most managers know how to deal with problems, but the process of transforming an organizational system into something new is a different ball game, and not an easy one to master. As one wag observed, "Turning a company completely around is not unlike turning a battleship in a small lake." Before launching a TQM effort, therefore, CEOs and their fellow executives find it useful to give careful thought to six key subjects, which we discuss in this chapter:

1. Understanding the dynamics of organizational transformation
2. Assessing your organization's readiness for change
3. Assessing your management team
4. Reviewing your own leadership style
5. Learning from other organizations' experience
6. Getting started

These six factors are discussed largely from the senior management point of view. At the end of the chapter we discuss what a lower-level manager or staff person in a non-TQManaged organization can do to bring TQM to the attention of an organization.

Understanding the Dynamics of Organizational Transformation

Organizations are always changing, especially in today's world of fast-moving technologies, takeovers, "arrangements" of convenience, emerging nationalism, and global competition. To survive, companies are constantly adjusting to the marketplace, public policy, and society. When something goes wrong with a product (before or after introduction), a competitor does the unexpected, or a new environmental regulation is enacted, the organization becomes imbalanced. Management acts to solve the problem and the system is brought back into balance. Changes may have been made in policy, strategy, or operating principles, but basically management has simply restored the organization to the state it was in prior to the problem. That is the usual definition of management's role—adapting to external and internal disruptions quickly and effectively by maintaining stability and confidence in the organization.

Unlike effecting simple change, however, *transforming* an organization into a TQManagement system is more fundamental. It is an active and ongoing process, more like the caterpillar's metamorphosis than a chameleon's color change. Unlike the chameleon, the butterfly will maintain its hue despite new circumstances. What sets transformation apart from a single change, or a series of changes, is continuous movement in which all parts of the organization adjust toward the same end, at the same time. It is important to know that without a plan and people's support, such a comprehensive shift of an organization's culture will almost certainly fail.

Fortunately we all know something about change and the dynamics of the change process. From the moment we are born, our lives are a potpourri of change. We live in a continuing cycle of new experiences and challenges, and of our physical and emotional adjustments to them. We find rest in the periods of stability between the stages of personal growth—plateaus of time in which we catch our breath, digest what has happened, and reassess our situation. Before long we learn that these plateaus can be very comfortable places. When we find one we like, we hold on. Challenges to these "old ways" evoke suspicion and caution. We readily find reasons for resisting such changes, even though they may be presented as logical and, in the long run, beneficial. Managers and researchers have pondered this resistance to change for many years and have developed some useful insights about how it affects organizational behavior.

One basic concept to keep in mind is that organizations

are social *systems*. Like other living organisms they take input from their environment (technology, marketing information, materials); process it, adding value, and deliver output in the form of products or services. Because these systems are made up of interdependent component parts, the shift or adjustment of one part affects all the others. Despite such constant flux, an organization's system is usually able to maintain its balance, but only by expending great amounts of energy.

It is no secret that the frequency of the changes impacting our organizations and the level of energy required to react is intensifying. Peter Vaill (1989) describes it as trying to survive in a "permanent white water society," where there are no quiet pools for recouping energy and perspective. Managing organizations today has become more like playing a basketball game where there are continual rapid adjustments between offensive and defensive strategies. When the offensive team misses a shot it switches to defense, and the defensive team must immediately go on offense. Coaches refer to this as the "transition game," in which the team reads the signs and actions of the opponents and quickly reposition themselves. Each player must be doing his job because a move by one player affects his teammates. A basketball team has much in common with an organizational system of interdependent elements, playing out the rules of cause and effect at a fast pace.

However, most organizational systems are more complex than basketball teams. Transforming an organization's culture requires the manipulation of many elements by forceful and continuous emphasis on new behaviors—totally adjusting the system to prevent its return to equilibrium. A basketball coach may modify the performance of the team during the game by signaling new offenses or defenses with which the players are familiar. However, to completely change the style of play (for example, from a fast-break style to a control game) requires a plan everyone understands, new skills and plays that have been practiced, and enthusiasm for the new style. In the same way, a substantial organizational change may require groups and individuals to abandon the experience, beliefs, and values that have guided their careers for many years, replacing them with values and beliefs that are as yet untested. One veteran of both the U.S. Army Airborne and Total Quality implementation quipped, "Parachuting may be the strategically correct thing to do, but *jumping out of a perfectly good airplane didn't always seem to make sense.* It was the same with Total Quality."

David Nadler, a quality consultant to such corporations as AT&T, Citicorp, Corning, Xerox, and GTE, champions an approach to managing organizational behavior and change based on general systems theory. The congruence model of organizational behavior shown in Figure 4.1 (Heilpern and Nadler, 1990) offers a pragmatic approach to understanding how organizations function that can be helpful in assessing an organization's readiness for change. It shows that a system's input falls into three categories: *environment*, which supplies a variety of limitations, requirements, and opportunities; the *resources* available to the organization; and the organization's *history* or experience. The match of resources to the environment's limitations, requirements, and opportunities, viewed through the eyes of an organization's history, shapes the *strategy*. The purpose of an organization is to transform that strategy into the activities and patterns of performance that will accomplish their *outputs*.

To accomplish the permutation from strategy to outputs, an organization depends upon four factors: (1) the *work*, or tasks, to be accomplished; (2) the *people* who perform the tasks; (3) the structures, systems, and processes an organization creates to aid people in doing the work, known as the *formal arrangements*; and (4) the *informal structures and processes* — the values, beliefs, organizational culture, and management styles that have evolved over time. An organization is at its most effective when these four components and the output are consistent with one another, or congruent with the goals of the strategy. This happens when the performance of the operating groups and individuals that make up the organization are in sync. As any experienced manager knows, this is easier said than done, but with the congruence model, management can assess the balance in their organization's behavior and evaluate how it might resist efforts to change. In struggling to stay in balance, an organization's system, like water, will seek its natural level and in

Figure 4.1. The Transformational Process—A Congruence Model of Organizational Behavior.

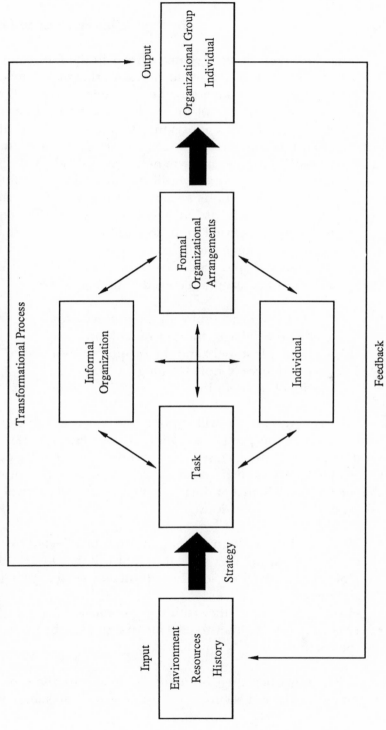

Source: Heilpern and Nadler, 1990, p. 185. Used by permission.

so doing cancel out isolated change efforts in the four components. Just knowing this is valuable in considering the content of
a TQM strategy. Said another way, the congruence model allows
managers a sort of blueprint for reading the relationship between their strategy and the organization's tasks, people, and
formal and informal processes. Managers are thus able to diagnose how transition initiatives will be received. Understanding
that a successful quality strategy will require addressing all the
elements of an organization's system is an important first step
that too many quality efforts in this country have failed to take.

   Anyone who has tried to make significant changes in an
organization knows that it is a difficult task. Because changes are
disruptive, many people naturally resist them. Some of the
factors that must be taken into consideration are these:

- The level of dissatisfaction with the present situation
- The cost of the change (short-term and long-term)
- How well people understand the proposed "future state"
- The consequences of not changing
- The clarity of the path for changing

   In general, people will support a change if (1) they are
convinced that the present situation is not desirable; (2) the
proposed "future" is clear, sensible, and desirable; (3) the path
toward the future is clear and realistic; and (4) the cost of the
change is not too high. For the planning executive, this involves
asking four critical questions:

- How will the people in the organization be affected by the
  change? What will they gain and what will they lose?
- How clearly do they see the advantages of the changed
  situation?
- How dissatisfied are they with the present situation?
- How prepared are they to take the first steps to bring about
  the change?

   Resistance to change is a natural human response. Most of
us want stability and security. The unknown creates anxieties

and an almost knee-jerk response of resistance. Change, especially change that is imposed, reduces our sense of control and autonomy and destabilizes our customary coping behaviors. Sometimes we resist change because it seems illogical (like parachuting from a perfectly good airplane), and sometimes we truly believe the old way is the right way and resist on philosophical grounds.

Change also affects organizational control, disrupting the normal course of events and undermining existing systems of management and control. As expectations, structures, and roles shift, it becomes increasingly difficult to monitor performance and make adjustments. Formal organizational arrangements are usually structured for stable conditions. Too often managers visualize the outcome of change, assume one simple step from today's organization, and fail to attend to the *process* of change. Because they see the change as movement from one steady state to another, they rely upon management systems that were designed for an organization *in place* and actually increase the difficulties for an organization in transition.

Then there is the matter of power. Organizations are political systems made up of individuals, groups, and coalitions competing for power. Political behavior is both natural and expected in any organization, but during periods of transition these dynamics become more intense because change upsets the balance of power among groups. The uncertainty of change creates ambiguity, which tends to increase political activity. Individuals and groups take action based on what they expect to happen to their power once the change has been fully implemented. It is only natural to try to influence power outcomes to maintain or increase one's position in the new order of things.

Although change is seldom made easily, it can be perceived by some as an opportunity — a chance to contribute and be recognized. That is the prescription for Total Quality: *Make quality an opportunity for people and reward them for it.* The key to a successful change lies in understanding expectations and engaging people in the process. In the most successful work-improvement efforts, a shared cultural objective will enhance both business performance and the quality of the human experience.

Now let's be more specific.

Assessing Your Organization's Readiness for Change

One of the most frequently expressed reactions to the Baldrige Award process in the business world and the President's Award process in the federal government has been: "It gave us the occasion to look at our organization in a systematic way." We will discuss the specific criteria of these two awards in Chapter Twelve, but we would like to suggest here some useful questions to ask about your organization and its readiness to become a Total Quality organization.

We believe that the two most basic questions for any organization are:

- What is our mission?
- Who are our customers?

Someone has said, "If you don't know where you're going, it makes no difference what road you take." And if you don't know who you're trying to serve, how can you ever find out whether you're doing a good job? It is surprising how many organizations lack a clear mission that is understood by everyone. We are reminded of the ancient story of the traveler who asked three masons, "What are you doing?" The first answered, "I'm laying stones." The second said, "I'm earning a living." The third replied, "I'm helping to build a cathedral!" Since quality is defined as "meeting the customer's needs," it is critically important that we know who those customers are and how they use whatever we produce. How would their lives be different if we weren't around?

If you are clear about your mission, other key questions come into focus:

- Who are the stakeholders in our organization—the people who are affected by what we do and who have an impact upon us?

- What are our strengths? (What do we brag about?)
- What are our weaknesses? (And how do we deal with them?)
- Who are our competitors? (What do they do better?)
- What kind of an organization do we hope to become?

In turbulent times like these, it is essential that we have a clear sense of our own identity. The bottom line only keeps score; it does not define what we do. The TQManagement organization is clear on what it is trying to do, and on what is helping and blocking its progress. It is a challenge for any organization just to keep strategies and goals in line, without even considering a major intervention like TQManagement. To completely alter, or dramatically adjust, the strategy and output of an organization requires more than a mere decree. It demands a clear understanding of where all the elements are in relation to the organization's current outputs (its *current state*) and a careful definition of where the organization is to move (its *future* or *desired state*) (Beckhard and Harris, 1977). To do this requires knowing what you want to create in the new organization. Since every decision and action an organization takes shapes its character, understanding clearly the future shape of the enterprise will indicate the kind and scope of changes required. Management will have to answer certain questions: What kind of enterprise will we be? What is our mission? How will our organization be structured? What will be its philosophy? How is it going to operate? What will be its strategy? Asking these questions begins to expose the vision of what management is trying to formulate. And because the current organization must be managed while it is being transformed, management will have to have a clear picture of the dynamics of the organization itself.

Creating an organization that's going to be more viable in the next five to ten years poses a new set of responsibilities, not only for managers, but for everyone in the organization. Everyone is expected to both make the current organization perform effectively and help turn it into something that will be more effective in the future (Delta Consulting Group, 1988a). It is useful to bear in mind that there are three key elements in the change process that must be understood and managed:

- The present state
- The transition
- The future (desired) state

The effective management of change involves (1) understanding the present state, (2) creating an image of the desired state, and (3) developing a strategy for making the change. After the initial diagnosis is completed, management's most challenging creative task is to state what will be done differently in the future. Here is where members of the senior management team have an opportunity to discuss their vision of the enterprise's mission. This vision may range from a set of principles or values to detailed papers outlining specific outputs, operating styles, and organizational structures. At a minimum it should address the question of values as well as performance. Because some companies have failed to take this step, their quality improvement campaigns have resulted in no significant change. Heilpern and Nadler (1990, p. 186) have developed five implications of TQM, which require the design and implementation of several initiatives that affect all components of the organization:

1. A change in strategy—in the definition of who we are and what we provide, as well as in the basis for being competitive
2. A change in the work—in what's important about the work and what the core requirements are for performing it
3. A change in people—in their roles, skills, capacities, and behavior
4. A change in organizational arrangements—in objectives, measures, structures, systems, training, and rewards
5. A change in the informal organization—in the beliefs, values, and assumptions that influence much of the day-to-day behavior that we see

Total Quality presents some new philosophical notions about the nature of work and how we go about the process of creating more effective organizations. One key element centers around the notion of *empowerment*. To truly empower people — enable them to make decisions based on their collective judgment and to solve problems — they must be given the capacity for action. This is not an abdication of management's responsibility, but the transfer of authority from one level or function down to another level or function. Employees are trained and coached to focus their attention on their outputs and customers. They are given the authority to stabilize and improve work processes and quantify the results. For most organizations this means a significant change in culture. In the Zytec Corporation (1991), for example, any employee can spend up to $1,000 to resolve a customer complaint without prior authority, hourly workers can make process changes with the agreement of only one other person, and salespeople are authorized to travel whenever they feel it is necessary for customer service.

Fortunately, the direction of the organizational change to TQManagement is one that makes sense to most people (although employees will sometimes test to see whether their empowerment is really solid). The three most commonly identified tasks are these:

1. To move *from* a vague understanding of customer requirements *to* a step-by-step approach to knowing and satisfying them
2. To make a transition *from* tolerating a certain margin of error followed by corrective action *to* a workplace where all employees strive to do things right the first time
3. To move *from* an environment where problem solving and decision making are done individually *to* one in which teams of people tackle problems and make decisions based on fact in a logical and consistent manner

Even though few would disagree with these changes, executives who would like to transform their organizations into Total Quality organizations should undertake the change with their eyes open, understanding that change is always a complex process and that it is likely to meet with some resistance. However, it can also mobilize new energy and commitment if it is undertaken in a thoughtful way!

Assessing Your Management Team

A second set of questions deals with your managers. These are the key players on whom you depend to forward the right messages and to exemplify the behavior that shapes the culture of your organization. Questions to ask include:

- How would you rate the competence of your managers?
- What is their level of commitment to the organization and its mission?
- How easily do they adjust to change?
- How willing would they be to explore new ways of managing?
- How receptive are they to receiving training?
- How well are they working together now, and what obstacles would have to be overcome for them to work together better?
- How would you describe the way they deal with their people?

The success of TQManagement depends on the wholehearted support, commitment, and teamwork of the management group. This is not a short-time effort that can be finessed by managers who are not really in agreement with the changes. The changes are too fundamental. The manager who does not trust his employees will not feel comfortable empowering them. The manager who is highly competitive will find it hard to work on a team with her colleagues. The key question is probably: "Are my managers open to change?"

The answers to these questions will give you a realistic picture of the support or resistance you can expect in launching TQManagement in your organization. It will also give you clues about who should be involved at different points and what roles they can best play in the conceptualizing, planning, and implementing processes. These are the colleagues you will need to help define the shape of the new organizational culture, to communicate it to their subordinates, and particularly to live it! For one thing, managers can help in *developing the support of key power groups.* Some groups of people may support the organization's changes based on their personal values and will require no attention; however, others are certain to oppose the new ways, no matter what they may be. Managers need to engage these people in the process and to take steps to negate the effects of their resistance. Fortunately, managers usually know who the key power groups are and can help develop a strategy for each group.

Subordinates may listen to what their boss tells them about finding better ways to serve customers, but they will *watch* what she does with their suggestions. They will hear the manager's words about empowerment, but they will *watch* how he reacts when they make an on-the-spot judgment call to meet some unexpected customer complaint. A management team's most powerful action is their *behavior that generates energy in support of the change*—the way they mobilize groups, create enthusiasm, and act as role models in support of the transition. Every Baldrige winner we have interviewed has mentioned the importance of executives and managers at every level "walking their talk."

A considerable body of evidence shows that employees treat customers the way their boss treats them. An employee who does not trust his boss will not take risks. An employee who has been disciplined by a surly boss will not put on a cheery smile for a customer. In its TQManagement effort, the city of Austin, Texas, stresses the importance of the "moments of truth" (those times when an employee is face-to-face with a customer) because a manager is not usually present when a front-line city employee is interacting with a citizen, *but the manager's influence is present.* And that's when the citizens of Austin form their impression of their city's government.

You will be counting on your managers to understand, communicate, and model the changes required by TQManagement. This means that they must be trainable. In some cases it may mean drastically changing their style of dealing with subordinates. Insecure managers who use their authority to keep their staff under control will have to learn how to coach. The managers who enjoy the power of decision making will have to learn to pass some of that responsibility on to their subordinates. Managers who pride themselves on being independent, decisive thinkers will have to learn the skills of teamwork and group decision making.

Your managers will also have a key role in *building stability* in the organization as it changes. An overload of uncertainty will cause some people to become defensive and resistant. Your managers will be central in providing the "anchors" people hold on to in order to maintain their identities and balance in the midst of turbulence. It will be a major responsibility of management to communicate and exemplify this stability.

Reviewing Your Own Leadership Style

A third set of questions is about you—the executive who would like to build a TQManagement culture. Your commitment must be clear and solid or you're headed for trouble. TQManagement is not a program that can be launched and then delegated to a subordinate. A major change effort can succeed only if the top person provides visible and consistent leadership. People throughout the organization will watch the CEO to get their clue as to the seriousness of the effort. They will not just listen to speeches and read articles in the organization's newsletter; they will watch how the boss spends time, gives rewards and recognition, takes risks, and exemplifies the principles she is advocating. Here is where actions speak louder than words—in spades!

Throughout the chapters that follow, we will be reporting some of the key actions CEOs took to launch and guide the TQManagement effort in their organizations. Your commitment must be real, or the enterprise will fail. Your colleagues will take their cue from you. To assess your commitment, you may want to reflect on these questions:

- What are my motives for considering this TQM effort?
- What am I willing to risk or give up to build a TQM organization?
- What is there about TQM that most excites me? (And can we achieve it without launching a TQM effort?)

- How comfortable will I feel "selling" TQM to my colleagues?
- How have I dealt with long-term commitments in the past?
- Am I willing to invest for a long time in the hope of a long-term return?
- How comfortable do I feel releasing authority and power to others? (Will I set the right example?)
- How will I deal with those who unrealistically expect quick returns on a high investment in training and experimentation?
- How comfortable will I be in a learning role — and seen by others as a learner?
- How well do I handle ambiguity and uncertainty?
- Am I willing to change my style of management if that is required to make TQM work?

As CEO you will be expected to exemplify Total Quality principles consistently and permanently. You cannot expect others to delegate and empower if you do not. You cannot count on others to view mistakes as opportunities for learning if you try to minimize your own misjudgments. You cannot look for others to take risks if you play it safe yourself. The time to clarify your own strengths, weaknesses, and personal flexibility is *before* you launch your organization in the direction of Total Quality. Nadler (1988, p. 20) has found that the principal reason for failure is a lack of appreciation by the CEO of the complexity, intensity, and gravity of the challenge: "When a CEO introduces a quality 'program' that falls short it is because he has failed to recognize that quality is not an event, not a decision, not a single action, and not a program with a start and finish. Quality is a commitment to a fundamental change in how the organization (and ultimately the CEO and his own senior management team) works, and that type of change doesn't occur by declaration or command."

The first action to motivate the change is *identifying and surfacing dissatisfaction with the current state.* The more satisfied people are with the current state, the greater their desire to keep it. The greater the pain and dissatisfaction with the current state, the greater the willingness to turn over a new leaf, and thus the less resistance. Most organizations considering Total Quality already are dissatisfied with their current state because of decreasing market share, reduced sales and revenues, and resulting manpower reductions. How well people understand such facts might well determine their levels of resistance or support. (Before launching its productivity and quality program, Westinghouse took a group of union leaders on a tour of Japanese plants to give them a better understanding of the competition they would be facing.)

A second action is *building participation into the change process*. Participation in the transition reduces the resistance, builds ownership, and motivates people to make the transformation work. It increases communication about the transition and the goals, as well as leading to a new source of information about the process that may well enhance the effectiveness of the future state. Of course, participation also entails relinquishing control, requires time and patience, and may create conflict. It will certainly involve situational diagnosis, planning, and feedback from all levels of the organization.

The third action step is *building in rewards for behavior in support of the change*. These should include both formal and informal rewards and recognition for the behaviors that are desired during both the transition and future states. In addition to using processes that affirm the transition, it is important to revisit the reward systems that exist in the current state to remove incentives for old (and often undesirable) behavior.

People will need time and opportunity to *disengage from the present state*. The feelings associated with the loss of the "good old days" are not unlike those associated with death. Nostalgia for the old way of doing things is a form of mourning, and management is wise not to be offended by the tales and myths of the past (even though the past may not have been so good) and to allow time for people to accept the fact that a new way is coming.

The CEO who can visualize the tasks and challenges involved in installing TQM must assess whether he and his colleagues are prepared to provide the leadership for this process.

Learning from Other Organizations' Experience

No one can be certain what any major organizational change will bring. Even the most carefully designed venture has unintended consequences. Fortunately, however, there is now a rapidly developing body of knowledge and experience dealing with TQManagement in both the private and public sectors. There are three ways you can tap into this experience: (1) by learning directly from executives and managers who have successfully guided their own organizations into TQManagement, (2) by reading the growing body of TQManagement literature, or (3) by engaging a consultant who has helped other organizations to make the change to Total Quality. Let us comment about each of these:

- Fortunately, those companies that have been successful in TQManagement—led by the Baldrige Award winners—are very willing to share their experience. Some of them present day-long seminars every week to describe what techniques have worked for them and what they have learned about TQManagement. (Contact persons and addresses of Baldrige Award winners are listed in Resource B of this book.) We can tell you from personal experience that these seminars are conducted in a first-class, professional manner.
- The growing TQManagement literature now includes a variety of books and journals. These publications are rich with concepts, experience, tools, and tips. (See the Annotated Bibliography.)
- The right consultant or consulting team can shorten the start-up and learning time considerably. The Federal Quality Institute (FQI) maintains a roster of consulting groups whose credentials have been examined carefully. (The FQI address is included in Resource B.)

Getting Started

After you and your key colleagues have done some of the soul-searching and taken the steps outlined above, you should be in a good position to make an informed decision to launch TQManagement in your organization. If you have visited a Baldrige winner you will have gained many new insights, and you will probably be enthusiastic about getting started. You are now ready to put into place the first piece of Total Quality –organization machinery: a top-level management team to plan and monitor the Total Quality effort. At Xerox they called it the Quality Improvement Team. Marlow Industries formed a TQM Quality Council. At Wallace Company CEO John W. Wallace headed a five-person Quality Management Steering Committee. And Milliken & Company named their key group the Policy Committee and Quality Council. The first task of this top team is to develop an overall strategy for initiating and managing the transition. In addition to the actions already noted, there are five key action steps the top team will need to consider (Delta Consulting Group, 1988a, pp. 9–11). A fuller discussion of these is presented in Chapter Five.

1. Develop and Communicate a Clear Image of the Future

This will serve as a guideline or goal of what is expected. A written statement or description will be valuable in clarifying the image and will serve in communicating the new direction to people. Communication of expectations should be accomplished both in written form and in group meetings (team and larger). It should be a prominent part of the organization's usual communication vehicles. In addition to letting people know what is expected, this will help to quell rumors, misconceptions, and the fantasies people sometimes act upon.

2. Use Multiple and Consistent Leverage Points

Structural changes, task changes, and changes in environment are all needed to effect the transition. These will include training, intervention to facilitate group behaviors, new structures, personnel changes, and perhaps organizational mergers. Whatever changes are planned, it is important to assure that they dovetail with other support changes, such as reward systems, reporting relationships, and job descriptions.

3. Use Symbols and Language to Create Energy

Symbols have tremendous emotional impact to create new power centers or bring together existing power centers under a common banner — witness the power of yellow ribbons and "Desert Shield" and "Desert Storm" pins and bumper stickers to mobilize public opinion. Xerox became "Team Xerox," Ford's "Quality Is Job One" TV slogan reaches employees and customers alike, and "Six Sigma" and Motorola have become synonymous. Language is most important both in creating common communication and in making the ambiguous real.

4. Make Organizational Arrangements for the Transition

These will vary by organization, but the following should be considered:

- *Designate a transition manager:* A senior manager should be responsible for making the transition happen — a person senior enough and respected enough to have linkage with the steady-state managers and those with a vision of the future.
- *Allocate resources for the transition:* Transitions in large organizations involve potential risk and therefore deserve to be done well. This means providing the transition manager with the personnel, training, time, money, and expertise (including consultative expertise) to get the job done.
- *Develop a transition plan:* Without a destination, almost any road will get you where you are going. However, when your destination is a clearly understood future state, you'll need a road map to make sure you arrive where you want, when you want. Such a transition road map should consist of specific objectives, benchmarks and measures, standards of performance, and roles and responsibilities for key persons and groups.

- *Create transition management structures:* It is difficult, if not impossible, for the hierarchy of an organization to manage the current state, plan for the future state, and control the transition simultaneously. It will almost certainly be necessary to use structures and processes outside the usual management process, such as task forces, pilot projects, internal and external consultants and specialists, and experimental units to support the transition initiatives.

5. Develop Feedback Mechanisms

Feedback mechanisms provide information on the effectiveness of the transition. Too often senior management orders changes and presumes they will be carried out, only to discover later that this direction has been ignored. It is important for transition managers to develop multiple, redundant, and sensitive mechanisms for gathering feedback about the transition. Some devices that could be used are surveys, focus groups, and consultant interviews, as well as the organization's customary communication channels, such as open doors and suggestion systems.

Once all the implications are understood, the next step is to develop the plan for the transition — the strategy for becoming a TQManagement organization. How will we know if our planning assumptions were correct? What are good measurement criteria for considering the effectiveness of the transition state's outcomes? Here are the signs of a successful change (Nadler, 1988):

- The organization is moved from the current state to the future state.
- The functioning of the organization in the future state meets expectations — that is, it works as planned.
- The transition is accomplished without undue cost to the organization.
- The transition is accomplished without undue cost to individuals.

The bottom line is simply that a CEO should not undertake a major organizational change like TQM without doing a great deal of soul-searching and diagnosing of the organization to be changed. To succeed, this change will involve risk and a high commitment of the CEO's time, energy, and resources. This investment must be weighed against the cost of continuing with "business as usual." But if you decide to move forward, there is much executive and consultant experience available to help you. The next part of this book will describe in more detail a systematic way to proceed.

If You're Not the CEO

A CEO who decides to make a major change toward quality is in a position to mobilize considerable support—brainpower, finances, and communication. But what can middle managers do—those who head a single division or department? Although Total Quality is generally conceived of as applying to a total organization, some of its features have been inserted with considerable success by managers whose organizations are operating in a pre-TQM manner. (The Quality Revolution has not touched most organizations yet, so these managers are still in the vanguard.) Here are some examples of individual efforts to create quality departments in larger organizations that operate in a traditional manner:

- The Communications Sector provided the quality role model for much of Motorola's success (Smith, 1989). Although Motorola had established quality improvement as a goal in 1981, it was the success of their Communications Sector with Total Defects per Unit as a quality goal and management process that led to Motorola's "Six Steps to Six Sigma" process.
- IBM also had an overall focus on quality since the early 1980s, but it was the example of IBM Rochester that has led the way. The Rochester (Minnesota) plant began in 1981 with a set of initiatives called PRIDE (People, Responsibly Involved in Developing Excellence) that focused on improving product reliability. They expanded this in 1984 with a focus shift from product to process efficiency, and in 1986

they moved from manufacturing-cycle time to development-cycle improvement. In 1989 (the year before they won the Baldrige Award) they established market-driven customer satisfaction goals taken from IBM Corporation's Quality Principles. Today the Rochester plant is IBM's benchmark for TQManagement (IBM Rochester, 1991).

- At Westinghouse, the Commercial Nuclear Fuel Division (Westinghouse Corporation, 1989b) led the way in recognizing that quality could give them a competitive edge in the marketplace. They published their first quality plan in 1983 and by 1985 a division-wide quality goal was published and a quantitative measurement system monitoring progress was implemented.

As a middle manager interested in bringing TQManagement to your part of the organization, you will want to review the same issues we have suggested for the CEO. You should also become as fully informed as possible about TQManagement and how it is working in various organizations. The Quality and Productivity Management Association and other organizations listed in Resource B of this book conduct conferences throughout the country where managers report on their innovations and experiences.

Like a CEO, your first task is to analyze your own situation. You need to know particularly who your customer is—who gets the products or services that your department provides? How well do you know this customer? How up-to-date are you on the customer's needs? How well are you meeting those needs—and what is the basis for your information? These questions are important whether the customer is outside or inside your organization.

You also will want to know more about your suppliers, the internal or external groups that provide your department with the information, supplies, equipment, or services you need to do your job. How are your relations with them? How much influence do you have, and is there a way of increasing that influence? Do they understand your needs? Can you develop a process by which those needs are kept up-to-date? How can you make them better partners?

The general thrust of your strategy should be to assess how much of your environment you can control or influence. How are your relations with your bosses? What is their general reaction to change and innovation? How fully do you enjoy their confidence? Do they understand what the nature of your job is— and are you agreed on what kind of performance they expect from your department?

Like a CEO, you will be in a much stronger position to initiate a new approach if you have first gotten together with colleagues to explore ideas and possibilities. If you decide to go forward with TQManagement in your department, you'll find the next chapters to be very useful.

If You're a Staff Person

There have been occasions when a CEO or key manager has called in a training director or organization development specialist to take the lead in launching a new program. He may have read about Total Quality and the Baldrige Award and decided: "We should go for that in our organization." Then, like an experienced executive, he delegates the job—to you!

You know from all that you have read that TQManagement is one process that cannot be launched from a staff position. It requires the wholehearted commitment of top management. Your task now becomes one of helping the leadership of your organization to understand what TQM is all about and to come to grips with the questions presented earlier in this chapter. Beware of overselling TQManagement or minimizing its requirements! Remember that this is a process that does not have an immediate payoff; it is intended for long-term results. Probably the best advice you can give to your top management is to contact Baldrige or President's Award winners to learn first-hand about their experience.

Key Actions to Consider in Planning

Throughout this chapter we have highlighted key action steps that anyone interested in TQManagement will have to consider in developing a plan. The size of the task will be based on an evaluation of the organization's readiness for change, the management team's capability to meet the challenge, the CEO's management style, and an assessment of what is needed in order to begin. This assessment is summarized in your organization's readiness to take twelve actions (Delta Consulting Group, 1988b):

1. Assure the support of key power groups.
2. Use leader behavior to generate energy in support of the change.
3. Use symbols and language.
4. Build in stability.
5. Surface dissatisfaction with the present state.
6. Participate in the change.
7. Supply rewards for behavior in support of the change.
8. Allow time and opportunity to disengage from the present state.
9. Develop and communicate a clear image of the future.
10. Use multiple and consistent leverage points.
11. Develop organizational arrangements for the transition.
12. Build in feedback mechanisms.

The evidence on the effectiveness of TQManagement that we have seen has been positive and impressive. So has a study by the U.S. General Accounting Office (1991), which reviewed twenty companies that were among the highest-scoring applicants for the Baldrige Award in 1988 and 1989. This study concluded: "Companies that adopted quality management practices experienced overall improvement in corporate performance. In nearly all cases, companies that used total quality management practices achieved better employee relations, higher productivity, greater customer satisfaction, increased market share, and improved profitability."

These are powerful and persuasive findings. It is easy to understand why some executives, organizations, and consultants have developed an almost missionary-like zeal to spread the word about Total Quality. But before "signing-up," it is critically important that key executives make a careful assessment of their own organization's need and readiness to undertake this long-term adventure of transformation.

The next chapters describe the strategies and key factors that have proved helpful in making the desired changes happen.

PART TWO

ENTERING THE RACE: STRATEGIES THAT WORK

Here we get more specific. We first discuss the problems and strategies of bringing about organizational change. We then describe how to lay the leadership foundation and use the five strategies that will support a TQManagement structure. The tools and techniques presented in these pages have proved to be effective in all the quality organizations we have studied, including the winners of the Baldrige National Quality Award and the President's Award for Productivity and Quality.

In Chapter Five we point up the importance of developing an overall strategy and show ways to deal with the problems that confront anyone attempting to change an organization's culture and method of operation.

In Chapter Six we discuss the kind of leadership required by a quality organization.

Chapter Seven describes Strategy No. 1 — creating the organizational machinery to initiate, monitor, and develop the Total Quality organization.

In Chapter Eight we deal with Strategy No. 2 — the tools and processes of TQManagement and how to use them.

Chapter Nine focuses on Strategy No. 3 — the education and training programs that equip managers and workers to handle their new TQManagement responsibilities.

In Chapter Ten we discuss Strategy No. 4 — the all-important recognition and reward strategies that will support the motivation of managers and workers to practice a philosophy of continuous improvement.

Chapter Eleven deals with the centrally important Strategy No. 5 — the communication system that keeps every member of the organization informed and involved with colleagues in accomplishing the purposes of the organization.

We have tried in this part to be specific enough to enable the reader to visualize the total process without presenting a cookbook of specific details. The key ideas are presented with examples from organizations where they have worked.

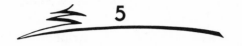

5

Planning for Change: Developing the Requirements

The best way to predict the future is to invent it.
— Alan Kay

Once senior management has completed a careful assessment of the organization's need and readiness to start the quality journey and has (1) established the future state it desires, (2) assessed its current state and the elements of the organization's system, and (3) identified the implications and action steps appropriate for making the transition to a Total Quality environment, their task is to translate those action steps into an implementation strategy. In this chapter we will discuss the prerequisites for developing a successful Total Quality strategy and give a rationale for the key factors that we found the Baldrige winners included in their implementation plans. We will explain why the development of a successful strategy is contingent on the level of senior management commitment and we will also discuss the process of choosing where the Total Quality emphasis should be placed. For some the greatest emphasis is placed on *statistical tools* and their application, while for others *changing behavior* is the paramount issue. We will identify some of the psychological challenges and benefits of launching a TQManagement effort, and we will explain why no Total Quality strategy will work without active employee involvement and a strong implementation plan. We will also explain why a good strategy must accommodate the different stages individuals and organizations pass through during the transition to Total Quality.

Quality as the First Business Principle

We cannot repeat too often that for quality to happen, a Total Quality strategy must begin at the top, with the commitment and leadership of the CEO and the organization's senior management committee or council. From the very beginning, every Baldrige winner's management showed its commitment to transforming the organization, communicating the quality objectives, and soliciting employee participation. One of the first steps was to create and publish a corporate quality statement to highlight quality as the organization's basic operating principle. The kind of policy we suggest avoids "round" words and does not delegate responsibility for quality. It is just the opposite—a straightforward, unambiguous commitment to establish a customer-driven management process. It does this by defining expectations that are realistic, measurable, and attainable for every job. It answers the questions that Warren Bennis (1976) asked in *The Unconscious Conspiracy:* How clear is the metaphor? How is it understood? How much energy are you devoting to it?

At Motorola (1987), Chairman Robert Galvin and his vice-chairs, CEO, and chief operating officer signed their names to this corporate quality policy:

> Dedication to quality is a way of life at our company, so much so that it goes far beyond rhetorical slogans. Our ongoing program of continued improvement reaches out for change, refinement and even revolution in our pursuit of quality excellence.
>
> It is the objective of Motorola, Inc., to produce and provide products and services of the highest quality. In its activities, Motorola will pursue goals aimed at the achievement of quality excel-

lence. These results will be derived from the dedicated efforts of each employee in conjunction with
supportive participation from management at all
levels of the corporation.

Xerox's (1983, p. 2) quality policy was written by the CEO,
David Kearns, and his senior management team, including the
operating heads of every major Xerox operation worldwide.
Their statement leaves no doubt where Xerox stands and what
management expects:

Xerox is a quality company. Quality is the basic
business principle for Xerox. Quality means
providing our external and internal customers with
innovative products and services that fully satisfy
their requirements. Quality improvement is the job
of every Xerox employee.

Both policies are clear, far-reaching in scope, and obviously no ordinary pronouncements from on high. Both herald
three significant new messages:

1. Customer satisfaction is the paramount concern.
2. Certain basic assumptions are made: management does not
    have all the answers; employees have ideas about how their
    work can be done more effectively; and employees are will-
    ing, even eager, to participate in developing solutions to
    business problems.
3. The intent is to fundamentally transform company culture.
    (For this reason alone, quality is the most significant strat-
    egy these organizations have ever embarked upon.)

Cultural Transformation — A Revolution

It would be nice if an organization were simply a big Lego toy so
its shape and form could be changed whenever we wished. But
organizations are made up of people, not Lego pieces, and the
task of transforming the behavior of the groups and individuals

who comprise an organization is not easy. As we described in
Chapter Four, changing an organization's culture requires (1) a
clear description of what will be expected once the desired, or
future state, has been reached and, of course, (2) implementing a
plan to bridge the gap from the current state.

All of the Baldrige winners had to ask the question, "What
will the future state look like after the transition to Total Quality
is completed?" An organization's answer will depend on what is
desired, the level of management's aspirations, and the needs of
the organization's customers. For most organizations the following are sanguine expectations:

- A business that consistently uses an incremental approach
  to knowing and satisfying a customer's requirements
- A workplace where *all* employees try to do things consistently right the first time
- An environment in which teams address problems and
  make decisions based on fact, in a logical and consistent
  manner

The main driver of TQManagement is employees focusing on their customers and work outputs. This is done by
empowering them to stabilize and improve work processes and by
giving them the tools to measure progress. For most organizations this means a total transformation of their work culture.

Management faces change every day, just to keep the
organization in balance. Viable organizations are sensitive to
the marketplace and public policy influences. Fortunately, this
sort of Darwinian process does, over time, cause some movement, because without adjustment the organization would be
overwhelmed by outside forces. However, as Peters and Waterman (1982, p. 15) noted in *In Search of Excellence*, "The evolutionary model does not support the occurrence of big leaps without
requiring . . . an all-knowing God or prescient planning." Given
our limited influence, we come down on the side of prescient
planning.

The Motorola policy describes the pursuit of quality as a
revolution. History teaches that revolutions are usually

launched by zealots who gather to themselves others who support their cause. They most often succeed by capturing and influencing six key elements of society. It is the same with TQManagement:

1. To bring about their vision for a new society, revolutionaries strive to control the laws and regulations that influence behavior. In TQManagement expectations are defined by the standards and measures employees use; these are the *tools and processes*.

2. Because there is power in money, revolutionaries who wish a new order will capture and use the banks and economic infrastructure to support their objective. So too the CEO who wants to effect change will use the organization's *recognition and reward systems* to facilitate the transition to Total Quality.

3. No self-respecting revolutionary would undertake the task of transforming a country without controlling the mass media to ensure that the new messages are heard by all. Similarly, the transition to Total Quality requires that *communication* plans and vehicles be engaged to carry the good news of quality.

4. Since many new ideas are developed and fostered in universities and schools, popular revolutions quickly harness these learning institutions and forums to spread the new way of thinking and ensure that newcomers understand what is expected of them. If employees do not understand the concepts, processes, and tools of Total Quality there is no hope of succeeding; this is why *educational programs* are such a key ingredient of any transition plan.

5. Of course the leaders of a revolution must themselves speak and practice the new gospel because without the support of leaders from top to bottom, no revolution can succeed. No single factor in a Total Quality strategy is more critical than is *management leadership and commitment*.

6. Finally, to help the revolution take root, there must be a junta, or revolutionary council, to implement the new plan—a select cadre of experts who fully understand the future state, are nearly fanatical in their quest, and are willing to oversee the other five objectives. TQManagement is not business as usual, and the transition process requires an infrastructure of experts

who can guide, cajole, and reinforce the objectives like military drill instructors. In TQManagement planning we refer to this as *organizational structures and roles.*

In summary, the transformation to TQManagement will not succeed without attention to these six strategic initiatives:

1. Management leadership and commitment
2. Supportive organizational structures and roles
3. Tools and processes
4. Educational programs
5. Reward strategies
6. Complete and regular communication

Statistics Versus Behavioral Change

The history of Total Quality in America has often focused on design specifications, manufacturing processes, and statistical tools, rather than on an organization's total management process and employee behavior. Quality professionals and associations have dealt mainly with the mechanical side of quality. We fully agree that no organization aspiring to TQManagement can survive without TQM's analytical and statistical tools and techniques. But our studies show that attention must also be given to the human side of the organization—the psychological and behavioral dimension. A CEO we know has said, "The soft stuff is the hard stuff."

All twelve Baldrige winners recognized the behavioral side of the quality issue: communicating the strategy and objectives, rallying people to the quality banner, and monitoring the required behavior. They recognized a simple fact—*people* make quality happen! Jeffrey Heilpern, managing director of the Delta Consulting Group, wrote in *The Quality Executive,* "We have come to the conclusion that the major barriers to quality superiority are not technical, they are behavioral" (Heilpern, 1989).

Walton (1986) reports Deming as saying that point 2 of his fourteen points "really means in my mind a transformation of management. Structures have been put in place in management that will have to be dismantled. They have not been suitable for two decades. They never were right, but in an expanding market you couldn't lose. The weaknesses showed up when competition came up."

Having realized that a successful TQManagement effort must recognize *both* the tools and processes of quality *and* the people who use them, successful TQM leaders assessed their organization's areas of strength and need in both areas. Employee actions need to coexist with processes and tools to form a comprehensive strategy. Since people tend to play to their own strengths and experiences, it may be necessary to allow one side of the equation to outweigh the other during the early stages of implementation.

Joiner (1988, p. 33) says, "You can't push statistics into an organization. You must work to create a pull for it. To create a pull for it, you have got to understand what other people's problems are and figure out how you can help them be more effective in doing their jobs well."

While the objective is to advance all of the six objectives of a TQManagement strategy, we have found that some companies, because of their unique culture, conclude that emphasis and discipline are best placed on the statistical side during the early stages. Other companies have seen that old values were so entrenched in their organization that much more attention to behavioral issues was required to move the organization toward the ultimate goal of Total Quality.

In 1981 Motorola (Smith, 1989, pp. 4–5) established "improvement of quality by ten times by 1986" as one of their Top Ten Corporate Goals, admitting at the time, "We don't know how to achieve such an ambitious goal." However, in 1986 their Communications Sector adopted a uniform metric— "Total Defects per Unit." Using this standard, the improvement rate achieved by the Communications Sector was much greater than had been possible in the "ten times" program; in 1987 Motorola revised their Total Quality effort (Management of the Quality Improvement Process) on management by measurement criteria, establishing three measurable goals:

- Improve ten times by 1989
- Improve one hundred times by 1991

- Achieve Six Sigma capability (3.4 defects per million parts produced) by 1992

Motorola's quality-improvement process was dubbed Six Steps to Six Sigma. By establishing a single metric for measuring the effectiveness of both outcomes and work processes, they found that supportive actions followed. Bill Smith (1989, p. 5), Motorola's senior quality assurance manager, says of the management by measurement style of management: "By establishing measurements which are correlated to the desired end result, and regularly reviewing the actual measurements, the organization will focus on those actions necessary to achieve the required improvement."

Xerox's (1983) Total Quality effort, known as Leadership Through Quality, also advanced the use of statistical measures, such as the seven statistical tools and statistical process control. But these were closely coupled with a heavy emphasis on the use of process tools and supportive behaviors from managers. Their implementation strategy was stated very clearly: "Every behavior and every action of the organization and its people — particularly senior management — must reinforce the basic principles of Leadership Through Quality. Our actions will be more important than our words." To encourage managers to become fully committed, Xerox leadership included two important planks to their strategy:

1. They stated their intent to "develop and promote supervisors and managers who exemplify the principles of Leadership Through Quality," adding: "Nothing will send a clearer message about our commitment than the hiring and promotion of people whose management style and practices are in step with the new culture" (1983, p. 24).
2. They established a Management Practices Survey, whereby the members of a manager's team provided confidential feedback on how effectively each manager exhibited the behaviors that support Total Quality.

Federal Express (1991) also has a well-developed and thoroughly deployed management evaluation system. Called SFA

(Survey/Feedback/Action), it involves an employee survey, analysis of each work group's results by their manager, and a discussion between the manager and the work group to develop written action plans to help the manager improve and become more effective. (A more detailed description of SFA is presented in Chapter Thirteen.)

Paul Vita, Houston sales manager for Wallace Company (1991) and one of Wallace's early quality champions, says that they investigated several quality philosophies, including those of Juran, Deming, and Feigenbaum. "We were multidenominational," he remarked. "We followed all of the major concepts that worked for us. You have to see the practicality for your own company" (Gilbert, 1991, p. 3).

Organizations embarking on TQManagement should be aware of the danger that a company already well versed in the use of statistical tools may view early successes as achievement of their goal, while under the surface the old behaviors linger, waiting for "this latest craze to pass." Still others must be on guard against becoming too enamored with early style changes, for example, collaborative meeting processes and the use of "soft" tools such as brainstorming; they too may see such fast results as success, while their "management of the facts" continues to be overshadowed by the same old decisions for the same old reasons.

The third reason the Baldrige winners' programs have succeeded where others have failed is that the Baldrige winners recognized that TQManagement is a continuous process. Unlike the usual change management programs to which employees are accustomed, like value analysis, the customer-of-the-month program, or zero defects, Total Quality is a metamorphosis to a new organizational culture based on customer requirements, and the transition requires patience and discipline.

Gilbert Rapaille (Lader, 1988, p. 35), a quality consultant to AT&T, likens the transformation process to a child's learning process. He describes a child at play in front of adults: "He is active. Suddenly something goes wrong. He fails. He does something that does not fit the adult expectations. He cries, is upset, ashamed, and he realizes he did not know exactly what to do.

Somebody is there—his teacher, his grandparents, perhaps. They say, 'It's all right that you made a mistake. I care about you, because you are somebody special and I trust you. I'm sure you are going to get better.' The child tries again and eventually succeeds. He feels good about what has happened. He is proud of succeeding, of having overcome the difficulties." Rapaille believes that this is how quality should work in America. He suggests that successful quality efforts recognize that results are secondary to the process and the breakthroughs that lead to success. "In fact," he says, "we could say that a result without the process is not quality. If we haven't stumbled, failed, and tried again, we haven't produced an internal feel for quality" (pp. 35–36).

Mead D'Amore, general manager of Westinghouse's Commercial Nuclear Fuel Division, said, "Quality improvement is a never-ending process. We cannot waver in our commitment to total quality" (Westinghouse, 1989b, p. 2).

Senior Management's Responsibility

TQManagement begins at the top, because the underpinning of Total Quality is senior management's resolve. In a brochure describing IBM's quality efforts (IBM Rochester, 1991), Chairman John Akers put it this way: "Market-driven quality . . . starts with making customer satisfaction an obsession and empowering our people to use their creative energy to satisfy and delight their customers. It is hard work. It is hard, grinding work and we will do it and we will do it to absolute perfection."

When successful TQManagement senior management teams first express their desire for Total Quality they are in effect making three value statements:

1.   We and our organization are committed to the principles, actions, and behaviors of Total Quality.
2.   We will meet our full responsibilities for implementation of our quality strategy.
3.   We will each, personally, practice the processes and use the tools of Total Quality.

Crafting a quality policy and setting strategic goals alone are not enough. Senior management must learn and internalize the principles of Total Quality. Wallace's (1991) top five officers underwent more than 200 hours of intensive training on the methods and philosophy of continuous-quality improvement. At Xerox (1990a), the Corporate Management Committee spent a year studying such authorities as Deming, Juran, and Crosby, as well as visiting companies with Total Quality programs in the United States, Japan, and Europe before deciding on a strategy of quality improvement. At Corning (Houghton, 1986), the first formal training program in quality concepts included the half-dozen top executives who make up their management committee.

And that's just the beginning. It isn't sufficient for top managers to simply endorse and support the culture-building efforts; they must lead them with enthusiasm and obvious determination. The daily behavior of successful managers shows a consistency of purpose that leaves no doubt about the priority they're giving to quality. To reach their goal, senior managers have to have the willingness to meet three challenges:

1. *They must translate their commitment into action.* Managers must have flexibility, a willingness to learn, and the ability to listen—and that commitment must be real, strong, and enduring. This may seem to take away some of their prerogative, but it does not—senior managers are still the boss, but a different kind of boss. Wallace's (1991) Vita points out, "When we began quality training, the top executives participated in all aspects of it. They weren't asking anyone to do something they themselves weren't totally embracing. The attitude was: 'If you're going to go through this training exercise, I don't want to hear about it. I want to do it too.' It took a lot of courage and wisdom to go back to zero and start all over again. But they were willing to do it."

2. *They must demonstrate patience.* There will be an enormous temptation to revert to old practices and quick fixes, but successful managers resist those temptations and go slowly. A Japanese expert on quality and employee involvement has likened the need for patience and discipline in TQManagement to that of the bamboo farmer. Once the bamboo seed is planted,

the farmer must water it every day *for four years* before the tree breaks ground. But when it finally does sprout, it grows sixty feet in ninety days. So it is with the pursuit of TQManagement.

3. *They must be relentless in the quest for quality.* Anything short of this will be interpreted as a sign of less than total commitment. Douglas MacArthur said, "It is fatal to enter any war without the will to win it." That kind of staying power can be difficult to maintain. When the light goes on in a manager's head that TQManagement is important, it feels great. Confidence turns into the enthusiasm of "We can make this happen!" The only problem is that the manager's spirit can dim once she gets into the nitty-gritty of a program; the initial enthusiasm can be terrific, but keeping it up means working hard at doing things in the Total Quality way and leading by example.

A management that is determined to change can never be satisfied with the status quo; error just is not acceptable. The expression "To err is human" comes from the Latin *Errare humanum est.* The next line is *perseverare diabolicum*, a loose translation of which means "It is dumb to repeat the same mistakes." It is management's responsibility to insist that errors are not repeated (McLaughlin, 1985). For TQManagement to take root and grow, people must be encouraged to take risks, knowing full well that mistakes will happen — and then to learn from those mistakes. The expectation of TQManagement is not perfection, but the *pursuit* of perfection. Employees work to the expectations of their leaders and if standards allow for error, that is what will happen. As Xerox's Kearns (1988, p. 30) said, "We must continually reset our expectation levels — expectation levels that today are above anything that people even thought about two or three years ago." The goal at Motorola (1990, p. 30) is the same. "Our overall goal is to achieve total customer satisfaction," said Dale Misczynski, corporate vice president and director of quality at Motorola's Communications Sector, the group that led the way for Motorola's Six Sigma quality goals. "Part of the culture is to set very high expectations. We don't always make them, but we come very close."

Employee Empowerment

If senior management's responsibility is the underpinning of Total Quality, then employee empowerment is its framework. The objective of TQManagement is to engage everyone in the organization — managers and individual contributors — in a totally integrated effort toward improving performance at all levels, in all functions. The successful TQManagement organizations we studied have done this by providing their people with greater influence over their work and by encouraging all employees to participate with their managers and peers in problem solving and quality improvement. These organizations realize that no one understands a worker's job better than the worker. Employee involvement challenges a person with work process authority, resulting in the worker having more influence about how the organization is run. In turn, the organization gains the benefit of the creativity, innovation, and commitment of the people closest to the action.

To be effective at managing their work, employees must have management's empowerment; they need training in the tools and processes necessary to improve work methods and quality (we will discuss this in more detail in Chapters Eight and Nine). Success depends upon the leadership and support of managers. Empowerment of employees begins with TQManagers accepting *their* responsibilities by (1) understanding and supporting the thrust and direction of the organization's Total Quality strategy; (2) facilitating, coaching, and supporting their team's activities; (3) attending training sessions to build their own skills in problem solving, quality improvement, and collaborative behaviors; (4) providing direction and guidance to their team; and (5) reviewing and acting upon their team's recommendations in a timely manner.

According to John O. Grettenberger (1991, p. 12), general manager of Cadillac Motor Car Division, Cadillac made the cultural change to Total Quality by emphasizing "teamwork and employee involvement" and expanding "the use of teams to nearly every facet of our business, increasing employee involve-

ment 600 percent. And we gave our people the system, knowledge, and empowerment to make things happen."

Individuals can, of course, improve work processes and
quality, but the real gains come when the collective efforts of
teams determine the best work process and solve problems. This
kind of teamwork requires collaboration through team meetings. Meetings are essential to employee empowerment, and
employee teams will need both the time and facilitation to
conduct collaborative sessions. For some employees, this may be
their first opportunity to discuss work-related issues at formal
sessions. But whether it is the first time or the four-thousandth
time, a productive meeting requires guidelines for process and
behavior because, as a pundit observed, "Meetings are often like
panda matings. The expectations are always high, but the results
are usually disappointing." By functioning as the team's facilitator, a manager provides guidance for the meeting process and
structure. (We review specific process recommendations for
meetings and collaborative skills in Chapter Eight.)

Union-Management Partnership

The Total Quality process will not work without the support and
leadership of an organization's bargaining group. The leadership of a union can make or break an organization's effort
because Total Quality requires that workers learn new skills,
focus beyond their immediate job tasks, and cooperate with
their managers. In addition, quality improvement will likely
necessitate changes in work rules and manpower allocations
that may not be covered by an organization's union contract.

Cadillac (1991) has benefited from a history of quality
cooperation between General Motors and the UAW. Since 1973,
GM and the UAW have worked together to jointly improve
quality of work life and product quality. In 1987 GM management and the UAW recognized that a consistent, joint quality-
improvement process was needed; as a result they formed the
UAW-GM Quality Network. Cadillac is a part of this network
through a divisional council made up of senior managers, plant
managers, and union leaders. The Cadillac council oversees all

quality improvement efforts and assists in the implementation of the division's business plan.

Xerox's quality effort has its roots in 1980 with an agreement between the company and the ACTWU, the union representing Xerox's hourly workers, to explore a joint management-labor problem-solving process. It was a quality-of-work-life program that addressed issues of worker satisfaction and shop-floor problems. When senior management decided to pursue Total Quality, one of their first steps was to bring in the ACTWU as a partner. During their 1983 contract negotiations, the ACTWU and Xerox agreed to sponsor joint study teams to examine noncompetitive, excessively costly operations (Xerox Corporation, 1990a).

Globe Metallurgical (Leach, n.d.) began their quality effort at two plants, each represented by a different union. At one plant the relationship was favorable and the implementation of Total Quality went smoothly and successfully. At the other, the relationship was acrimonious and, although it was ultimately successful, the implementation was long and hard and had to survive an economic strike that resulted in a decertification of the union. Today both plants, one union and one nonunion, operate employee-involvement and quality-improvement identically.

Implementation Plan

Having reviewed the prerequisites of a TQManagement strategy — senior management responsibilities and employee empowerment — the next step is to review the elements that make up an implementation strategy. Earlier in this chapter we identified six key strategic objectives as common to the Baldrige winners. We selected these six for our TQManagement strategy because they include both the leadership of people and the management and statistical processes that a Total Quality effort requires at all levels of an organization. We found that all twelve Baldrige winners included these initiatives in their overall strategy with varying degrees of emphasis.

Once an organization's senior management team has

hammered out their quality policy and formulated the outlines of their desired state as a Total Quality organization, the next step is to create a plan to get there. This may be a formal document or a series of strategic steps taken in increments. As an example, at Xerox a Quality Implementation Team of senior managers from all major operating groups devoted the whole of 1983 to forging a comprehensive, ninety-page planning document. Known affectionately as the Green Book because of its cover's color, it outlined tools, modeled processes, detailed instructions, and established annual goals from launch in 1984 through 1987 (Xerox, 1983). Westinghouse's Commercial Nuclear Fuel Division (CNFD) (Westinghouse Corporation, 1989b) launched their effort differently. They established a Quality Council made up of the same people who manage the business every day. The council set annual quality goals for the division and monitored and reported on progress. They have published an annual Quality Plan every year since 1983, each year focusing on a different theme consistent with the division's progress toward Total Quality. The Wallace Company's (1991) management developed sixteen Quality Strategic Objectives to guide business decision making—in fact, business and quality aims are one and the same in Wallace's Quality Business Plan. Using the Baldrige criteria to assess their progress toward the sixteen objectives, management conducted periodic retreats to rate themselves and developed a two-year improvement plan, which was later condensed to a one-year process.

The point is that the level of planning required and the timeline for implementation depend upon the needs of the organization. The management of change requires thoughtful assessment and planning. Whether you require the detail of a Xerox or the flexibility of a Westinghouse, we believe that you will need to focus to some degree on the six mechanisms for transformation. We think of these as the essential supports for a TQManagement structure. Although the level of emphasis that management assigns to each factor will be the level that is uniquely suited to their organization, the architecture of the plan should be consistent with the principles of TQManagement and the strategy your senior management has approved. In the next six chapters we will detail the implementation requirements for each building block, but for now we will limit ourselves to a general description of each. (See Figure 5.1.)

The Foundation of TQM:
Management Leadership and Commitment

We have written at length about the importance of *senior* management's behavior, but this is also true of managers throughout the organization. The behavior of the management team at all

Figure 5.1. Building Blocks of the TQManagement Organization.

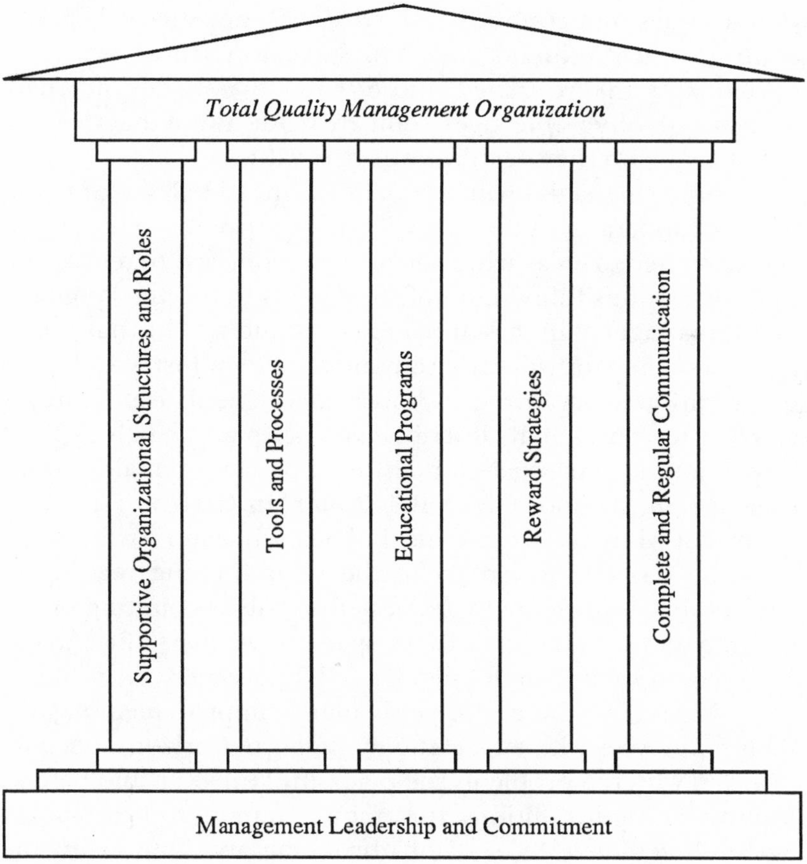

levels of the organization provides the necessary leadership, sets the tone, and acts as an example for the successful implementation of Total Quality. Any successful organizational transformation effort relies on the competence and support of local management. Managers who practice the principles of quality day in and day out are those who thoroughly understand and have complete ownership of the quality concepts and tools, and who possess the skills to take those concepts into action. Obviously it is much easier for line managers to take a chance on changing process for quality's sake in a company committed to Total Quality than in one where the first rule is "Don't rock the boat." It's hard enough to get commitment, but follow-up behavior is even more difficult. It is also important to remember that declared values that contradict practices will not succeed. In the Baldrige and President's Award organizations, those who support quality are rewarded; those who do not, despite their success with other objectives, soon are made aware that they are out of step with the organization's new values.

Some managers will see quality as an "added" factor to the organization, rather than being their responsibility. Since managers are used to measuring performance, one way to reduce the "not my responsibility" kind of thinking is to use the language many managers understand best — numbers. The nature of numbers called for will vary from industry to industry and from organization to organization; however, in general, useful categories are measures that describe *outgoing* quality, such as final inspection, as a surrogate for customer-perceived quality. As an example, in his book *Moments of Truth*, Jan Carlzon (1987) reports that when he became head of Scandinavian Airlines Systems, he was concerned about the poor on-time record. To correct this, he personally requested a daily accounting of the on-time status of all flights. In the space of two years, the SAS on-time record went from 83 percent to 97 percent.

Managers who desire performance improvement engage their employees with expectations similar to Carlzon's, become involved with the problems such measures uncover, and help in finding the right solutions. It is not uncommon to hear a manager telling an employee, "Don't bring me problems, bring me solutions," but this can be short-sighted. Employees usually solve problems if they can, but many problems are beyond their abilities, resources, or authority (McLaughlin, 1985). The quality-conscious manager looks for problems, but then helps employees to uncover solutions. In short, managers support TQManagement by (1) becoming role models of Total Quality; (2) being trained and showing leadership in the use of the processes; (3) ensuring that quality is a key criterion in selecting individuals for promotion; (4) obtaining feedback from employees on their own management style, behavior, and support for total quality; and (5) inspecting for Total Quality—not just results, but the processes used to obtain results. "Expect what you inspect" is a hallmark of TQManagement. If managers do not routinely follow up on *all* the plans they have set in motion, their quality effort will die a slow death.

Management leadership and commitment is the bedrock of Total Quality. It is the first of the six strategic objectives because it is the foundation upon which the other five objectives can stand, like strategic pillars supporting the structure of TQManagement.

Pillar No. 1: Supportive Organizational Structures and Roles

The pursuit of TQManagement is not without its price: successful organizations make investments, and a *quality infrastructure* is one of them. Although successful implementation of Total Quality is fundamentally dependent upon the activities of management throughout the organization (the operating unit head and the senior management team are always responsible for implementing Total Quality!), one person—preferably a peer of the senior management team—is usually accountable for assisting senior management in implementing the strategy and keeping it updated. In assessing what is needed to achieve the organization's quality strategy, management should begin with identifying the resources and support services available within the company. Not all Baldrige winners chose to establish a quality office or designate a quality officer. However, most did. The roles of senior managers and the quality office need to be

clearly defined so that the quality officer is free of other responsibilities and can maintain a broad view of the organization's
goals and quality progress. In this way the quality officer is better
able to facilitate the transition from the present to the desired
state of TQManagement.

Larger organizations also established quality officers at
the division or group level. As an example, Xerox's Systems
Group had a vice president of quality on the group staff. Additionally, each of the five divisions that made up the Systems
Group had quality officers. Within the functions of each division another level of managers was devoted to quality implementation full- or part-time, based on the size of the function. In
addition to supporting their line organizations, the divisions'
quality officers were gathered into an "implementation team" to
guide implementation throughout the entire group. However,
such assignments need not be based on organizational structure. At IBM Rochester (1991) each senior manager "owns" one
of six critical factors and is responsible for the plans and implementation of that factor.

TQManagement organizations require training; after
training, employees will most likely need assistance at their
work sites. Training can be purchased, and trainers, of course,
can be "rented." The size of the organization determines
whether additional expert advice is required to supplement the
available in-house training resources. As we pointed out, successful revolutions usually have a junta of zealots. For this reason
there is value in placing "quality specialists" throughout the
organization, who can act as subject-matter experts on the tools,
methods, and processes of Total Quality. They are internal,
posttraining consultants. These services, too, can be purchased,
although internal "experts" have the advantage of leveraging
identification with internal role models, as well as supporting
participation goals. It is important to remember that in addition
to quality experts, organizations need support from the personnel department to assure that both communication and
recognition and reward systems are dovetailed to the implementation plan.

Another valuable role quality officers play is that of fostering and facilitating a network of all the organization's "specialists" battling in the trenches of quality implementation. Such a network can share experiences, synthesize what works well, learn from what has not worked, discuss state-of-the-art methodologies, and develop tactical and strategic actions to move the organization closer to the desired state.

Pillar No. 2: Tools and Processes

Tools and processes are the machinery of Total Quality, providing people with new methods of assessing and performing their work, solving problems, and improving quality. Common instruments include a problem-solving process, a quality improvement process, the seven statistical tools, benchmarking, and techniques for collaboration activities. We will expand on the detail and use of these and other tools and processes in Chapter Eight, but for now we will touch on their significance to a TQManagement strategy.

Phil Crosby (1979) and many other TQM experts have stated that the cost of poor quality, or the lack of conformance to quality, is at least 20 percent of sales. From our experience, we agree that it is at least that high, not including lost sales opportunities, which, admittedly, can be very difficult to measure. Since most companies only measure the number and kind of customer complaints they receive, they don't know how many customers or potential customers really don't like their products or services, because these customers go someplace else to do business.

Federal Express (1991) measures its quality performance by twelve Service Quality Indicators (SQIs) that comprehensively describe how its performance is viewed by customers. Each SQI item is weighted to reflect how significantly it affects overall satisfaction, and each SQI has a cross-functional team, headed by a senior executive and involving front-line employees, support personnel, and managers from all parts of the corporation. The SQI measurements are directly linked to the corporate planning process, which begins with the CEO, the COO, and an executive planning committee. SQIs form the basis on which corporate executives are evaluated. Individual performance objectives are established and monitored, and executive bonuses rest upon the performance of the *whole corporation* in meeting performance improvement goals. (Senior executives at Federal Express did not get bonuses the year they won the Baldrige Award because the company's goals had not been met!)

It is easy to see how quality improvement can facilitate the achievement of business goals. Quality improvement is a strategic tool with emphasis on the use of the process to achieve "improved" results rather than results alone. The key is understanding what has to be improved, the customer for the work, and the customer's requirements. Numerous models for quality improvement exist. At Motorola (1989) it's the Six Steps to Six Sigma Quality Program. At Xerox (1990a) it's a nine-step quality improvement process. At Westinghouse (1989b) its eight key measures are called Pulse Points, which include key indicators of customer satisfaction such as fuel reliability and error-free documentation, and internal quality measures such as first-time-through yield of manufactured components.

Within any quality-improvement effort there is also the need for a common method of solving problems. In many organizations it is not uncommon for six or more people to sit down for a meeting, "each with a specific solution in search of a common problem." A problem-solving model has enormous power to cut through a lot of the pointless and fruitless debate that is so often typical of unstructured problem-solving meetings. A structured method can greatly enhance the quest for quality: identifying, selecting, and analyzing problems; generating and planning solutions; and implementing and evaluating the solutions. Whatever the model or specific process for quality improvement or problem solving, most are based on Deming's (1986) PDCA (Plan-Do-Check-Act) model, and the whole purpose is to provide a road map employees can follow to produce quality products and deliver quality services, by showing them where to begin and what questions to ask.

The most common tools used with both quality improvement processes and problem-solving methods are the seven statistical tools: *histograms, Pareto charts, cause-and-effect diagrams (fishbones), control charts, check sheets, flow charts,* and *scatter diagrams.* These are discussed more fully in Chapter Eight.

Another method for determining the direction of quality-improvement efforts is *benchmarking,* a structured process for measuring products, services, and practices against the organization's toughest competitors, or against companies recognized as leaders. Xerox is probably the nation's leader in advancing this process as a quality tool, but it is also employed extensively by other Baldrige winners, especially Cadillac and IBM Rochester, where strategic targets are derived from their comprehensive benchmarking process. Benchmarking metrics provide focus for business-planning and quality-improvement strategies. (The creation of the International Benchmark Clearing House is described in Chapter Fourteen.)

Pillar No. 3: Educational Programs

TQManagement begins with education and ends with education. Training provides every employee with an understanding of quality and a working knowledge of the tools and techniques of quality improvement. Training has proved to be a powerful investment for the Baldrige winners; when their people were adequately trained to use the tools of quality, they required very little supervision to understand the root causes of their problems and the steps required to resolve them. Training employees significantly reduces the amount of management involvement needed in daily tasks, and it empowers individuals to resolve issues and allows employees to continually improve their own outputs and processes.

Training is perhaps the most important change agent in the early phases of TQManagement implementation. Many training modules are available, but whatever the organization chooses, it is best to customize the training for the organization's needs, because the training content and implementation structure are of critical importance to the success of Total Quality. In developing a training plan, we found that the quality-transition planning team should consider the following:

1.　A simple curriculum, tailored to the organization's needs, which can be applied consistently across all operating units.
2.　Thorough, but easy to grasp, core modules to teach quality concepts, the organization's goals and expectations, and the tools of quality. A modular design allows teams to receive training in single sessions or staggered classes, based on their unique requirements.
3.　An employee orientation module to be delivered to all operating units as soon after the kickoff of the quality effort as possible. The purpose is to explain the objective and the training delivery process and to let people know when they can expect to participate.
4.　A training delivery plan that cascades from the top down and allows work groups to receive their training as a team.
5.　The use of work group managers to actually teach some portions of the training. Nothing will show commitment faster and lock managers into the "walk your talk" habit.
6.　On-the-job application of both the quality-improvement and participative problem-solving processes as part of the learning process. Completion does not occur until mastery has been shown. This can be a powerful demonstration of commitment, especially in a top-down delivery process.

Pillar No. 4: Reward Strategies

The world of work is prominent in most of our lives. In fact, many of us spend more waking hours in our work environments than we do at home with our families. The implications of this are threefold: First, and fundamentally, the way people are treated at work powerfully impacts the way they feel about themselves as individuals. Second, their treatment on the job clearly affects their work performance. And third, people usually want and need to "belong" and thus seek close team relationships with their peers and boss.

These factors underscore the importance of establishing a work atmosphere characterized by confidence, respect, and mutual trust, one that fosters the development of personally satisfying work relationships. These relationships are especially critical to an organization engaged in TQManagement, because a positive work environment ensures that people will be encouraged and motivated to practice Total Quality behaviors. Establishing a work climate that goes beyond "labor for hire" will promote employee loyalty and belonging. In turn, employees have expectations about how they should be treated as part of the Total Quality team. In TQManagement it is part of the manager's job to meet these expectations by acknowledging and appreciating employee support for Total Quality, teamwork, and commitment and by fostering a work environment that values interpersonal relations.

We will explore this subject further in Chapter Ten, but for now let us make a few key points. *Recognition* by itself is an intangible activity through which the organization and its management express appreciation for a person's value. It may take the form of a simple "thank you" or an honorary title like team captain, but its power should not be underestimated. It is amazing to us how little managers make use of such a readily available tool. *Reward,* on the other hand, is tangible, taking the form of money, a plaque, or a gift. It is important to note that reward without recognition has little lasting value. Any recognition and reward strategy should be aimed at both individuals and groups who contribute to quality improvements, whether the appreciation takes the form of symbols or dollars.

Some elements we found among Total Quality organizations that are worth considering are (1) special awards and cash bonuses for teams and individuals, (2) assurance that promotion decisions take into account demonstrated use of the principles of Total Quality, (3) management incentive plans to promote the use of quality processes as well as the achievement of results, and (4) a general bonus plan, or other group plans (gainsharing), that enable employees to participate in the financial benefits of Total Quality.

One significant difference between TQManagement organizations and the rest of the pack is that their reward and incentive system is consistent with their quality objectives and principles. Traditionally, production quotas, sales figures, and other productivity-oriented bases are the yardsticks of achievement, but the Total Quality organization that uses such measures alone is sending conflicting messages about its goals. In the eleventh of his fourteen points, Deming (1986, pp. 78–80) advocates elimination of work standards and numerical quotas. His argument is that work standards and quotas are values that have no bearing on process capability and serve only to create variability in performance by obscuring an employee's understanding of the job. Rather than focusing on standards, successful managers focus on stabilizing and improving the work process.

Pillar No. 5: Complete and Regular Communication

Success in TQManagement is dependent on consistent and credible communication in the broadest sense of the word. Formal communication—no matter how carefully worded or creatively crafted—will not succeed if it is at odds with the organization's behavior. Messages that are formally communicated internally and to the public must be consistent with the organization's progress toward complete implementation of Total Quality. In the Baldrige companies every behavior and every action of the organization and its people—particularly senior management—reinforces the basic principles of Total Quality. Actions are always more important than words. Some examples of actions we found that communicate this principle most forcefully include:

- Decision making at all levels that follows Total Quality principles, such as participative problem solving and actions based on statistical evidence
- Recognition, reward, and promotion for team players and individuals who exemplify Total Quality behaviors
- Requiring employees to have a clear definition of their customer, a thorough understanding of their customer's requirements, agreement with the customer on how these requirements will be met, and the means and resources necessary to meet them
- From the boardroom down, meetings that reflect Total Qual-

ity by the use of quality-improvement and problem-solving processes and statistical tools
- Visible and consistent evidence that quality overrides all other management considerations in deciding how the organization and its individuals behave

TQManagement will flounder unless employees are continually informed of the overall objectives of the organization and their Total Quality progress. Some of the steps we observed among Total Quality organizations in their communication strategies are (1) including quality objectives in the organization's business plans, (2) soliciting employee feedback (there must be good communication in all directions to ensure that people learn from what's happening locally), (3) engaging all current communication vehicles (including management speeches) in spreading the word of Total Quality, and (4) requiring operating units to prepare annual communication plans in support of the process.

The TQManagement Strategy and the Twelve Action Steps

On the basis of what we learned from the Baldrige Award winners and others, we believe the foundation and pillars of the TQManagement strategy represent a comprehensive structure upon which an organization can plan a transition to Total Quality. In Chapter Four we described twelve actions an organization must take if a change strategy is to succeed (Delta Consulting Group, 1988a). Table 5.1 shows how the six strategic objectives (the foundation and five pillars) support each of the action steps.

Stages of Change

TQManagement is based on the idea that by establishing quality as their key business principle, organizations will be able to achieve their business objectives, such as market share, an effective cost structure, and sufficient profit to ensure the long-term health of the enterprise. We have stressed throughout this chap-

Table 5.1. Relationship of the Strategy Structure to the Twelve Action Steps.

Action Step	Management Leadership and Commitment	Organizational Structures and Roles	Tools and Processes	Educational Programs	Recognition and Reward Strategies	Communications
1. Assure the support of key power groups	•	•			•	•
2. Use leader behavior to generate energy in support of the change	•				•	
3. Use symbols and language	•	•	•	•		•
4. Build in stability	•		•			•
5. Surface dissatisfaction with the present state	•	•		•	•	•
6. Participate in the change	•	•	•		•	•
7. Supply rewards for behavior in support of the change	•				•	
8. Allow time and opportunity to disengage from the present state	•	•		•		•
9. Develop and communicate a clear image of the future	•	•	•	•		•
10. Use multiple and consistent leverage points	•	•		•	•	•
11. Develop organizational arrangements for the transition	•	•				
12. Build in feedback mechanisms	•	•		•		•

Source: Delta Consulting Group, 1988a. Used by permission.

ter that accomplishing these business goals requires fundamental changes in the behavior and actions of *everyone,* individually and collectively. This demands a positive attitude in the pursuit of customer satisfaction and continuous-quality improvement. In short, these goals demand a quality strategy that drives toward improving the environment by changing it!

Reaching the new environment is neither easy nor quick. We have emphasized the importance of patience during TQManagement implementation because transformation to the new culture requires time and learning. Writing in *The Quality Review,* Nadler (1988, pp. 21–22) says the typical organization passes through six stages that take from four to six years to complete:

- *Stage 1:* Management becomes aware of quality and takes some tentative steps.
- *Stage 2:* The senior executive realizes the need for a firm commitment and investment of manpower and time, which in turn builds both a constituency and a feeling of urgency.
- *Stage 3:* Large numbers of people are trained in the tools and concepts.
- *Stage 4:* People have mastered the tools and are applying them to a high order of projects and activities.
- *Stage 5:* The tools, processes, and quality language are integrated into day-to-day work operations.
- *Stage 6:* The last phase is characterized by continual improvement where higher standards are established, systems are perfected, and the organization is alert to competition and changing customer requirements.

Nadler's observation is consistent with what we found in the organizations we examined. Nearly all of the Baldrige winners came to quality because of threats to their business from overseas or domestic competitors or from customers who were already committed to Total Quality. John Wallace, CEO of Wallace Company (1991, p. 24), noted: "In our case embracing quality as a way of doing business literally meant our survival."

All of the quality leaders began by having their senior

management study and become familiar with quality. The senior management of all the Baldrige winners attended one or more seminars conducted by America's quality gurus (Deming, Juran, Feigenbaum, and Crosby). Milliken (1990) began its quality effort in 1980; since that time, at the monthly senior management review, the first half of the day is devoted entirely to quality discussions on process, measures, and progress. Xerox (1990b) began its training cascade with its senior management teams.

The goal of organizational maturity in quality — the point when everyone is using the tools and processes — is slow to arrive, because internalization takes time. Corning's James Houghton (1987, p. 22) describes it this way: "If there is commitment at the top, the people at the bottom quickly become committed themselves. They're saying, 'Where have you guys been all my life? We know how to do the job. Give us the tools and let us get on with it.' Once you've got commitment at the top and at the bottom, the big problem is then getting commitment in the middle. That takes a lot of effort. Eventually, commitment must exist throughout the organization. But it goes top down, bottom up, and then eventually hits in the middle."

The flow through the stages is not sequential. Like water flowing down a hill, some streams will move faster than others; pools may form until they overflow and catch up with the rest of the flow; and some lines may switch back, crisscrossing in slow paths before finding their way to the larger streams. The road map to guide an organization through these stages is a comprehensive implementation plan that defines the future state and spells out what must be done to get there. The strategy an organization selects for itself will reflect the unique needs and operations of the organization, but it should include at a minimum these six elements:

1. Management leadership and commitment
2. Establishing supportive organizational structures and roles
3. Using the right tools and processes
4. Developing and implementing educational programs

5. Creating meaningful recognition and reward strategies
6. Encouraging complete and regular communication

    In the six chapters that follow we expand on these elements and offer the experience of the Baldrige and President's Award winners and others to demonstrate the power of the TQManagement structure.

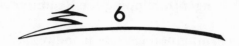

6

Leadership and Commitment: Laying the Foundation

*There's nothing more difficult to take in hand, more perilous to
conduct, or more uncertain in its success than to take the lead
in the introduction of a new order of things.*
— Niccolo Machiavelli

Without a genuine, hands-on commitment from an organization's managers, TQManagement cannot succeed! The behavior
and actions of managers—at all levels—provide the necessary
leadership, set the proper tone, and demonstrate the examples
for successful implementation of Total Quality. It is management's leadership and commitment to Total Quality that lays the
foundation upon which the pillars of a TQManagement strategy
can be built.

The senior managements of all the Baldrige Award winners recognized that the successful implementation of
TQManagement demands explicit affirmation and involvement
from all managers of the organization. Each of the senior staffs
attended quality training, struggled with the development of
their organization's quality policy, and committed the time and
effort to "walk their talk." More important, by personal example—employing continuous communication, using employee

148

feedback surveys, and setting clear objectives—these senior TQManagers established an expectation that managers throughout their organizations would also exhibit leadership and commitment to Total Quality.

The style changes required to advance TQManagement are extensive and actually constitute a new scheme for managing. Deming (Walton, 1986, p. 59) says that this is essential: "We will have to undergo total demolition of American style of management, which unfortunately has spread to just about the whole western world."

Nevertheless, Total Quality does not change traditional management responsibilities and accountability. Decision making still belongs to the manager, as do planning, organizing, communicating, and evaluating performance. What *does* change, however, is that the manager's capacity as a teacher and team leader is enlivened, because TQManagers must work with their employees to establish work processes that are consistent with the principles and guidelines of TQManagement. In this chapter we will examine the manager's new role and the way quality organizations adapt to meet the TQManagement requirements. We have consolidated our findings into six goals for management leadership and commitment that are consistent with all twelve change initiatives (see Table 5.1). Management leadership and commitment are essential if an organization is to establish a solid foundation for the rest of the TQManagement strategy.

The Manager's New Role

In successful TQManagement operations managers continue to be responsible for the functional requirements of their management job. But TQManagers must also be more attentive to the capacity of their work group, its functions, and each team member's readiness for participating in Total Quality activities. Traditionally, managers have been responsible for (1) establishing a system, (2) making assignments, (3) directing work, (4) setting work standards and goals, (5) evaluating performance, and (6) providing training for poor performers or replacing them. When managers do these things, they believe they are creating the most efficient work system possible. However, the experience of the Baldrige winners and others indicates that there are better ways to accomplish the same tasks. More important, the TQManagement approach moderates the inherently adversarial relationship between management and employees that is so often part of a traditional management style. In TQManagement a manager's new role includes:

- Providing the team with a consistent and clear purpose based on the customer requirements for his team's outputs
- Finding innovative means to involve people in solving their work problems
- Identifying the cost benefits of her team's solutions and work process improvements
- Taking ownership of continual improvement of the work system
- Making certain the team knows and applies the tools and processes of Total Quality and coaches the team by (1) monitoring their efforts, (2) making suggestions for improvement, (3) helping with TQManagement implementation, and (4) evaluating their results
- Being a role model for TQManagement by learning and using its tools and processes

This new role is obviously very different from traditional concepts. David Bradford, who with Allan Cohen, coauthored *Managing for Excellence: The Guide to Developing High Performance in Contemporary Organizations* (Bradford and Cohen, 1984, p. 26), makes use of the mythical Lone Ranger in describing the traditional American heroic manager:

> The Lone Ranger, an imposing masked figure, rides up on a white horse to overcome great odds in solving the problems of the day. This model of the vanquishing leader—a bit mysterious, generous, but aloof—is a very common theme. Think of the setting: helpless, disorganized townsfolk are being threatened by some bad guys. The Lone Ranger,

helped just by his trusty and loyal sidekick, arrives in the nick of time, with the right blend of courage and cunning, faces down the bad guys by being just a little quicker, smarter, and tougher, leaves a silver bullet as a symbol of his having solved the problem, and at the end, rides stoically off into the sunset. The grateful townspeople wonder who that masked man is—and wish he could stay—but are left to go about their mundane tasks no wiser or better prepared to deal with the next big problem. When again faced with a major crisis, they'll just have to hope for a return of the thundering hoofbeats and another last-minute rescue by the daring hero.

Bradford and Cohen (1984, pp. 10–11) identify four "myths" about American managers that are important to note here because they are emblematic of the Lone Ranger style of managing and because that style is the antithesis of what TQManagement is about:

- *Myth 1:* The good manager knows at all times what is going on in the department.
- *Myth 2:* The good manager should have more technical expertise than any subordinate.
- *Myth 3:* The good manager should be able to solve any problem that comes up.
- *Myth 4:* The good manager should be the primary person responsible for how the department is working.

Unlike the "Lone Rangers," successful TQManagers possess the skills and characteristics of coaches. They have learned how to facilitate collaborative processes and develop their work groups into *teams* that understand their customers' real requirements. TQManagers know that creating a team means that each team member's interpersonal skills and work process skills have been developed to their full potential. This requires teaching, feedback, and counseling. A TQManager will ask: "Have I communicated my expectations?" "Does each individual understand the skills and processes?" "Do I treat my team as mature adults?" "Do they treat each other the same way?"

Robert Swiggett of Kollmorgen, a Connecticut-based printed-circuit-board manufacturer, described the significance of the new management style to John Naisbitt and Patricia Aburdene (1985) in *Re-inventing the Corporation:* "The role of a leader is the servant's role. It's supporting his people, running interference for them. It's coming out with an atmosphere of understanding and love. You want people to feel they have complete control over their destiny at every level. Tyranny is not tolerated here. People who want to manage in the traditional sense are cast off by their peers like dandruff."

Even Jack Welch, General Electric's chairman, who acquired and disposed of businesses without seeming to worry about the effect on employees (earning him the nickname "Neutron Jack"—buildings were left standing, but the people were gone), has seen the need for a new management style. During the 1980s Welch changed GE's traditional portfolio of business and in the process doubled revenue to $60 billion and trebled profits to $4.4 billion. Now he is concerned about maintaining those gains and believes that productivity by empowering people is the answer. In the company's 1991 report Welch and vice chairman and executive officer Edward Hood cosigned a statement that called for managers to have "the self confidence to empower others and behave in a boundaryless fashion" ("A Balance Between Values and Numbers," 1992, p. C1). Welch says that GE must have the values to "take this company forward, rapidly, through the 1990s and beyond" and he adds that mangers must be "open to ideas from anywhere" ("A Soft New Edge for Neutron Jack," 1992, p. C1). There are several reasons for Welch's newfound confidence in employee empowerment, but one is GE's $1 billion investment in its Louisville kitchen appliance plant, which includes Total Quality on the assembly line. "Yes, it's hard to hold back a $100 million line at 10 percent production until you get zero rejects," Welch says. "But once you do, productivity just explodes because you eliminate rework, which in some cases used to take up a third of the plant" (Flanigan, 1992a, p. D1503).

Once the TQManager has established and trained her team she will focus on lifting the barriers that block performance improvement. She does this by working with the team collaboratively and using periodic inspection of the team's work processes and results as the data source to help identify the barriers to be removed.

Managing in a TQManagement Organization

Before an organization's managers can make the kind of changes we are talking about, each individual manager must first accept and internalize four suppositions about managing in a TQManagement organization:

1. The manager is responsible for setting team and individual performance standards that are based on customer requirements.
2. The methods for reviewing objectives and planning variances have to be consistent with quality improvement and based on facts.
3. Employees are better able to improve the work system than is management, because problems primarily come from the system, not the workers.
4. Performance improvement is not accomplished by slogans, exhortation, punishment, or unrealistic goals.

Setting Performance Standards

A TQManager must first make certain that the team understands their mission and outputs and has identified the customers for their outputs. Next he facilitates his team's dialogue with their customers to validate the requirements. He then ensures that the team has the data and resources available to meet the requirements.

At Federal Express (1991), the quality measure is customer satisfaction, which is tracked in terms of progress against the twelve-component Service Quality Indicators. Data from these tracking systems, including bar code scanning of packages

every time they change hands, provides facts that allow managers and employee teams to conduct an analysis of SQIs on a
daily, weekly, monthly, and annual basis and thereby identify
current problems. There is a cross-functional team for each of
SQI's service components. A senior manager heads each team
and ensures the involvement of all the employees and managers
necessary to deal with the issues. Two of these teams have a
network of over 1,000 employees throughout the corporation.

Mort Topfer (1989, p. 10), a senior vice president with
Motorola, puts their expectation succinctly, but directly: "Managers at Motorola are as accountable for achieving quality improvement goals as they are for any other business goal. It is part
of the job's requirements, and as such, partly determines career
advancement."

Reviewing Objectives and Planning Variances

A team's work system and performance should be constantly
monitored, and these examinations must be based on hard
evidence. Not only must the facts be identified and validated,
but the causes behind the facts must be determined by knowing
the *how, why,* and *what.* Only in this way can a manager and her
team be absolutely certain that they can meet their customers'
requirements and be able to take corrective action when the
outcomes are in danger of not meeting requirements.

All quality-improvement efforts at Milliken (1990) are solidly based on such factual information, obtained from an array
of standardized data bases accessible from all facilities. Most
manufacturing processes are under the scrutiny of real-time
monitoring systems that detect errors and help pinpoint causes.
The resultant data (some analyzed with the aid of computerized
expert systems) supports process-improvement efforts to predict
and prevent the causes of errors. Milliken's work teams are able
to access these data bases as necessary.

Encouraging Employees to Improve the Work System

When management accepts the premise that employees are
better able to improve the work system than they are, they go a

long way toward reducing the adversarial role between managers and employees. This enables employees to speak freely and builds the belief that managers, although they are accountable for the business, can be influenced to make changes. This supposition not only promotes teamwork; it also fosters continuous performance improvement.

Federal Express's Fred Smith (Karabatsas, 1990) says, "I think that most of the employees of Federal Express know that our company is run by a team of individuals, from the first-line, customer-contact people to the senior management group. . . . I don't think they have any mistaken impressions about the fact that it takes the entire team, everyday, to make our system work."

IBM Rochester (1991, pp. 4–5) identified six critical success factors in reaching their published vision: "Customer—the final arbiter; Products and services—first with the best; Quality—excellence in execution; and People—enabled, empowered, excited, and rewarded" and in achieving their strategic goal of being undisputed leader in customer satisfaction. The six critical factors are product strategy, requirements, Six-Sigma strategy, education, employee involvement, and cycle improvement. The quality objectives that support these six critical success factors are integrated into each employee's performance plan and are agreed upon by both the manager and the employee. This sort of deployment of objectives not only builds employee participation; it also makes empowerment an operational reality. In this way each quality-improvement achievement by IBM's employees is directly linked to the achievement of their business objectives.

Improving Performance

TQManagers believe that performance improvement can only be achieved by removing the barriers in the system and identifying the hidden opportunities for breakthroughs that improve work processes and performance. In TQManagement *inspiration* has its place, but it is the *perspiration* of fact-based assessment that produces the results. Deming (Walton, 1986, p. 77) often remarks during his seminars, "You can beat the horses; they run faster for a while. Goals are like hay somebody ties in front of the horse's snout. The horse is smart enough to discover no matter whether he canters or gallops, trots or walks or stands still, he can't catch up with the hay. Might as well stand still."

Corning's Houghton (1987, p. 23) says that to support Total Quality a manager must have "flexibility, a willingness to learn, and the ability to listen. You don't get the job done by yourself. The only way to get the job done is by working as a team. We must listen and learn to be more participative. The throwing of thunderbolts down the mountain won't work. The collective wisdom must be applied."

Evolutionary Phases and Barriers to Change

It is, of course, unrealistic to expect a management metamorphosis overnight. All of the Baldrige winners stress the need for patience and agree that change occurs in an evolutionary fashion. Their experience suggests that it takes four or five years of hard work before all managers are routinely practicing the principles of Total Quality. Xerox's Kearns (1988, p. 30) says, "Quality improvement is a long term proposition that takes a lot of patience . . . and a lot of discipline. . . . There are no short cuts, no panaceas; and large organizations do, in fact, change slowly."

In Chapter Five we noted six stages an organization passes through on the road to Total Quality. Within these stages, among TQManagement organizations, it is generally accepted that employees, but especially managers, personally experience the change in four phases:

1.   The desired behaviors are not well understood and not well practiced — people are *unconsciously incompetent.*
2.   The desired behaviors are understood, and with much conscious effort they are practiced consistently — people are *consciously incompetent.*
3.   The desired behaviors are practiced well, but only with conscious effort — people are *consciously competent.*
4.   In the final phase the desired behaviors are practiced con-

sistently, as part of a person's natural style—people are *unconsciously competent*.

Knowing that these phases exist, and that individuals and work groups pass through them at different paces, allows TQManagers to appreciate and accept the importance of patience. Managers are better able to cope with the change process within their work groups and to recognize the *real* and *imagined* barriers that invariably crop up. By understanding the phase process, managers can plan actions to match the needs of their organization and thus counter the barriers to progress. This is extremely important because these barriers can be very discouraging in the early years. All of the Baldrige winners experienced the following barriers to some degree:

- Total Quality is seen as just another cost-reduction program.
- Employees do not believe management has long-range commitment.
- Employees do believe that "when push comes to shove," short-term marketplace problems and profit pressures will take precedence over Total Quality.
- Consistent priorities are absent during implementation.
- Cultural resistance exists.
- Senior people are not available, or too busy, to be trained or to practice Total Quality tools and processes.
- Results are expected too fast.
- Management won't free work groups for training.
- There is a "not invented here" attitude regarding Total Quality processes and tools.
- The organization has insufficient resources or funds to implement changes or is told to "do it within existing budgets."
- The perception exists that the process takes too long or that "we are already doing that."
- There is no perceived change in management behavior.

The surest way for an organization to overcome these barriers is to have the senior management team openly become involved in the implementation and establish a style that *uses, teaches, inspects,* and *promotes* TQManagement. All of the organizations we examined told us that achieving a supportive management style throughout the organization was directly linked to the *role model* set by their senior management team. To create an environment that makes quality happen, lets it happen, and helps it happen, a senior management team needs to set four personal objectives: (1) to learn the required processes and tools, (2) to use the processes and tools, (3) to teach by example and demonstrate direct involvement in TQManagement, and (4) to inspect the use of the processes and implementation of the TQManagement plan.

Six Strategic Goals for Management Leadership and Commitment

In describing the office of president of the United States, Lyndon Johnson said that the "hardest task is not to know what is right, but to do what is right." The same can be said of the new management role in Total Quality. Intellectualizing TQManagement is the easy part; translating those beliefs and desires into tangible actions is a whole different challenge. A look at America's quality leaders provides an insight into what is required. Our studies revealed several common characteristics these organizations have adopted to establish and maintain their TQManagement styles. We have consolidated these observations into six key goals for laying the foundation for management leadership and commitment:

1. Senior officers and executives act as the role models, promoters, and inspectors of TQManagement.
2. Employee involvement and teamwork are established as an integral part of Total Quality.
3. Quality improvement is promoted by managers personally using their quality processes to improve the organization's business processes.
4. TQManagers maintain a style of openness, patience, and trust.
5. The evaluation of TQManagement support is included in

the methods used to identify future supervisors and managers.

6. TQManagers reinforce and encourage Total Quality as a never-ending task.

Adopting a TQManagement Style

No matter how much exposure we may have to management theory and training, in the final analysis most of us develop our management style by emulating our favorite boss. We reason that if it worked for him, and it feels comfortable, then it is good enough for us. If for no other reason, this is why it is important for senior managers to personally adopt a TQManagement style. The managers who work for you want to be like you because they want to be as successful as you are.

In order to master the skills that let them effectively use quality processes, senior managers must participate in their organization's quality training and regularly consult with their quality officer or consultant. Only when managers have mastered the quality processes are they able to tell their organization with credibility how they intend to modify their behavior and management style. To reinforce their commitment to a personal change strategy, managers must first be open to feedback on ways they can improve their use of the quality techniques. They cannot hope to provide constructive criticism to their team members until they have demonstrated a personal commitment to change. Once such a commitment has been shown, however, they can speak from a platform of experience.

Specifically, we found that successful TQManagers do five things:

1. They participate in quality training and learn as much as possible about Total Quality.
2. They work with their organization's quality officer or consultant to be sure the requirements for supporting the implementation plan are clearly understood.
3. They continually speak of Total Quality as a long-term commitment, not a short-term program.

4. They develop specific actions for their own personal in-
    volvement with their team for coaching and inspecting
    quality implementation.
5. They adopt a process and plan for receiving feedback on
    their personal use of quality processes and tools.

Lew Hatala (Lader, 1988, p. 36), quality engineering manager at AT&T's Atlanta Works, said of their quality efforts, "We
started telling our production specialists that we really wanted
to hear their ideas. It took them about a year before they began
to believe us. In the process, managers began acting less like
bosses and more like leaders. Many of them were surprised to
learn what good ideas their subordinates had. And some subordinates got to know their managers as people for the first time."

Establishing Employee Involvement and Teamwork

Since the people who do the work know it better than those who
supervise, it is imperative that employees become involved in
solving their own work problems. TQManagers facilitate their
employees' involvement by continually initiating and building
their team's skills at implementing TQManagement. The managers of the organizations we studied work at accomplishing three
team development objectives: (1) communicating their team's
Total Quality progress and achievements by both written messages and personal contact, (2) recognizing and rewarding their
teams for problem solving and quality improvement, and (3)
identifying strategic or tactical problems as opportunities for
their team to pursue and, having done that, joining their team
as a participant/leader.

In *Tools and Methods for the Improvement of Quality* (Gitlow,
Gitlow, Oppenheim, and Oppenheim, 1989, p. 14) the authors
describe the quality environment as one where "a true cooperative spirit prevails. . . as teamwork is a prerequisite for the firm
to function and constantly improve the extended process. The
corporate culture changes so that workers are no longer afraid
to point out problems in the system, and management is actively
involved in the never-ending improvement of the extended pro-

cess with workers. Workers and management learn to speak the same language, the language of statistics and process control. Workers are responsible for communicating to management the information they have about the system so that management can act."

Teamwork cannot survive without interteam and intra-team communication. First, as in any team, members must be able to dialogue with one another. Second, as they develop this new way of working they will need contact with other teams for both data on comparable work processes and reinforcement. To facilitate these needs, managers should participate in team activities, encourage team meetings, share timely performance feedback, and stimulate cross-functional team development. Successful Total Quality organizations also support open communication by establishing jointly held but noncompetitive goals for teams.

Naisbitt and Aburdene (1985, p. 52) described the importance of managers' developing their teams in *Re-inventing the Corporation*: "We used to think that the manager's job was to know all the answers. But in the 1980s, the new manager ought, rather, to know the questions, to be concerned about them and involve others in finding answers. Today's manager needs to be more of a facilitator—someone skilled in eliciting answers from others, perhaps from people who do not even know that they know."

TQManagers have embraced their new role when they are competently doing the following (*consciously* or *unconsciously*):

1. Learning, reinforcing, and personally using the tools and processes of Total Quality.
2. Preparing their team for collaboration by discussing, individually and collectively, their expectations, personal styles, and work processes and by using team-building techniques.
3. Learning, reinforcing, and personally using effective meeting skills. TQManagers invite trained observers to attend their team meetings and make suggestions for improvement.
4. Looking for opportunities for their teams to work on com-

mon problems that have been identified by individual suggestions, team brainstorming, or benchmarking data.
5. Recognizing that however many times people are informed
    about the state of the business and the organization's suc-
    cesses, it is never enough. TQManagers know that informa-
    tion and affirmation about the organization's progress (and
    a team's progress) must be provided on an ongoing basis.

Houghton (1986, p. 18) says, "To implement total quality,
we've got to have faith in the ability of our organizations to do
more than they have in the past. People are capable of accepting
much more responsibility than they've been given credit for.
People of every rank are clearly an important part of the drive
and decision-making process. They are smarter, more knowledgeable, and more capable than you may think. Give them the
tools, the knowledge, and let them do the job."

Cadillac's (1991) partnership with the UAW has been a
catalyst in their transformation. The Cadillac Quality Network
includes councils at each of their seven major facilities, which
are supported by nearly 600 work teams and cross-functional
teams, each composed of from ten to fifteen hourly and salaried
employees. Cadillac solicits the views of employee teams during
preparation of its annual business plans, which embody short-
and long-term quality-improvement goals. This open, yet disciplined, planning process, guided by analyses of information in
more than fifty data bases, culminates with the completion of
detailed quality plans for plants and staff units.

Promoting Quality Improvement

It is obvious to us that organizations have the most impact when
they integrate the TQManagement processes and tools into
their normal business processes, such as planning sessions,
operation reviews, and long-range planning. When this happens management demonstrates that Total Quality is the process for managing the organization's business—today! The message is that it is not a greenfield exercise, where everything has to
be started over. In addition, searching for the root causes of

issues—not being satisfied with easy or simplistic answers until the *why* of a problem is answered—further demonstrates that TQManagement is the organization's new style of operating. Continuously asking *why* becomes a powerful tool allowing managers to uncover the real causes of problems in their group's work process. This not only reveals opportunities for improvement, but forcefully demonstrates what Total Quality is all about.

Kearns (1988, p. 30) said, "There is no question that top management must drive this process. And employee involvement is absolutely key. It is the people who do the work [who] know how to do it best, but they must be trained and given all the information that senior executives have if they are to be effective in helping us run our business."

James Harrington (1991, p. 16) warns in his book *Business Process Improvement,* "Expending much more effort to improve business processes during the 1990s will be a major factor in being competitive in the twenty-first century." He goes on to suggest that failure to improve business processes may result in undesirable effects: "Processes left unregulated will change, but that change will be for the convenience of the people in the process rather than for the best interest of the organization or the customer."

Maintaining Openness, Patience, and Trust

This is no easy task for most managers, but the return on this investment in style change can be very powerful. TQManagers demonstrate their new style by using quality tools, participating in their team's work process, soliciting employee feedback, and communicating regularly. Managers reinforce their commitment to Total Quality by continuously monitoring their own behavior and seeking feedback on their progress. By committing time and attention to her team now, a TQManager can expect the team members to increase ownership for their jobs, take on a deeper commitment to the organization's goals, and demonstrate increased competence in the use of the tools and processes of quality. Openness will not only foster feedback opportunities for both the employee and the manager, but provide the team accessibility to their primary resource for information, tools, and help: the manager.

By demonstrating trust the manager encourages employees to state their needs. This stimulates learning and builds self-confidence, which in turn makes employees more responsible. When a manager actively joins with his team in learning and applying the tools of Total Quality, he shows his commitment to teamwork. The team of such a manager will soon identify with their interdependence and the value of teamwork, which will in turn lead to team creativity and the discovery of new and improved work processes. That is when the manager sees the real return for his new management style!

But to adopt this new style a manager will need encouragement and help from senior management. An organization's senior management provides their managers with the motivation to strive for the desired kind of personal changes by taking four actions: (1) sponsoring feedback tools that measure a manager's style and are tied directly to TQManagement behaviors; (2) conducting an annual survey of employee attitudes and satisfaction with the organization's quality effort and management processes; (3) inspecting how managers, as individuals, manage their teams and the quality processes, and especially how they use feedback to adjust their management style; and (4) conducting two-way communication at all levels of the organization, including roundtables, one-on-one interviews, and "managing by walking around."

Identifying Future Supervisors and Managers

If Total Quality is to receive the proper attention of managers and become the organization's management style, it will be necessary to establish a cadre of TQManagers both for today and for tomorrow. Baldrige Award winners not only evaluate management candidates on their functional expertise; they also measure a candidate's support of Total Quality. This includes the candidate's absolute knowledge of basic quality improvement and ability to teach quality skills and tools. The candidate's quality-improvement achievements are given equal priority with her functional accomplishments. Successful TQManagement organizations have modified their succession-planning processes to include quality measures and to use such techniques as selection interviews, panel interviews, and premanagement workshops that include selection standards or modules based on TQManagement. Simply stated, a candidate for promotion in a TQManagement organization must demonstrate personal behavior that is supportive of Total Quality. These revised criteria for management selection are then communicated throughout the organization and incorporated in all management training. This is a powerful means of communicating the organization's commitment to Total Quality that underscores the seriousness of senior management's commitment to building a new culture.

It is also clear that in TQManagement organizations the greatest long-term contribution of senior managers to the organization's quality investments is the excellence that they build into future leadership at all levels. Building leadership that is firmly committed to quality is essential for long-term, continuous improvement. In the words of Deming (Walton, 1990, p. 237): "The aim of leadership should be to improve the performance of man and machine, to improve quality, to increase output, and simultaneously to bring pride of workmanship to people."

Reinforcing and Encouraging Total Quality

TQManagers know that changing an organization's culture is a long-term commitment. For that reason TQManagement organizations use every form of recognition and reward at their disposal to encourage the new behaviors. At the same time all of the Baldrige Award winners were careful to use their recognition and reward plans realistically during the initial phase of their quality implementation. They guarded against overuse so that such rewards did not become commonplace or add to the skepticism that often exists in organizations. These managers gave serious thought to the following goals:

Recognizing the Activities of Individuals. The TQManagement organizations we examined provided recognition in a variety of ways, from congratulatory notes and personal achievement presentations to plaques, team T-shirts, quality bulletin boards, and team recognition days. But perhaps the most powerful thing TQManagers do is remembering to say "thank you." Whatever the recognition these managers provide, it is delivered in a genuine manner; done often enough, it overcomes the skepticism that sometimes permeates the recognition programs of less effective organizations.

Rewarding Deserving Teams or Individuals. Cash awards and significant prizes for support of Total Quality help to highlight the outstanding accomplishments and behaviors that send the message: "Quality is important." However, the *who, what,* and *how* of such rewards should not be determined without careful thought and planning. Successful TQManagers recognize the power of systematic reward plans that encourage desired behaviors and build in the policies and guidelines that ensure their use on an ongoing basis. In addition, the senior management of a TQManagement organization will want to consider an incentive plan to support their managers' efforts. (See Chapter Ten.)

A Foundation for TQManagement

The management of an organization that focuses on these six goals not only supports the twelve action points for strategic change but also establishes a bedrock foundation that will support the rest of their TQManagement strategy. Like the winners of the Baldrige Award, these organizations demonstrate a commitment to Total Quality that starts with top management and flows from the CEO's office to the broom closet. TQManagers understand all the intellectual arguments for giving their employees the capacity to make quality happen, but at the same time they know that this alone will not create a workplace where quality happens consistently; instead, they must establish and maintain their own personal involvement. Henry Milewski, project director at the American Suppliers Institute, says that Total

Quality makes "obsolete much of what we have believed [about management] for the last seventy years" (MacFarland, 1990, p. 31). He compares the impact of Total Quality on American business leaders to the effect of Einstein's discovery of the theory of relativity on the scientific community. He says that it is turning all we have believed about management and business upside down. "It's a whole new way of thinking; we're looking at an entirely new belief system."

John S. Lloyd, president of Witt Associates, put it well: "Quality is not an accidental outcome. It is always the end result of visionary leadership. People create quality through intelligent effort, desire, and skill. The organization that takes aim at quality as a target and makes the deep commitment to strive for quality in its products and services must have outstanding leadership if it is to succeed" (Naval, 1989, p. 112).

If a foundation of management leadership and commitment is carefully laid, the pillars of the TQManagement strategy will stand firmly. Only then can management hope to make the desired state a reality.

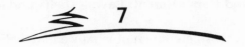

Strategy No. 1: Establish Supportive Organizational Roles and Structures

It can be very difficult to make significant changes, especially when you have been in the habit of doing things differently for decades, and especially when the very success that brought you to the positions you now hold is rooted in doing some things, frankly, the wrong way.

—W. Edwards Deming

While the transition to Total Quality is certain to yield a return, it is not without its price. TQManagement organizations have to invest time, effort, energy, and dollars. One focus for these investments is an infrastructure to facilitate the process of change. Although the kind of supportive structures and roles an organization develops should consider all of the relative action steps (Table 5.1), three strategy initiatives must receive special attention:

1. Developing and communicating a clear image of the future state
2. Using multiple and consistent leverage points to manage the transition

3. Implementing organizational arrangements for the transition

Each of these initiatives will require some level of incremental or redirected manpower, organizational restructuring, and redefinition of roles. In this chapter we will look at ways of facilitating these three change initiatives and will examine several opportunities for providing organizational support to a TQManagement strategy.

Clear Image of the Future

One of the first and most important steps to take on the road to TQManagement is that of developing and communicating *a clear image of the future*. Such a description is essential for clarifying the gaps between the organization's current and future states, because it is these gaps that form the basis for the transition strategy. Descriptions of the future can have a powerful effect upon people. John Kennedy's 1961 vision for placing a man on the moon and returning him safely to earth "in this decade" was not only a national goal, but a specific future event for which an entire industry was built.

When Winston Churchill and Franklin Roosevelt emerged from their 1943 Cairo conference proclaiming that only by "unconditional surrender" could the Axis nations obtain peace, it mattered little that there was no political or military precedent for their pronouncement. "Unconditional surrender" became a banner cry for Allied commitment to a total victory (Hicks, 1949). When people can clearly visualize a future goal they are better able to see their own part in the required commitments and investments.

In addition to letting people know what is expected, communicating the future state helps to quell the rumors, misconceptions, and fantasies people often imagine about Total Quality. The importance of employees' understanding what is expected of them cannot be stressed too strongly. For one thing, a clear description of the future state is certain to encourage dissatisfaction with the way things are, and the greater the dissatisfaction with the organization's current processes, the less resistance there will be to the change effort.

The future-state description must provide a clear, far-reaching, and challenging picture of where the organization will be in five or more years. It should describe the behaviors and conditions that must be initiated in the organization, in language everyone can relate to and understand. Table 7.1 represents the "vision" of Total Quality in the U.S. Department of Defense (U.S. Department of Defense, 1990). It is a simple outline of what will be different in various areas.

Mary LoSardo, quality manager for Metropolitan Life, described their quality vision, Achieving Personal Quality, for Jerry Bowles and Joshua Hammond (1991, p. 93): "The core of the cycle is a positive vision, a dream of what it is that we want to be. This is then broken down into specific goals pinpointing the behaviors that will lead you to that positive vision."

Once senior management has identified the gaps between the current state and the future state, they must determine whether they or a transition team should craft the plan to close the gaps. They must also decide who will own the task responsibility for managing the organization toward the desired state. We'll discuss these considerations later in this chapter, but for now it is important to recognize that communicating the organization's vision is a key management role. That vision must consist of a clear articulation of the organization's future state and a plan for closing the gaps, including specific targets to measure progress. This fits with what Deming refers to as "constancy of purpose." No company will stay in business without a plan, he says (Walton, 1986, p. 57).

Management's commitment and support is significant, but it is their leadership that really counts. Employees will look to senior management to determine whether their new direction is being managed with the same care and attention that is given to the organization's other business goals. Robert Cowley, the plant manager at AT&T's Merrimack Valley Works when Deming introduced his methods there, says: "If you're really going to have an impact, you really need to get a critical mass of

Table 7.1. Vision for a New Culture.

Category	Current State	Future State
Mission	Maximum return on investment/management by objectives (ROI/MBO)	Ethical behavior and customer satisfaction; climate for continuous improvement; ROI a performance measure
Customer requirements	Incomplete or ambiguous understanding of customer requirements	Use of systematic approach to seek out, understand, and satisfy both internal and external customer requirements
Supplier objectives	Undirectional relationship	Partnership
	Orientation to short-term objectives and actions with limited long-term perspective	Deliberate balance of long-term goals with successive short-term objectives
Improvement	Acceptance of process variability and subsequent corrective action assigning blame as the norm	Understanding and continually improving the process
Problem solving	Unstructured individualistic problem solving and decision making	Predominantly participative and interdisciplinary problem solving and decision making based on subsequent data
Jobs and people	Functional, narrow scope; management-controlled	Management and employee involvement; work teams; integrated functions
Management style	Management style with uncertain objectives, which instills fear of failure	Open style with clear and consistent objectives, which encourages group-derived continuous improvement
Role of the manager	Plan, organize, assign, control, and enforce	Communicate, consult, delegate, coach, mentor, remove barriers, and establish trust
Rewards and recognition	Pay by job; few team incentives	Individual and group recognition and rewards; negotiated criteria
Measurement	Orientation toward data gathering for problem identification	Data used to understand and continuously improve processes

Source: U.S. Department of Defense, 1990.

people. . . talking the same language, understanding the same concepts, so that these folks can really have an influence on the way we do business" (Walton,1986, p. 182). At Nashua Corporation, the company Deming featured in the 1980 NBC documentary, *If Japan Can, Why Can't We,* CEO Charles Clough believes that the focus on management is crucial. "There has to be training at several levels, especially for managers," he told Andrea Gabor (1990, p. 114). "See, the workers pick this up very fast, they understand what's going on."

Multiple and Consistent Leverage Points

Captains of the tugboats that move large seagoing ships around harbors know that applying leverage at only one point of a ship will not get the job done. A single tug might be able to turn a ship, but to do so it has to move frequently, pushing from different sides and at different leverage points. It is easier to move a large ship when more than one tug is used, each applying a different level of pressure at a different point. So it is with implementing Total Quality: it takes multiple actions and the leveraging of multiple issues. That is why the second key initiative for managing the transition is the use of *multiple and consistent leverage points.*

For example, since changes in tasks and the work environment are areas that will have to be leveraged to move the organization toward Total Quality, quality training and facilitation skills are new tasks that will be required. Still other leverage requirements may be new structures, organizational mergers, or personnel changes. Whatever innovations are necessary, it is important that they dovetail with the organization's other systems, such as reward programs, reporting relationships, and manpower management (including staffing and job descriptions).

As we have stressed, the transition to TQManagement is largely contingent upon significant behavioral change on the part of everyone in the organization. To provide this kind of help can be challenging, which is why many organizations have found that there is value in establishing subject matter experts (quality specialists) for the tools, methods, and processes of

Total Quality throughout the organization. For one thing, all the Baldrige winners report that Total Quality will not survive without training. (We will discuss a training strategy in Chapter Nine, but for now we will confine ourselves to the posttraining need.) After an organization's employees have been trained on the quality processes and tools, they will most likely need on-the-job assistance, including encouragement, reinforcement, and group facilitation skills and advanced statistical processes. Quality experts can be an excellent investment as a means of leveraging posttraining learning and on-the-job behavior.

All of the Baldrige winners consulted with at least one of America's premier *sensei* (Japanese for "counselors")—Deming, Juran, Feigenbaum, and Crosby—either by direct contact or by attending their seminars. Many visited numerous Japanese *sensei* and the industrial practitioners of Total Quality throughout the world. But when the time came to launch their own efforts, they either used the premier consultants to help them to develop their own "experts" or turned to lesser known quality specialists. Wallace Company utilized the services of Sanders & Associates to train and consult their employees. Xerox employed the Delta Consulting Group to assist them in developing their own internal network. Globe Metallurgical retained the American Suppliers Institute before investing in their own training cadre.

In addition to quality specialists, the transition also will need the assistance of the organization's human resources department. There are several significant support systems usually managed by Human Resources that are essential to TQManagement, such as communication, recognition and reward systems, and management training. Because of their expertise, we recommend that Human Resources representatives be included in the strategy design. However, we should tell you that several successful TQManagement efforts have gone out of their way to avoid identification with Human Resources for fear that Total Quality would be seen only as a human resources program. Because some organizations have a history of using Personnel as the fulcrum for myriad marginally successful "motivational" programs, this can be a valid concern, but we hasten to point out that without engaging Human Resources, an organization runs the risk of losing an important source of ideas and support. We'll say more about this a little later in this chapter.

Organizational Arrangements

The third key initiative is establishing *organizational arrangements for the transition.* Although these will vary by organization, based on size, management style, and resources, the principal tasks and roles that have to be considered are a *transition plan,* a *transition manager,* and *transition management structures.*

Transition Plan

As noted in Chapter Five, the transition plan, or strategy, is the road map to make sure you arrive at your future state. The kind of transition road map we suggest consists of specific objectives for TQManagement, benchmarks, and measures to establish performance standards for the organization and its operating units, as well as the roles and responsibilities for key persons and groups. (Chapters Six through Eleven describe the elements of a transition plan.)

Motorola is synonymous with Six Steps to Six Sigma, but their quality efforts actually began with a planning document titled *Rise to the Challenge,* their plan for achieving customer satisfaction (Dobyns and Crawford-Mason, 1991). Xerox's (1983) *Leadership Through Quality* is a ninety-two-page document describing their change strategy with very clear guidelines, milestones, and measures. At New United Motor Manufacturing, Inc. (NUMMI), the quality strategy is spelled out in the seven goals of the *NUMMI Team Members' Handbook* (Bowles and Hammond, 1991). The IBM (1991) quality activities began with Market Driven Quality, a five-step plan that is the basis for their continuous-improvement activities. Milliken's (1990) basis for quality is their Pursuit of Excellence plan.

Transition Manager

Who will make the transition happen? As we have noted earlier, senior management is ultimately responsible for implementing the quality strategy. However, most TQManagement organizations appoint a senior person who is respected enough to have linkage with the "steady-state" managers and who has the visibility and vision to be able to describe the organization when the transition is complete and in the future state. Several Baldrige winners created transition managers, or quality officers, at the division or group level. As an example, Xerox had a vice president of quality for each group staff, as well as for each of the major divisions. The functions of each division had yet another level of managers assigned to quality implementation full-time or part-time, based on the size of the function.

Transition Management Structures

It is a very difficult task for senior management teams to keep their organization focused on its current challenges while simultaneously planning for the future and controlling the organization's transition. To bring it off, most organizations require structures and processes outside their usual management systems, such as task forces, internal and external consultants or specialists, and pilot programs. Several of the Baldrige winners formed special teams to develop their quality transition plans and manage their implementation. At IBM Rochester, Motorola, and Wallace Company, the transition teams were composed of senior executives who integrated their transition-team role with their regular tasks. At Xerox a team of vice presidents and vice presidential candidates were released from their assignments and spent over a year on an "implementation team" that developed and managed a quality strategy. There are advantages and disadvantages to both approaches. The use of senior managers who are still serving in their executive roles allows for easier assimilation of quality into the organization and demonstrates a high level of commitment. But on the flip side, when the senior staff and implementation team are one and the same, TQManagement may be seen by employees as an executive program. The dedicated-team approach avoids that problem but has the disadvantage of appearing too elite, with the members becoming so expert in the new culture that their advocacy alienates others in the organization. Both approaches have proven to work; senior management should choose an approach based on their organization's environment. Keep in mind, however, that the primary advantage to the dedicated team approach is that it *builds participation into the change*.

Expanding employee participation in transition planning and implementation should be carefully considered because it aids in reducing resistance, builds ownership, and motivates people to make the transformation work. Participation helps increase communication about the transition and the goals throughout the organization; in turn, it usually leads to new sources of information about the process that will enhance the effectiveness of the new organization. At Milliken (1990), they value a program called Opportunity for Improvement. When Milliken's quality efforts began in 1988 they received half a suggestion per employee—in 1990 the average had jumped to nineteen per employee (Bowles and Hammond, 1991). TQManagement planners should be aware, however, that involving employees in the transition also entails relinquishing control, requires big investments of employee time, and demands patience from senior management. Because extensive participation may create conflict within the organization, it will also require situational diagnosis, planning, and feedback from the participants.

Figure 7.1 represents a dedicated infrastructure that was used by one large organization in their transition to Total Quality. It is offered here as one example for transition planners to consider.

Whatever approach an organization chooses for building an infrastructure to implement TQManagement, its success will depend on the clearly identified and understood roles of key persons. Make no mistake—changing an organization's culture and operating processes is complex, hard work; confusion about responsibilities and "turf wars" will only add to that complexity. The more that participants accept and understand their roles and responsibilities, the easier the transformation will be. All the organizations we studied were concerned about *who* should do *what*, and *when* they should do it. To help themselves KISS ("Keep it simple, stupid") their plans, they all addressed, in

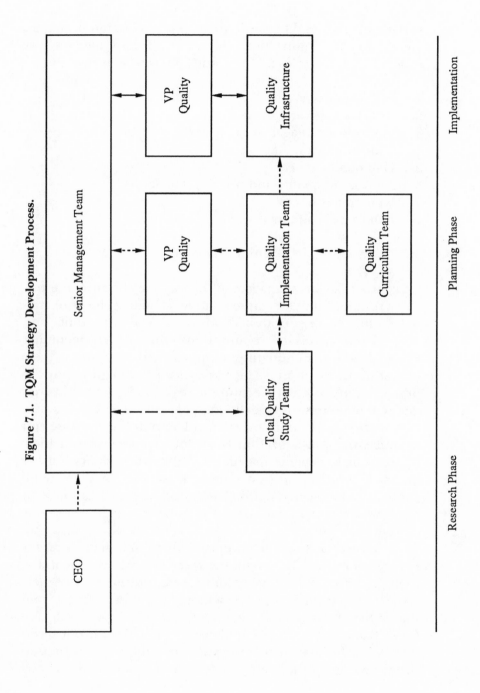

Figure 7.1. TQM Strategy Development Process.

varying degrees, eight roles in their implementation strategies. We think any organization planning a Total Quality effort should give these roles and responsibilities serious thought:

1. Senior manager
2. Unit manager and team
3. Transition manager or quality officer
4. Transition team
5. Unit quality officer
6. Network of quality and training specialists
7. Human Resources
8. External consultants

Senior Managers

Of course, like any management process or objective, the primary responsibility for implementing TQManagement rests finally with the organization's individual operating units and teams. However, it is the organization's senior management that has the lead role in initiating, supporting, and sustaining their operating units' efforts. The road to quality begins with the organization's vision of the future state of Total Quality, but even before that vision can be defined, senior management must be certain they agree on the mission and outputs (the purpose and products) of the organization. Ford Motor Company began their effort to make "quality job one" in 1984 when Henry Ford II announced a new mission statement for the company. It included the following (Walton,1986, p.135): "Our mission is to improve continually our products and services to meet our customers' needs."

With their mission, outputs, and vision in hand a senior management team can begin the race to TQManagement. For their part, it will be necessary for the senior team to revisit their own role as a team: What is the senior team's mission apart from that of the organization? What are the team's outputs? Why are they a team, what purpose do they serve, and what products do they deliver? It may be that the mission of the senior team is to "lead the organization and satisfy their customers." Their outputs might be a "strategic plan and a business plan," or they might consist of Deming's fourteen points. What is important here is that once the senior team knows what products they produce as a team, they can begin to apply the processes of quality improvement to their own work and thus showcase those processes. Also, senior management must implement quality at the corporate level, which means leading the organization's senior staffs in incorporating the tools and processes in the work they do.

As we have said, senior managers of successful transitions to TQManagement are willing to make investments in the change — *especially investments of their own time!* The top executives of every organization committed to a Total Quality transition are involved in a whole range of activities that are necessary to lead the change. These activities will generally fall into four areas: (1) using the quality processes in their senior team meetings; (2) conducting presentations and communication meetings on quality objectives throughout the organization; (3) attending quality events such as reviews of unit quality progress and quality celebrations, and (4) participating in their own education and training. The scope of the organization's change task will dictate how significant an investment of time is necessary, but launching a new culture will certainly increase the amount of time the senior team must spend together. We know from research (Delta Consulting Group, 1988b) that the less successful transitions to TQManagement are those where the investments of time were delayed or avoided because senior managers felt so overloaded with change activity that they could not do their work.

The dilemma is that while the senior staff's time is essential to TQManagement implementation, it is going to cut into the time the team needs to spend leading the rest of the organization. This can result in charges that the senior team is too insular or too absorbed in its "own process." This Catch-22 cannot be avoided — the challenge is to manage the balance of the two demands until the organization sees quality and its business process as one and the same. This is not easy, but more and more executive teams are learning how to do it effectively.

(In Chapter Fourteen we'll discuss more about the development of executive teams.)

In successful organizations the senior staffs work hard at making the change an integral part of their work. The U.S. General Accounting Office (1991, p. 31) noted: "We often heard from corporate executives that quality improvement is a difficult, long-term process. Consequently, senior managers led the process, demonstrating their commitment to quality throughout their daily actions and working to build quality values throughout the organization. Among the companies we studied, an effective leadership effort eventually resulted in a quality program that was integrated into all key business processes."

Westinghouse's Commercial Nuclear Fuel Division's Quality Council (Westinghouse Corporation, 1989a) (also their senior transition team) has been from the outset composed of the division's senior management, plant managers, and quality-assurance managers. The Quality Council establishes the general goals and guidelines for continuous-quality improvement throughout the division; each of the specific goals is led by a member of the council. In this way they demonstrate management leadership but also spearhead the integration of quality objectives into the daily operations of the business.

Total Quality success is fundamentally dependent upon the activities of managers throughout the organization, and the operating-unit heads and the senior management team are always responsible for implementing Total Quality. However, there is a value in having one person, the transition manager — preferably a senior management peer — assist the senior management team in implementing the strategy and keeping it updated. This kind of role sharing allows the senior management team to avoid the "nitty-gritty" of the organization-wide transition and to better focus on the strategic issues of moving from the present to the desired state of TQManagement. It is important that the division of responsibilities between the senior management team and a transition manager or quality officer are clearly defined to avoid confusion and overlap. It is also important that the transition manager be free of other responsibilities in order to maintain a broad view of the organization's quality goals and implementation progress. With this kind of visibility the quality officer can advise the senior management team where they can best place their focus, both individually and collectively. We'll discuss the role of the transition manager in somewhat greater detail a little later in this chapter.

Unit Manager and Team

It is a fact that if Total Quality doesn't happen at the operating-unit level, *it will not happen!* Every organization that has launched a quality effort knows that the line organizations are where "the rubber meets the road" for continuous-quality improvement. It is in the engineering, manufacturing, and sales departments that the work processes and practices can be improved, increasing the organization's product quality and ensuring that customer requirements are met. But before this can happen, operating management must implement the organization's quality policy within their units, create an environment that will allow TQManagement to thrive, and provide leadership and role models that their employees can emulate.

Unit managers start by developing a climate of teamwork and helpfulness within their own management team. An operating unit's management team begins by accepting their responsibility for incorporating the TQManagement strategy in their product, business, and operating plans and activities. Like the senior managers above them, they must learn and master the quality tools and processes in order to be able to demonstrate their continuous and consistent use of quality improvement in managing their own unit.

As a team, the task of an operating unit's senior management is to manage the implementation of Total Quality within their division or department and to develop plans and goals to improve the quality of their products, work processes, operations, and management practices. This means reviewing and monitoring their unit's plans for achieving TQManagement— implementing the quality strategy, assisting in the design of the unit's quality processes, setting objectives for quality, and measuring progress in achieving quality.

In 1986 Motorola began work on a new pager (Bowles and Hammond, 1991). At that time their usual development cycle was three to five years. But when they set up their Boynton Beach "Bandit" plant to produce a new pager, they cut their best plan estimate in half, to eighteen months. They then set out to find ways to make it happen. A twenty-four-person cross-functional team literally scanned the world looking for process ideas and existing technology. They "borrowed" what they saw as "best" from other Motorola plants, Honda, Seiko, Xerox, and others (thus the name "Bandit"). The tools they chose read like a quality textbook: benchmarking, concurrent engineering, Just-In-Time, supplier reduction, design for manufacturability, design for assembly, and flexible manufacturing. The outcome was a state-of-the-art robotic production line that went on-line within plan, producing high-quality pagers (when a customer in the same area is "beeped," it does not interfere with another customer's pager) in record time at a price better than that of their competitors. When an order for a pager is placed at the Schaumberg, Illinois, headquarters, a customized pager comes off the line two hours later.

If organizations are to have successes like that of the "Bandit" plant, their senior teams must incorporate TQManagement in their list of tasks for all their units' operating reviews and business plans. Most important, a unit's senior team must demonstrate their commitment through their personal actions. They must be prepared to teach the quality tools and processes, use and inspect the processes within their teams, be visible to their people, and take the time to regularly update their employees on the unit's performance, progress, and plans.

A significant responsibility of unit management is defining and implementing the "next customer" concept within their teams. As we discussed earlier, for TQManagement to be "total" in an organization means establishing the idea of customer-supplier relationships between work groups and workers. Only when an organization's workers begin seeing one another as customers and suppliers in the work process chain can the organization put in place systems to identify and satisfy their internal customers' requirements. It is this internal customer–

supplier concept that is the foundation for continuous-process improvement. Of course, the focus on the ultimate consumer (the one who buys the product or service) cannot be forgotten.

At Federal Express (1991), the customer-supplier concept is regarded as extremely important in Total Quality. Their process assumes that everyone within the organization is both a customer and a supplier; this builds effective working relationships between operating units. The process seeks to balance the needs of internal customers (what is expected) and the capabilities of internal suppliers (what is delivered). In this framework, each group in the customer-supplier chain negotiates performance expectations. Districts negotiate with metroplexes about package movement requirements; metroplexes then negotiate with the hubs and air operations. This "alignment process" provides everyone with an opportunity to influence how the work is done so that the end user's expectations are met. Federal Express's COO, Jim Barksdale, describes it this way: "When you stop to think of all the ways people rely on one another throughout our operation, you can see that everyone's job really is to support someone else so they can keep their 'customers' satisfied within the organization" (Federal Express, 1991).

Promoting and communicating their support for TQManagement is not only a vital action for the unit management team but also one that will make their overall task easier. The most visible actions they should plan are the incorporation of local communication vehicles and reinforcement of quality improvement through appropriate recognition and rewards. They should also further reinforce Total Quality within their unit by ensuring the selection and promotion of managers who support Total Quality and who demonstrate the behaviors and values inherent in TQManagement. Like the organization as a whole, this will send a clear, unambiguous signal to everyone in the unit that management is serious about TQManagement.

Another significant decision the unit's senior management team will have to make is whether they want to establish a local quality officer to oversee their implementation plan.

Transition Manager or Quality Officer

We have stressed over and over again (because it is so vitally important) that successful implementation of Total Quality requires management support throughout the organization. However, there is significant value in having one executive accountable for assisting senior management in implementing the strategy and keeping it updated. We have found that several Baldrige winners elected to follow this strategy by appointing a senior manager as their quality officer. From these examples it is apparent that in such cases the roles of the senior management team and the quality officer should be distinct to avoid misunderstanding and miscommunication. In addition to a corporate quality officer, some large organizations also established quality officers at their division or group levels. As explained earlier, Xerox had vice presidents of quality on their group staffs and quality managers at the unit level. In addition to supporting their line organizations, these dedicated line managers were gathered into an "implementation team" to guide the process throughout the entire group. However, such assignments need not be based on the organizational structure.

At IBM Rochester (1991), each senior manager "owns" one of the six critical factors of the quality effort: (1) improved products and definition of service requirements, (2) an enhanced product strategy, (3) a Six Sigma defect elimination strategy, (4) further cycle-time reductions, (5) improved education, and (6) increased employee involvement and ownership. Each executive assumes responsibility for leading the plans and implementation of the critical factor for which he is accountable. Laurence Osterwise (Dobyns and Crawford-Mason, 1991, p. 157) of IBM Rochester explains that "people would rather be led than managed and empowered as opposed to controlled." He says that empowerment "starts with the authority, the responsibility, then the accountability. It causes people to be more thoughtful when they really get that authority and responsibility and more dedicated and committed."

A good quality officer provides leadership and a unifying focus for the organization's quality-improvement effort. A quality office can be an umbrella for coordinating all aspects of TQManagement, including (1) strategy implementation, (2) employee empowerment, (3) continuous-quality improvement tools and technology, (4) quality deployment into business planning and work processes, and (5) monitoring of progress toward the achievement of Total Quality. But perhaps a quality officer's most important function is to keep the organization's senior executives and operating units regularly informed on progress in the implementation plan and to facilitate corrective actions and interventions to keep the organization on-track toward its future state.

A quality office should exist in both a narrow and a broad sense. In its narrow sense, a quality office provides implementation support, strategy planning, project coordination, and quality technology; it works closely with the human resources department in the areas of communication, training, and employee involvement. In its broad sense, the quality office consists of the "transition team" (the people throughout the organization who have oversight responsibility for making TQManagement happen in their units and who come together as a network of implementation experts) and the organization's quality-training operations. Any organization considering a quality office has to realize that the most effective functions of such an office can only be fulfilled if they are understood in the wider context.

Since a quality officer's primary purpose is to assist the senior management team in designing and facilitating the processes that support TQManagement—especially ensuring that quality tools and processes are an integral part of the senior management team's work style—the quality officer has to become familiar with those tools and processes and develop her organization development and facilitator skills. Because of the unique line experiences and process skills a quality officer must possess, the senior management team that chooses to establish a quality office should *select their quality officer early in their planning* to allow their selectee time to acquire the training and skills necessary for the job.

A key responsibility in a quality officer's job description is assisting operating units in the development of their Total Quality implementation plans, and reviewing and monitoring their progress. A sure way to accomplish this is for a quality officer to help the senior management team define strategic goals for each year of the implementation period that can be cascaded to the organization's operating units. Strategic goals should include specific targets for training, proliferation of the use of quality-improvement and problem-solving processes, and senior management's participation in the first round of the training. In short, the quality office must make certain that the processes of TQManagement are in place and being used throughout the organization. This is best accomplished by regular inspections of the implementation by the quality officer and senior managers. At Xerox they say, "You can *ex*pect what you *in*spect."

To support both the organization's and the unit's goals, the quality officer must also be accountable for establishing communication requirements for Total Quality. Simply put, the quality officer should determine what is to be communicated, when it is communicated, and how it is communicated. The quality officer will have to engage the organization's communication resources to ensure that these professional services are fully utilized to support the TQManagement requirements.

A key, but sometimes overlooked, task of the transition manager is to get the participation of Human Resources in developing a recognition and reward system that supports TQManagement and to coordinate other applicable human resource functions, such as communication and training. While some companies we studied steadfastly guarded against Total Quality being identified as a "Personnel program," they also worked staunchly to make Human Resources a partner in their efforts.

Another valuable role a quality officer can play is to foster and facilitate a network of all the "specialists" who battle in the trenches of quality implementation. Such a network can share experiences, synthesize what works well, learn from what has not worked, discuss state-of-the-art methodologies, and develop tactical and strategic actions that will move the organization closer to the desired state. A wise quality officer uses such a network to test whether employee involvement in team activities is receiving continued emphasis, is understood, and is appropriately linked to the organization's Total Quality goals. Through a network of internal practitioners, the transition manager is able to serve as a quality resource for the operating units and facilitate the training of unit quality officers.

Houghton (1987) credited Forest Behm, Corning's first quality officer, with getting them off to a fast start in 1983 and Dave Luther, who followed Behm, for keeping the effort focused and on-track. Luther made it a practice to meet regularly with people from other quality companies to share ideas and progress. Houghton encouraged this "because nobody has the best ideas. You learn from doing" (p. 20).

Transition Team

It was Robert Burns who cautioned that the best-laid schemes of mice and men often go awry. And so it can be with quality-implementation plans. Not all operating units will progress at the same pace. Some groups require more emphasis on certain elements of the strategy than others, while other units will acquire valuable lessons that should be shared with other groups. For all of these reasons, and to focus on the overriding goal of maintaining a constancy of purpose, most Baldrige winners have established transition teams to guide and monitor operating-unit and organizational progress.

The Westinghouse Quality Council with wide involvement from all parts of the organization, establishes the CNFD's Quality Plan initiatives in the areas of management leadership, product/process leadership, human resource excellence, and customer orientation. (These are also the four imperatives for Total Quality in Westinghouse's model.) Each of the actions under these initiatives is assigned to a member of the council, who is responsible for advancing Total Quality processes, allocating personnel, reviewing and reporting on progress to the full council, and maintaining open and frequent communication with employees on progress.

Another model for transition teams is to form the organization's quality officer and the local unit quality officers into an oversight committee. Xerox used such a model. An example of a similar structure is shown in Figure 7.2. At a minimum the implementation team is responsible for oversight of these functional activities:

- Implementation plan assessment and inspection
- Updating of quality tools and processes as organizational maturity allows
- Policy recommendations
- Quality-training curriculum and introduction
- Team development
- Communication strategies and plans

Unit Quality Officer

As a member of the operating unit's senior management team, the unit quality officer is responsible for the quality-implementation plan and for facilitating the transition to Total Quality, in much the same way as is the organization's quality officer. From a task description view, it can be said that a unit quality officer is responsible for (1) establishing training requirements and curriculum and participating in the unit's quality-training activities, (2) developing a recognition and reward system to support TQManagement, (3) establishing links between employee teams in the operating unit and ensuring that their role in TQManagement is understood, (4) serving as the unit's quality-resource person, (5) participating as an ongoing member of the corporate quality network, and (6) establishing a unit quality-implementation team or network. Newt Hardie, Milliken's vice president for quality, sums it up well: "Our role as leaders is not to catch people doing things wrong but to create an environment in which people can become heroes" (Bowles and Hammond, 1991, p.159).

The unit quality officer's biggest challenge is to engage the senior staff in participating in the establishment of quality objectives and to set standards and measurements for the operating unit. At this level it is vital that management receive ongoing assistance in defining and implementing the "next

Figure 7.2. Quality Support Organization (Infrastructure).

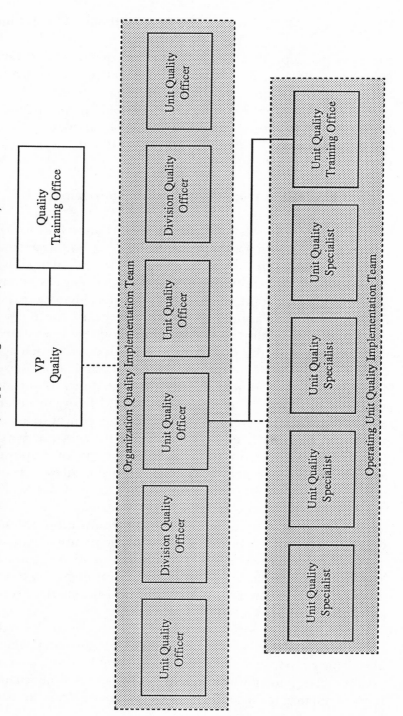

customer" concept. This means that the unit quality officer must help the senior staff, as a team and as leaders of the next tier of teams, to identify their key outputs, customers, and work processes. The quality officer will have to do assessments, provide feedback, and facilitate remedial learning of the organization's quality concepts, continuous-improvement process, and problem-solving capabilities.

Network of Quality and Training Specialists

All the quality leaders stated that an organization's teams will need training, and that after the initial training, employees and teams will still require assistance at their work sites. An organization's size will determine whether external resources are required to provide training; however, remember that successful revolutions require a junta of zealots. For this reason there is value in having quality specialists throughout the operational units to help with the posttraining reinforcement. Such specialists act as experts on the tools, methods, and processes of Total Quality. Most commonly, such internal, posttraining consulting is provided by an employee cadre. For organizations with minimal training resources, the necessary educational programs can be purchased and consultant trainers can be retained. For example, in addition to a handful of employee experts, Wallace Company (1991) utilized the services of a consultant to provide training and start-up help. Although training can be obtained from external sources, internal "experts" have the advantage of being able to leverage identification with the organization and support employee participation goals, because they themselves are local employees—and role models. The U.S. Navy has launched an intensive training program to prepare 3,000 command trainers, who will become TQM experts dispersed throughout the navy.

These quality specialists and quality officers also form the nucleus of an internal network of experts who can help facilitate an ongoing functional relationship between the organization's quality office and the local quality officers, once the quality-implementation team completes its work. As an example, as we have previously mentioned, a joint Quality Network of UAW and General Motors managers has been in existence since 1987, formalizing a working arrangement that started in 1973. At Cadillac (1991) the Quality Network is composed of councils at all levels of the organization that oversee all quality-improvement efforts and assist in the implementation of the Division Business Plan. The Quality Network focuses the entire organization's attention and effort on customer satisfaction as the "master plan" achieved through people, teamwork, and continuous improvement.

The reporting relationships of the quality specialists to the quality officer, as shown in Figure 7.2, can be represented by either a dotted or solid line, based on the needs of the operating unit. For example, in units where employee-involvement activities (such as quality circles and task forces) and continuous-improvement processes are already firmly established in the functional areas, the reporting relationship would probably be represented by a dotted line (meaning that although they are a direct report within their line organization, they also have functional accountability to the quality officer). However, in operating units where these two activities are in their early stages, organizations should give serious consideration to a solid-line relationship as a means for providing a central focal point until these activities are solidly established in the unit's business and management processes. Of course, the unit quality-implementation team members who come from major functions will likely have a strong dotted-line relationship to the quality officer, but they are primarily direct reports to their functional directors or vice presidents, because the ultimate accountability for the implementation of TQManagement rests with the unit managers.

The role of operating-unit quality specialists is to support their managers by being the on-site experts on tools, methods, and processes. As such, they support the organization in seven ways: (1) assisting managers in planning the implementation of Total Quality; (2) assisting managers in training their employees and implementing the processes; (3) supporting managers in the development of quality objectives, standards, and measurements; (4) supporting ongoing quality-improvement efforts by providing feedback to senior management and recommending new approaches; (5) facilitating the identification, management, and successful achievement of quality-improvement projects; (6) assisting managers in the delivery of specialized skills and management processes that support Total Quality in their functional area; and (7) providing the methodology to measure the effectiveness of Total Quality in their unit.

An organization's network of quality experts shares experiences, synthesizes what has worked well, learns from what has not worked well, discusses state-of-the-art methodologies and activities in the functional areas of quality, and plans tactical and strategic actions to move the organization closer to its mature future state. It also helps if quality trainers establish a formal network to share training experiences, curricular enhancements, and training technologies. Xerox (1983) found that it was valuable to hold some of the meetings of their Quality Training Network jointly with the organization's implementation team, especially in the early days.

Another excellent opportunity for developing the organization's quality competence is to have the quality office encourage and foster participation in external quality networks. There are several such networks, composed of senior representatives of world-class companies, who actively pursue and promote TQManagement within their own organizations. They include the American Society for Quality Control, the Association for Quality and Participation, the American Society for Training and Development, the Quality and Productivity Management Association, and numerous regional organizations linked through National Productivity Network.

Human Resources

Robert Dodson (1991, p. 91) wrote, "Total quality is a marriage of business strategy and human resource development at the altar of customer satisfaction." Certainly, in addition to quality experts, organizations committed to quality need support from their Human Resources department to ensure that communication and reward systems are dovetailed to their implementation plan. Even though a TQManagement effort should not be seen as a Personnel program, without engaging Human Resources an organization runs the risk of losing a valuable support group. Not only does the Human Resources staff provide valuable skills in communication, reward systems, and management training, but most HR groups also provide organization development expertise.

As an organization's experience with Total Quality grows, and competition demands even greater returns from quality investments, management will need to develop new processes and approaches to ensure that customer requirements are met with even greater accuracy and timeliness. When this occurs the role of the organization's human resources community will become vital. If the HR professionals are not familiar with quality goals and methods, or they do not feel ownership of the quality outcomes, there is a danger of conflict between HR and quality strategies. This would probably mean even greater reliance upon outside consultants, which not only is costly, but in the long run works against the organization "owning" its TQManagement effort.

External Consultants

External consultants can be a vital asset to management in starting up a TQManagement effort. Not only can they provide important resources in training and TQManagement orientation, but they can also act as process architects who help to build the in-house constituency that is so vital to long-term success. As we described in Chapter Five, consultants can bring the tools and techniques needed for planning and implementing the strategies for change. Perhaps even more important, a worthy consultant can also fill the role of an objective assessor for the senior management team and can act as the CEO's personal sounding board on progress.

In selecting a quality consultant it is wise to select a person or firm with whom the senior team will be comfortable — a person who is a good listener and flexible, but who is professionally sound in Total Quality and able to be firm when necessary. A CEO will want a person who clearly shares his values and who will take the time to learn about the organization and determine how those values might best be incorporated in a quality strategy. It is important, therefore, that the "chemistry" between the senior team (especially the CEO) and the consultant be good. It is equally important for the consultant to be as committed to the organization's success as is the team. (You can find that out by having the consultant identify her quality expectations for the organization and what values she believes are important.) Be wary of the consultant who can do anything and everything and who has all the answers, rather than one who expects the senior management to develop their own visions and expertise. Selecting the best consultant for your organization is a decision equal in importance to deciding to pursue Total Quality. The right selection can make the journey more successful than it might otherwise have been.

However, be cautious. If quality is seen as consultant-driven, it will most certainly fail. Success will be achieved only when the basic leadership talent and capacity exist within the organization. Consultants can help the organization develop effective leaders for the transition, but they can't compensate for fundamentally ineffective leadership (Nadler, 1988).

TQManagement is not business as usual. To achieve an organization's vision for the future requires not only doing things a new way, but using new structures and roles to facilitate the change. The transition to Total Quality will need special support for communicating the future state, use of many and varied leverages, and new organizational arrangements. Without these investments a vital pillar of the TQManagement strategy will be lost. The investment in time, effort, energy, and dollars may be difficult to make, but the return in process improvements, employee satisfaction, and product service quality will more than pay back the wise investor.

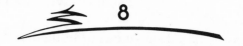

8

Strategy No. 2: Use the Right Tools and Processes

It has been said that figures rule the world. Maybe. But I am sure that figures show us whether it is being ruled well or badly.

—Johann Wolfgang von Goethe

On May 15, 1981, twelve Ford Motor Company executives visited Nashua Corporation, the small carbonless-paper manufacturer in Nashua, New Hampshire, which had suddenly become famous after the NBC TV documentary, *If Japan Can, Why Can't We?* Their purpose was to learn what W. Edwards Deming had done for Nashua. William Conway, then Nashua's CEO, shook his audience when he told them, "The only way you're going to do it is to use the technical tools of statistics. No other way. You've got to train all your people from A to Z, people have to understand the power of (controlling) variation." Conway said to the Ford executives that the only way Total Quality could work was if they used statistics themselves, got into the program, and pushed and sold it every way possible. He said, "It won't fly if someone wants to do it down below, without the strong support of top management." He added, "Get in your mind, right from the first, that the whole program is based on one simple theory, that is, you're going to help people" (Gabor, 1990, pp. 104–106).

TQManagement goes to the very heart of an organization's culture by establishing quality as the organization's basic operating principle. The ultimate goal is to assist the organization in anticipating and responding to its customers' needs in the design and manufacture of its products and services. This compels the organization to acquire the best possible understanding of what the customer desires, how their product or service is to be used, and how it is perceived relative to other suppliers. Quality improvement becomes the job of every employee, and to accomplish their jobs all employees must possess the tools of TQManagement. Total Quality requires a work environment in which every behavior and action is designed to provide external and internal customers with innovative products and services that fully satisfy their requirements.

All Baldrige winners and the other quality leaders we studied provide their employees with a common set of tools and techniques to enable them as individuals and work groups (1) to identify their customers' requirements, (2) to continuously evaluate and improve their work processes and the outputs they deliver, and (3) to do this collaboratively. Such tools and processes allow employees to form teams and to track key performance indicators by applying quality at the critical steps of their work processes. The goal is error prevention and doing things right the first time, but with the knowledge that continuous improvement is the realistic goal. Measuring the checkpoints in a work process will provide a team with three benefits: (1) it permits objective evaluation of a work process, (2) it allows early identification of problems and supports the actions required to meet the output, and (3) it helps to prevent errors.

The primary objective of measurement is process control and defect prevention. By measuring key indicators, TQManagement organizations are able to identify likely outcomes and to initiate action when their work process does not meet the requirements. The emphasis is on in-process control rather than inspection at the end of the process. Deming says, "Continual reduction in mistakes, continual improvement of quality, mean lower and lower costs. Less rework in manufacturing. Less waste of materials, machine time, tools, human effort" (Walton, 1986, p. 26).

In this chapter we will review the most common tools and processes of TQManagement:

- A process for solving problems
- A structured methodology for continuous improvement of quality
- A method for measuring the cost of quality
- Process control and the seven most common statistical tools
- A method for benchmarking competitors and functional leaders
- Additional tools and processes
- Methods for facilitating collaborative behaviors

Problem Solving

There are many problem-solving models in use by America's quality leaders; all of these models are designed to offer a systematic approach to resolving questions, issues, or problems by allowing employees to focus on three activities: (1) enabling individuals and work groups to conduct careful analysis based on numerical and other data and to explore potential solutions, (2) planning for the implementation of optimal solutions, and (3) monitoring the results of their corrective actions.

It is in the context of a systematic problem-solving process that the application of statistical tools most commonly occurs. By using a standard problem-solving process, regardless of the functional background of the team members, an organization enjoys a common method and language for analyzing variabilities, determining true causes, and planning optimal solutions. The operation of cross-functional problem-solving teams and the general management of problem resolution are therefore more easily facilitated by having all employees use the same process. A typical problem-solving process follows six steps (see Figure 8.1).

1. *Identify and select a problem to solve.* The objective of this

Figure 8.1. Six Steps to Problem Solving.

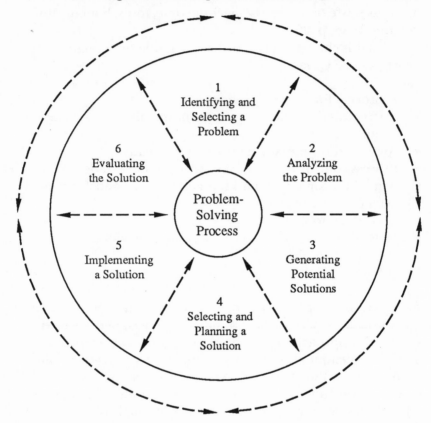

step is to explore, clarify, and describe a problem so that the team develops a clear understanding of it. Problems to be solved typically are work-related and within the team's responsibilities; they can be identified either by the work group (self-directed) or by management (management-directed). Some sources of variability are the key indicators of a work process, feedback from customers, and competitive benchmarking data.

2. *Analyze the problem.* Here is where most of the statistical tools have application. This step involves stating what is wrong, gathering and interpreting factual data, investigating possible causes, and zeroing in on the real problem. Analysis also in-

cludes stating the solution in the form of objectives or desired outcomes and noting any restrictions or limitations of a solution.

3. *Generate potential solutions.* The purpose here is to produce as many ways as possible to solve the problem. It is useful to start by reviewing the problem statement (step 1) and the data generated in step 2. Research has shown that the ultimate solution of a problem is improved by the generation of as many alternatives as possible. (Linus Pauling once said that the best way to get a good idea is to have lots of ideas.)

4. *Select and plan a solution.* In this step a work group evaluates their ideas and agrees on a recommendation to solve the problem. Even though a given idea may not work on its own, some of its elements might be valuable, so time should be taken to combine the best ideas and to carefully but critically evaluate each alternative. Ideally, the team will arrive at its recommendation through consensus. Once a solution is known, the team develops the plan to implement the solution.

5. *Implement a solution.* A solution is more likely to work smoothly if the actions needed to put it into operation are carefully planned. This involves anticipating implementation problems, planning to include the people whose support will be necessary, and assigning and accepting responsibilities for actions. This step should be relatively easy, because solutions derived by participative means are usually subject to much less resistance, in turn making implementation smoother and less time-consuming.

6. *Evaluate the solution.* In reality, most solutions are a mixed bag. They are neither tremendous flops nor stellar successes, but the team must know just how successful they are; therefore, the team is responsible for following up on their recommendations to determine whether a solution actually solves the problem. Knowing exactly what is happening lets the team make the improvements that will help solve the problem. Most often this means reapplying the statistical tools used in the analysis to allow before-and-after comparisons.

A statistical approach to problem solving is essential to continuous improvement, because without knowing the facts of a problem and its root cause, a solution is a crapshoot. Using a structured problem-solving process gives employee teams a set of required gates to pass through before they invest time and energy in gathering data, using tools, or implementing corrective actions.

Quality-Improvement Process

A process of continuous quality improvement provides a road map the organization can follow to keep headed in the direction of producing quality products and services. It shows where to begin and what questions to ask along the way in order to stay on track. It helps keep the focus on customer requirements and avoids costly side trips and wasteful backtracking. The emphasis is on continuous improvement rather than results, because this approach focuses employee creativity and innovation on the work *processes* that produce quality products and services, and on identifying ways to improve them. What a problem-solving process is to problem resolution, a quality-improvement process is to meeting customer requirements; it helps employees change the way they do their work to improve the quality of the services and products they provide their internal or external customers. The effect of a disciplined, well-practiced quality-improvement process has been shown to be a more timely response to the needs of the marketplace and improved business results, including better profit margins.

Problem solving is a vital part of the quality-improvement process, since quality improvement is designed to surface potential problems at the earliest possible point in the production of an output. It may not always be immediately obvious which of the two processes should be used to tackle a particular work issue; it takes a little skill and experience to know which process is most appropriate. Regardless of which process is selected, once a team starts work on a process they soon learn whether it is helping to accomplish the objective. However, it helps to know the basic differences between problem solving and quality improvement:

1. While problem solving is a general method for fixing

variations in systems, work processes, or results, quality improvement is a tightly focused process for ensuring conformity to the customer requirements of a specific product or service.

2. Problem solving assists with problem identification, data analysis, understanding root causes, and finding solutions and alternatives. Quality improvement assists with eliminating unnecessary work; preventing problems; and improving supplier-customer communication, work process evaluation, critical measurements, and confidence in results.

3. Problem solving is appropriate when there is a gap between what is happening and what is wanted — to move from vague dissatisfaction to a clearly defined problem — or when you are not sure how to approach an issue. Quality improvement is appropriate when you are starting a new work process or you need to improve an existing work process, but you don't have clear customer requirements.

4. The two processes support one another. You would move from problem solving to quality improvement when the problem you have identified is a lack of quality (meeting customer requirements) or an inability to assess quality, or when the proposed solution involves producing a specific output. You would move from quality improvement to problem solving when an evaluation of the work process capability shows that it cannot produce an output that will meet the customer's requirements, or when an evaluation of results indicates that the work process did not produce a quality output.

There is no single quality-improvement process that is better than any other; nearly all derive from Deming's "Plan-Do-Check-Act" model. There are two that are more commonly used than the others: (1) Xerox (1983) uses a nine-step model that has become a standard for many other Total Quality organizations and (2) Motorola's six-step method, known as Six Steps to Six Sigma, is now used by many organizations throughout the country. A good quality-improvement model is general enough to apply to the different sorts of products or services that people create. It is a guide, not a rigid set of directions. In selecting a process, successful organizations consider what would be best for all their people and functions, so that the model can be easily adapted to their particular work. Regardless of the process used, quality improvement is approached from the viewpoint of the supplier who is responsible for producing the work—while remembering that suppliers are also customers for someone else's work. The power of a quality-improvement process lies in this kind of open communication between supplier and customer, and in their shared responsibility.

The Nine-Step Quality-Improvement Model

The objective of the nine-step quality-improvement model is to help individuals and work groups identify their customers' requirements, determine the capability of their work process to meet those requirements, and continuously evaluate and improve the quality of their work. The nine steps in this continuous-quality-improvement process follow.

1. *Identify the work to be done.* In this step the team, or employees, identify the product or service to be produced as part of their job: What output is passed on to the next person or persons in the work process? To be effective, the work output should be neither too broadly nor too narrowly described. It is best expressed in a noun-verb style. The first word of the description—the noun—should be quite specific and as tangible as possible. The second part is phrased as a verb—a word expressing what is done to produce the output, for example, *report written, invoices generated, customer information data base updated.*

2. *Identify the customer for the work, using real names.* Because quality means meeting agreed-upon customer requirements, it is important to know who the customer is for the work. Usually this is the next person in the work process, the receiver of the work output and the next to act on it. (As was stressed earlier, a customer may be either external or internal.) The customer should be identified by name, since people, not departments or divisions, identify and agree upon requirements. (As an example, if you are to supply a financial report for marketing, don't stop there; find out what individual in marketing uses your report.) Where there are multiple customers, it is easier if there is a surrogate who can speak for all of the others. There may also

be secondary customers—persons beyond the next step in the process—who receive or make use of the output and who may influence the requirements. In addition, there may be end users, those who ultimately use the product. As an example, a curriculum developer's product may be produced for a national sales manager (primary customer), who provides the course to field sales managers (secondary customers), who then deliver it to sales representatives (end users). It is also important to remember that a team's manager is often not the customer for the group's work; in this case the manager's role is to facilitate dialogue between the team and the real customer.

3. *Identify the customer's requirements (dialogue).* Requirements are nothing more than what the customer wants, needs, or expects of the output. Customer requirements range from general to very specific (the latter is better than the former) and should relate directly to the customer's objectives. Requirements can and should be negotiable, but a supplier should push for specificity when determining what the customer wants. As an example, a customer who wants a "green sweater" will have to provide more information to the supplier, while the customer who wants a "green, cashmere, crew-neck, 4-ply, size 40 sweater" may have to negotiate if green is not in stock—or the price is too high! Even before a discussion about customer requirements begins, the customers must describe the outputs they need as clearly as possible and provide potential suppliers with a detailed description of what it is needed.

4. *Convert customer requirements into the supplier specifications required and renegotiate with the customer as necessary.* Specifications are the detailed description of outputs as stated in the supplier's terms. Supplier specifications must be achievable and matched with a measurable specification, such as time, money, or the physical attributes of the output. Supplier specifications have to be reviewed with the customer to show that they will produce an output that meets expectations, or to renegotiate when specification's don't meet requirements. As an example, a customer requirement may be a "report published" in two weeks, while the supplier's capability may be one week, or two—or three. The supplier needs to know what will be acceptable to the customer.

5. *Identify a work process that will meet the requirements.* Once requirements and specifications are in sync, the next step is to establish a systematic way of defining what has to be done to produce the output. A number of formal techniques can be used to help with this task, such as flow charts, PERT charts, and other project-planning processes. At a minimum, the work process steps must include the major activities and identify the major milestones and measurement points. You can avoid "reinventing the wheel" by finding out what documentation already exists for similar work processes, but keep in mind that complex work requires more detailed information than does simple work. Although organizing the work process is primarily the responsibility of the supplier, the customer should be involved if possible. (Often the customer is more knowledgeable than the supplier.)

6. *Select measurements for the critical steps in the process.* In quality improvement, the emphasis is on prevention of errors, rather than on detection and correction. This will require a systematic plan for collecting data about the work process, using measurements derived from customer requirements and supplier specifications. What is going to be measured, and how it is going to be measured, has to be decided before the work process begins. A comprehensive plan will include three categories of measurements: (1) *process capability measurements,* to indicate if the work process is capable of meeting the requirements; (2) *in-process measurements,* to indicate at a given point how well you are doing; and (3) *evaluation measurements,* to be applied after the work is complete. In selecting measures, it helps to focus on the vital few that will provide essential information. Begin by finding out what measurements already exist for this or similar work processes. If this is a new process, it is useful to find out if there are comparable data or processes from which you can generalize. It helps to remember that the customer, better than anyone else, can help to determine which measurements are the critical ones for ensuring a quality output. (The customer can also help the supplier understand why the key measurements are important.)

7. *Determine the capability of the process to deliver the expected*

outcomes. The purpose here is to determine if the process you have selected is capable of producing the desired output, one that meets the specifications agreed to by both the customer and the supplier. The focus is on the outcome, to determine if the work process will produce the customer's requirements. Here is where the process capability measurements are tested to ensure that the process will actually work. If the measures do not leave you confident, revise the work process before you begin. If repeated attempts to revise it still leave you with a process that is not capable of producing an output that meets the customer's requirements, talk with the customer and if necessary renegotiate the requirements. Or the customer may need to acquire a different supplier!

8. *Evaluate the results and identify steps for improving the process.* Evaluation of results must be based on the specifications the customer and supplier agreed to as part of determining supplier specifications. In a sense, these specs represent a template against which the results are measured, although the emphasis is on results rather than process. The customer has an important role here; the supplier can check some of the results against the specs, but other requirements, such as style, effectiveness, relevance, and courtesy, may be more subjective and require the customer's input.

9. *Decide on the next steps.* If a problem has emerged with the output, a problem-solving process will have to be applied to determine where the work process has failed. If the process has produced the desired results, the evaluation from step 8 will allow you to gauge the opportunity for further quality improvement. Of course, it is necessary to continue to monitor the work process and results on a regular basis to ensure that you maintain quality. It is also important to keep in mind that an output that meets today's requirements may not be a quality output tomorrow. That is why it is good to stay in touch with your customer.

Six Steps to Six Sigma

Six Sigma is Motorola's (Norling, 1989) quality-measurement system. It means virtually zero defects. Sigma indicates how often defects are likely to occur; the higher the Sigma level, the lower the defect rate. As an example: 1 Sigma = 32 percent defect rate, 2 Sigma = 5 percent defect rate, and 6 Sigma = 0.0000002 percent defect rate or $^3/_{14}$ defect per million. This metric is used in all Motorola operations, and because it is a common one, it has become their only true measure for eliminating defects.

To help operations reach Six Sigma levels, Motorola devised a six-stage methodology called the Six Steps to Six Sigma, a process not unlike the nine-step quality-improvement process we have just described. The methodology is used proactively in two ways. First, it is used to prevent defects before they can occur, that is, to change the way work is done so that defects are not produced. Second, it is used to anticipate customer requirements. As performance improves, customer expectations rise, and the definition of a defect becomes increasingly stringent. This ongoing iteration is implicit in the Six Steps to Six Sigma methodology. The six steps are as follows:

1. *Identify the product or service you provide.* Like the nine-step process, the objective here is to identify the specific output.

2. *Identify the customers for your product or service, and determine what they consider important.* Ask for whom you do your work, then determine exactly what the customer satisfaction requirements are for that work. Any failure to meet these requirements is considered a defect. The message here is that only by actively seeking and listening to each customer's voice can you know how defects should be defined. (This step combines steps 2 and 3 of the nine-step process.)

3. *Identify your needs to provide a product or service that satisfies the customer.* In other words, what do you need to do your work? With this step you complete a macrolevel system map or flow chart that describes how required inputs are converted by the work process to create outputs that totally satisfy the customer.

4. *Define the process for doing the work.* By definition, a process is an ordered sequence of human or machine operations designed to produce a desired result. This analysis is taken to the task level, with tasks defined by those who perform or manage the process.

5. *Mistake-proof the process and eliminate wasted effort.* The objective is to identify how you can do your work better. To mistake-proof the process, first identify the types of errors, or potential defects, that occur at each step of each task. Then, the challenge is to find ways to lower the probability that those errors will occur. Some methods to use include simplifying key tasks, training to eliminate specific errors, providing work aids, standardizing procedures and formats, and instituting failure-free methodologies. Draw a map of the revised process, specifying measurement points for both defects and cycle time; in addition, look closely at essential inputs to determine when they are needed. Based on process revision, it may also be necessary to redefine the requirements for those inputs. The redefinition is done in such a way that the inputs correlate to the customer-satisfaction requirements. Changes must be communicated to both internal and external suppliers, and all parties must reach mutual agreement on how the changes are going to be fulfilled. (This step combines steps 6 and 7 of the nine-step process.)

6. *Ensure continuous improvement by measuring, analyzing, and controlling the improved process.* This step is intended to answer the question: How perfectly are you doing your customer-focused work? It involves formulating and publicizing actual performance versus goals for both defects per unit and the established sigma level. (This step combines steps 8 and 9 of the nine-step process.)

Cost of Quality

The *cost of quality* measurement was developed by noted quality consultant Phil Crosby (1979) and stands out as a dramatic way to help people in the continuous improvement of quality. Simply, cost of quality can be defined as the cost of nonconformance to customer requirements plus the cost of conforming to customer requirements. The aggregate cost of quality can be used to create awareness, prioritize opportunities, and broadly assess progress in all functions and operations. Crosby estimates that large companies spend 15 to 20 percent of their sales on nonconformance alone. Capturing even a small amount of these nonconformance costs would have a profound effect on any organization's bottom line. These are six elements to the cost of quality:

1. *Cost of prevention.* The cost of up-front activities to prevent failure from happening. Examples are training and capital expenditures.

2. *Cost of appraisal.* The costs incurred to determine conformance with quality standards. Inspection and auditing are the most common examples.

3. *Cost of internal failure.* The costs of correcting products or services that do not meet quality standards prior to delivery to a customer, such as engineering design changes and invoice errors.

4. *Cost of external failure.* The costs incurred to correct products or services after delivery to the customer. Field retrofits, sales commission adjustments, and service expenses fall into this category.

5. *Cost of exceeding requirements.* Costs incurred to provide information or services that are unnecessary or unimportant to the customer (or for which no known requirement has been established). Unread reports, product features a customer does not use, or sales calls with no purpose are common examples.

6. *Cost of lost opportunity.* Lost revenues can result from customers choosing competitive products or services and from cancellations when products and services do not meet the customers' requirements. Many organizations would argue that lost opportunity is impossible to measure; however, most sales representatives are usually able to gauge the reasons they lose to competitors. In addition, incremental incentives, such as the automotive industry's cost of rebates, would be counted here.

Process Control and Seven Statistical Tools

In defining statistical control for Japanese managers in 1950, Deming said: "The statistical control of quality is a system of application that embraces all formal quantitative aspects of planning, design, purchase, production, services, marketing, and re-design of product. It helps to find problems, to state them in meaningful terms, and to solve them. It provides a plan, a road-map, that leads to a better competitive position."

The heart of process control is the control circle Deming adapted from Walter Shewhart (see Figure 2.1). The elements of the control circle are: P—establishing a plan or standard for achieving your goal; D—enacting the plan, or doing; C—measuring and analyzing the results, or checking; and A—implementing the necessary reforms when the results are not as originally planned. But the heart of the process will not beat without the blood of statistical tools.

Solving problems and pursuing quality improvement requires not only teamwork, but the use of a basic set of statistical tools. The advantage of statistical tools is that they allow people to differentiate between *common* causes and *special* causes of problems. Common causes constitute 85 percent of the problems encountered in most work; they are faults of the system. They affect the members of a team equally and will remain until they are identified and removed by management. On the other hand, special causes are specific to a particular employee, machine, or work practice. Special causes can be detected by statistical signals and are usually identified and corrected by the individual.

Another way to look at it is that common causes are usually related to *effectiveness*—not whether the organization is doing things right, but whether they are doing the right things. Special causes are related to *efficiency*—how well things are being done. To succeed, an organization must be *both* effective and efficient. This means identifying the right problems and fixing them the right way.

Organizations pursuing quality in their outputs have learned that in order to solve problems, they must distinguish between common and special causes through the use of statistical tools. Attempts to improve individual performance are useless when the problem lies in the system, where only management can eliminate or reduce the impact of the problem. But the use of statistical tools by all employees provides a common method of identifying and understanding critical problems and managing their solution by the facts. The seven most commonly used statistical tools are (1) check sheets, (2) Pareto charts, (3) cause-and-effect diagrams, (4) histograms, (5) run charts, (6) scatter diagrams, and (7) control charts.

Check Sheets

Check sheets (Figure 8.2) are used to gather data based on sample observations in order *to identify patterns*. This data is the logical starting point in most problem-solving cycles. A check sheet is an easy-to-understand method to learn how often certain events happen. Constructing a check sheet involves four steps:

1. Agree on what you want to know. (Everyone on the team has to be looking at the same thing.)
2. Decide on the most reliable way to collect the data.
3. Design a format for recording data.
4. Make sure time is available for gathering the data.

Figure 8.2. Check Sheet.

Problem	Month			
	1	2	3	Total
A	II	II	I	5
B	I	I	I	3
C	IHT	II	IHT	12
Total	8	5	7	20

Pareto Charts

A Pareto chart (Figure 8.3) is used *to display the relative importance of problems or conditions* in order to choose the starting point for problem solving, identify the basic cause of a problem, or monitor a solution. This tool, named for Vilfredo Pareto, a nineteenth-century economist, was made popular by Juran. It is a special form of vertical bar graph designed to help determine which problems to solve and in what order to solve them. A Pareto chart based upon check sheets or other forms of data collection helps to direct attention and effort to the critical problems. The use of Pareto charts has given rise to the "80-20" rule, which suggests that 80 percent of an organization's problems come from 20 percent of its tasks. Constructing a Pareto chart requires nine steps:

1. Use a check sheet or "brainstorm" to obtain data.
2. Arrange the data in order from the largest category to the smallest.
3. Calculate the total.
4. Compute the percentage of the total that each category represents.
5. Compute the cumulative percentage.
6. Scale the vertical axis for frequency (zero to total).
7. From left to right construct a bar for each category, with height indicating the frequency. Start with the largest category and add them in descending order (combine the cate-

Figure 8.3. Pareto Chart.

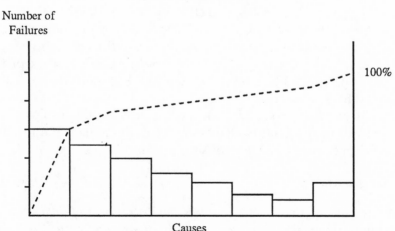

gories containing the fewest items into an "other" category and put it on the extreme right, as the last bar).
8. Draw a vertical scale on the right and add a percentage (0 to 100 percent) scale.
9. Plot a cumulative-percentage line.

Cause-and-Effect Diagrams

The cause-and-effect diagram (Figure 8.4) is useful for *displaying all the possible causes of a specific problem or condition.* Kaoru Ishikawa is credited with inventing "cause-and-effect" analysis; this is why the charts are most commonly known as "Ishikawa" diagrams (or "fishbone" charts because of their appearance). The problem, or effect, is stated on the right side of the chart and the major influences, or causes, are listed to the left. The diagram illustrates the various causes affecting a process by sorting and relating them. For every effect there are likely to be several major categories of causes (the bones of the fish). The major causes are usually listed as the four "M's": manpower, machines, methods, and materials (although any major category that helps people think creatively can be used). The fishbone takes shape as possible causes are listed on each of the major bones. The objective is to cure the cause and not merely list the symptoms. There are four key steps in constructing a cause-and-effect diagram:

1. Begin by agreeing on the effect (problem statement).
2. Generate the causes by check-sheet data or brainstorming.
3. Place the problem statement in a box to the right, draw the four major cause categories (or the steps in the work process), and add brainstormed ideas. For each cause, ask, "Why does this happen?"
4. Identify the root (most basic) causes of the problem by finding the factors that are repeated. Collect additional data to verify the relationship of causes to effect.

Histograms

A histogram (Figure 8.5) *displays the distribution of data by bar graphing the number of units of anything in separate categories.* As with

Figure 8.4. Cause-and-Effect Diagram (Fishbone or Ishikawa Diagram).

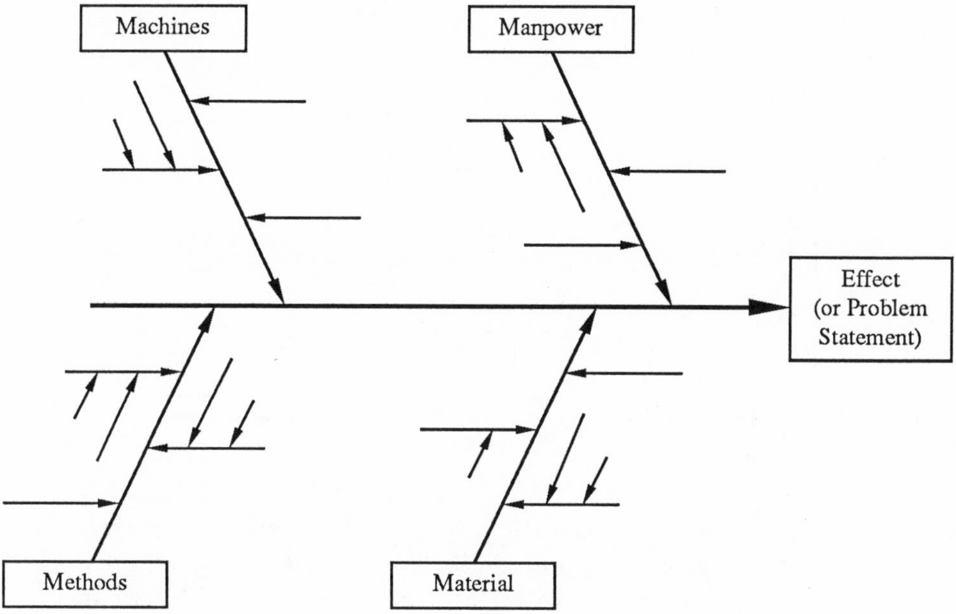

a Pareto chart, a histogram displays in bar-graph form the frequency with which events occur, but it goes beyond Pareto by taking measurement data and displaying its distribution. This is critical since the repetition of events will produce results that vary over time. Since random samples of data under statistical control normally follow the pattern of the "bell-shaped" curve, the shape of a histogram's distribution is helpful. The first thing a histogram can show is the negative or positive deviation from normal, or *skewness,* of the curve. It also can show *variability,* or how much spread there is in the curve. Histograms start with an unorganized set of numbers, followed by four steps:

1. If data is not already arranged by frequency, make a check sheet.
2. Determine the range (R) for the entire data set by subtracting the smallest value in the set from the largest value; divide the range value into a certain number of classes (K);

Figure 8.5. Histogram.

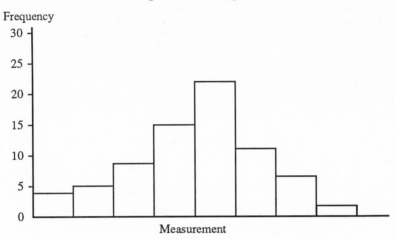

determine the class width (H): $H = R/K$; determine the class boundary, or end points. Take the smallest individual measurement in the data set and add the class width to it. Consecutively add the class width to each class boundary until the correct number of classes is obtained.

3. Construct a frequency table based on the values computed in step 5.
4. Using the frequency distribution table, construct vertical bars for each of the values, with height corresponding to frequency.

Run Charts

A run chart (Figure 8.6) *provides the simplest possible display of trends within observation points over a specified period of time.* Run charts are most often used to monitor a system to determine if the long-range average is changing. Points are plotted on the graph in the order in which they become available. Typical examples of processes that can be graphed are machine downtime, yield, scrap, typographical errors, and productivity over time. There is a caution: Be alert to the tendency to see every variation in data as significant. The purpose of a run chart is not to identify all problems, but to focus attention on the truly vital changes in the system.

Scatter Diagrams

A scatter diagram (Figure 8.7) provides a tool with which to study the possible relationship between one variable and another. Scatter diagrams are *used to test for possible cause-and-effect relationships.* Although they cannot prove that one variable causes another, they do help to show whether a relationship exists and the strength of that correlation. A scatter diagram consists of a horizontal axis representing the measurement values of one variable, and a vertical axis representing the measurements of a second variable. There are three steps to building a scatter diagram:

1. Collect 50 to 100 paired samples of related data and construct a data sheet.
2. Draw the horizontal and vertical axes of the diagram, increasing values as you move up and to the right on each axis. Place the cause variable on the horizontal axis and the effect variable on the vertical axis.

Figure 8.6. Run Chart.

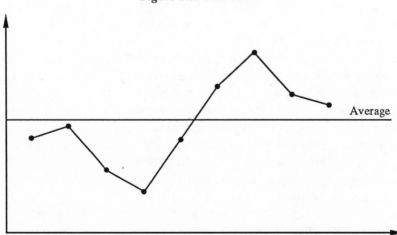

Average

Figure 8.7. Scatter Diagram.

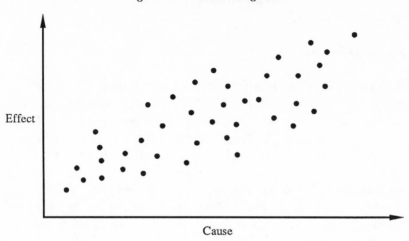

3. Plot the data on the diagram and circle the values that are repeated as many times as appropriate.

Control Charts

A control chart (Figure 8.8) can be *used to discover how much variability in a process is due to random variation and how much is due to unique events,* in order to determine if a process is in statistical control. Control charts were developed by Shewhart in the 1920s, but it was Deming who perfected their use. Deming's research with control charts led him to his conclusion that 85 percent of improvement opportunities come from changes in the system, which are management's responsibility, while only 15 percent are within an individual employee's control. A control chart is simply a run chart with statistically determined upper control limit (UCL) and lower control limit (LCL) lines on either side of the process average. The limits are calculated by allowing a process to run untouched, sampling the process, and plugging the sample averages into the appropriate formula. Then sample averages are plotted onto a chart to determine if these points fall within or outside of the limits, or if they form "unnatural" patterns. If either of these conditions exist, the process is "out of control." The fluctuation of points within the limits results from variation in the process, indicating common causes within the system; these can only be corrected by changing the system. Points outside of the limits usually come from special causes, or exceptions to how the process normally operates. Such special causes must be eliminated before a control chart can be used as a monitoring tool. Only when special causes are corrected can the process be in control; sampling will make sure that the process doesn't fundamentally change. There are two types of control charts:

1. *Variable control chart.* Samples are expressed in quantitative units of measurement, such as length, weight, and time.
2. *Attributes control chart.* Samples reflect qualitative characteristics, such as "is defective/is not defective," or "go/no go."

Additional Tools and Processes

In addition to the seven statistical tools, TQManagement organizations find three other tools helpful in improving their work process.

Figure 8.8. Control Chart.

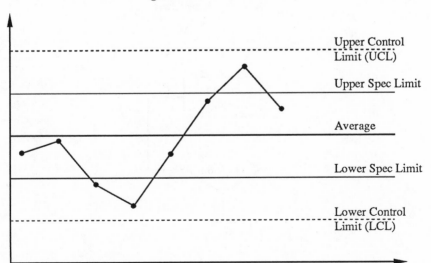

Flow Charts

A flow chart (Figure 8.9) is a pictorial representation showing all of the steps of a work process. Flow charts are helpful for *identifying deviations between the actual and ideal paths of any product or service*. They provide excellent documentation that can be a useful tool for evaluating how the various steps of a process relate to one another, and they can uncover loopholes that are potential sources of trouble. Flow charts can be used to document anything from the route of an invoice or the flow of materials to the steps in a sales cycle or servicing of a product. There are three steps in developing a flow chart:

1. Identify the major activities to be completed and decisions to be made.
2. Use the simplest symbols possible.
3. Check the logic of the plan by following all the possible routes through the chart to ensure that you have planned for all contingencies.

Figure 8.9. Flow Chart.

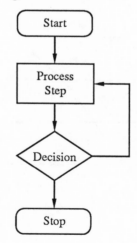

Force Fields

How does change occur, either personally or organizationally? Change is a dynamic process, suggesting movement from either "time A" to "time B" or from "condition X" to "condition Y." Where does the energy for this "movement" come from? One approach is to view change as the result of a struggle between forces seeking to upset the status quo—"driving forces" that move a situation toward change while "restraining forces" block the movement. When the opposing forces are equal or the restraining forces are too strong to allow movement, there is no change. It stands to reason that some change will occur when the driving forces are more powerful than those on the restraining side. Force field analysis (Figure 8.10) was developed by Kurt Lewin to help groups facilitate change in three ways: (1) by causing people to think together about all the facets of a desired change and encouraging creative thinking, (2) by encouraging people to reach consensus about the relative priority of factors on each side of the "balance sheet," and (3) by providing a starting point for action.

Figure 8.10. Force Field Analysis.

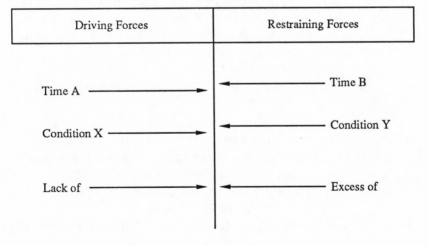

Brainstorming

All of the above tools facilitate thinking by *focusing* attention on the truly important dimensions of a problem. It is equally important, however, to *expand* thinking to include all of the dimensions of a problem or solution. Brainstorming helps a group to create as many ideas as possible in as short a time as possible. Originally developed in 1963 by advertising executive Alex Osborn, brainstorming was conceived as a systematic method for solving problems in relatively little time. Osborn maintained that four principles must be followed for brainstorming to be effective: (1) criticism is ruled out, (2) freewheeling is welcome — the wilder the idea the better, (3) quantity is encouraged (the greater the number of ideas generated, the higher the quality of the final solution), and (4) combination and improvements are desired. There are two common methods for brainstorming:

1. *Structured.* Every person in a group must give an idea as their turn arises during a rotation of the group or "pass" until the next round. This method (called the "Nominal Group" technique) encourages shy people to participate but it can also create a certain amount of pressure to contribute.
2. *Unstructured.* Team members simply give ideas as they come to mind. This method tends to create a more relaxed atmosphere but also risks domination by the most vocal members (and requires attention to control them).

Both methods follow these generally accepted guidelines:

- Never criticize ideas.
- Write every idea on a flip chart or blackboard. Having the words visible to everyone at the same time avoids misunderstandings and acts as a stimulus for new ideas.
- Make sure that everyone agrees on the question or issue being brainstormed. Write it down too.
- Record on the flip chart the speaker's words; don't interpret.
- Keep the session to five to fifteen minutes.

Benchmarking

Over a thousand years ago the Chinese general Sun Tzu (1963, p. 84) wrote in his treatise *The Art of War:* "Know your enemy and know yourself; in a hundred battles you will never be in peril." Throughout history successful leaders have used this advice to achieve superiority. Establishing operating targets based on the best possible industry practices is a critical component in the success of every business, and benchmarking is a tool an organization can use to search for the practices that can lead to superior performance. The Japanese term *dantotsu* means striving to be the "best of the best" and represents the essence of the process they have used to establish competitive advantage. In the United States the process that has evolved as America's *dantotsu* was first developed and championed by Xerox Corporation (1983) beginning in 1979. Quite simply, it is a process designed to allow organizations to assess their competition and themselves and, using that knowledge, to develop and implement a plan to gain superiority. Benchmarking is a straightforward, dynamic process adaptable to the functions of an organization. In his book *Benchmarking,* Robert Camp (1989) describes four basic steps:

1. *Know your operation.* To know what to benchmark requires that you know your organization's strengths and weaknesses compared to those of your competitors. If you don't know your operation's strengths and weaknesses you won't be able to defend yourself; you won't know which operations to stress and which to improve.

2. *Know the industry leaders or competitors.* You need to know the dimensions of any gap — negative or positive — between your competitors and yourself. You must also assess your competitors' potential performance so that the dimensions of any gaps can be projected over time. In this way you can identify the best practices of industry or functional leaders to ensure your superiority.

3. *Incorporate the best.* Once you have acquired the hard data you can start to use it to set your goals, to gain or maintain

superiority and to weave these goals into the organization's formal planning process. The key is to uncover why some operations are better and how they got that way. Finally, communicate formal action plans through the various levels of the organization.

4. *Gain superiority.* Having incorporated the best of the best, by continuously improving against that standard, the organization should gain superiority. Follow up by measuring process periodically, constantly updating your position. The ultimate goal is to achieve superiority in all areas by using the data to direct employee efforts for continuous improvement.

Quality Function Deployment

Quality Function Deployment (QFD) is a system developed in Japan for designing quality into a product at a lower cost and in a shortened development cycle. First used at Mitsubishi's shipyard in Kobe in 1972, it subsequently was introduced into the United States by Don Clausing of M.I.T. as the Makabe Method and by Bob King of Goal/QPC as the Akao Method. It translates the "voice of the customer" into design characteristics and target values that can be disseminated horizontally through an organization's product planning, engineering, manufacturing, quality assurance, and service operations. It emphasizes early involvement of all functions of the company and therefore is a natural adjunct of simultaneous engineering because it provides systematic methodology for integrating interdisciplinary inputs while facilitating better interdepartmental communication.

Sometimes called "the house of quality" because its structured format of sequential matrices resembles the drawing of a house with a pointed roof, QFD provides guidance in converting the customer's requirements into the manufactured product. The advantages of QFD are that (1) it provides a framework for simultaneous engineering, (2) it identifies conflicting design requirements and the critical characteristics to be controlled, (3) it reduces product development cycle time while improving quality and lowering cost, (4) it decreases the number of down-stream engineering changes, and (5) it provides a comparison with competitive products.

Simultaneous or Concurrent Engineering

Simultaneous or concurrent engineering is a product design process employed by many quality organizations, Cadillac being a prominent example. Simultaneous engineering is an integrated product-development and quality-design process—a systematic approach to the integrated, concurrent design of products and their related processes, including manufacture and support. It is intended to cause the developers to consider, from the outset, all elements of the product life cycle from conception through disposal, including quality, cost, schedule, and user requirements. In addition to bringing together benchmarking data, a focus on customer requirements, supplier partnerships, and design tools (like PDCA, Design for Competitiveness, QFD, and Taguchi methods), concurrent engineering requires cross-functional teams, and the development of cross-functional teams requires an active use of team processes.

Collaborative Skills and Processes

The glue of Total Quality is teamwork, from the senior management team to the shop floor. After all the processes and tools have been learned, it will have all been for nothing if people cannot work together. "None of us is as smart as all of us" is a cliché often cited to show the value of teamwork. But harnessing the power of groups takes more than a catchy phrase and the mere formation of a team. Most Americans are raised to be team players, from youth soccer and Little League to the NFL's Sunday TV lineup. However, sports metaphors often work against building productive work teams in organizations. Too often we see teamwork as "playing" our position better than anyone else and sacrificing ourselves to the team's goals, but when we believe someone else can play our position better, rather than representing our assets to the team, we too often question our ability to contribute at all. That kind of thinking just won't work in TQManagement.

Teams require a balance of authority and collaboration to achieve empowerment; in teams, people do not merely value conformity and getting along, but instead recognize that they must coordinate their efforts through openness and honesty. This means that people must use, rather than suppress, their thoughts and feelings to accomplish defined objectives. As an example, to accelerate the rate of product development, design engineers, marketing people, and manufacturing managers must be able to shape their shared boundary conditions and understand the strategy and operating philosophy while maintaining a flexible system based on *negotiated* roles and responsibilities. To do so requires skills and tools to help the group overcome its dependency and develop self-management.

The organizations we studied strive for collaboration among their people by stressing four areas: (1) team start-up, (2) decision-making processes, (3) meeting processes, and (4) interpersonal behaviors.

Team Start-Up

A team is a transforming mechanism that takes inputs from external and internal suppliers, provides added value, and produces outputs. The team's mechanism is composed of the vision and direction of the organization, the procedures and processes under which the team operates, the relationships of the members, and their roles. All of these must be negotiated and understood by all the members (and renegotiated when necessary) in order to obtain the correct inputs and provide outputs that meet the customer's requirements. A good start-up process will document the inputs, the outputs, and the elements of the mechanism and will establish contractual agreements between the members to identify their roles and outputs (Kayser, 1989).

When a team is first formed, before undertaking their work they should take time to review a few basic needs. This is best done with the help of a trained facilitator and begins with reviewing five key factors about the team:

1. The team must understand their charter—their reason for working together.
2. The members must recognize their interdependence; they need one another's knowledge, skills, abilities, and experience in order to achieve mutual goals.
3. Members must be committed to the idea that working together as a team will lead to more effective outputs than working in isolation.
4. The team has responsibility for delivering an identified output (a good or service).
5. Their effectiveness is based on synergy, interdependence, and a support base.

All of this begins with the team developing a core mission statement—a succinct description of what the team is in place to do. It should identify the team's reason for existing in the larger organization (who they are, what they do, for whom, and why). Also a good start-up process will include a force field analysis of the mission. The driving and hindering forces should be plotted for the external environment, the internal environment, human resources, systems, policies and procedures, and whatever else is significant.

In negotiating roles a team must realize that a lack of clarification, understanding, and acceptance of one another's responsibilities will likely create role conflict and ambiguity. Both research and experience have demonstrated that when either role conflict or ambiguity is high, team effectiveness suffers.

Synergy in a team is always potentially greater than the sum of the combined energies of its members. What energy is to an individual, synergy is to a team. Effective teams are made up of independent individuals who must combine their separate efforts in order to produce the organizational result; this is the basis of collaboration. For this reason a team's focus should be on *combining* rather than *coordinating* their efforts. Team members should recognize their potential for supporting one another. As individuals we carry our needs with us all the time; therefore, teams have the potential to provide their members both social and emotional support. When this happens, a more satisfying and productive environment results.

Decision-Making Processes (Consensus)

Decision making in groups can be tough. Ideally a team strives to find a position acceptable enough so that no member opposes it, a decision "everyone can live with"—in other words, *consensus.* This does not mean a unanimous vote, since the team decision may not represent everyone's first priority. Similarly, it does not mean a majority vote because when majority rules, only the majority get what they are happy with, leaving the minority with something they may not want. Instead, consensus is a state of affairs where communication has been open, the group climate has been sufficiently supportive, and everyone in the group feels they have had a fair chance to influence the decision. Consensus means that there is a clear course of action to which most members subscribe, one the dissenters will support because they feel they have had their chance to influence the outcome. Of course, the logically perfect—but realistically least attainable—kind of decision is the one where everyone truly agrees on the course of action to be taken.

One method for facilitating a consensus decision is multi-voting, a series of votes that reduces the number of alternatives on a list. This is accomplished by numbering the items on a list, combining similar items, renumbering items if necessary, and then allowing members to choose several (up to one-third of the total number of items). After the votes are tallied, items with the fewest votes are eliminated. Each member then makes three choices and assigns a point value to them (first = 3 points, second = 2 points, third = 1 point). Point values are recorded on a flip chart and the rank order determines the voting outcome.

Finally, each team member is asked to state aloud whether she can support the decision once the session has ended and everyone has left the room. If she cannot make such a commitment, her reasons need to be stated and openly and honestly discussed. It is better to take more time to ensure group support for the decision than to rush to adjournment and certain disaster later.

Meeting Processes

Meetings are an essential element of any organization's life, but as we commented earlier, like panda matings, the results are usually disappointing. However, without meetings, collaboration becomes nearly impossible, because there must be a way for groups to conduct business. Successful organizations have found that having their teams use the following ten questions provides the group with guidance on the most efficient use of their meeting time (Finnigan, 1991; Kayser, 1990).

1. *Why hold the meeting?* Too often teams meet only because it is the "weekly team meeting" or the "monthly activity review." Team members should test their need for a meeting by completing this sentence: "We are having this meeting in order to _____." They might then ask if some other means of communication might do just as well; getting together will undoubtedly get them talking, but a memo or telephone call would have saved time and money. It is important to remember that unnecessary meetings have an adverse effect when a clear purpose is not identified, because when people believe that their time and talent have been wasted, the resulting resentment will hinder prospects for future involvement activities.

2. *What is the expected outcome?* During the time invested, what is to be accomplished? Establishing a desired outcome for team meetings does two things: first, it gives the meeting a focus, and second, it establishes a benchmark against which actual outcomes can be measured. There may be more than one outcome for the meeting and each one should be described using the noun-verb method described earlier. This will provide a precise and useful expectation.

3. *What type of meeting is it?* A group's mission and responsibilities will usually dictate the purpose and type of session required, but it is important for everyone to understand what to expect. Meetings should be planned for problem solving, information sharing, data gathering, or decision making.

4. *On the basis of the type of meeting planned, have the right people been invited?* An information-sharing meeting requires people with the right information. Similarly, group decisions can only be made by attendees who are empowered to make the decisions, and problem-solving activities will only be as good as the knowledge and expertise present. Also, was anyone not invited who might later reverse or hinder the outcomes? If so, make them part of the group, or least make them aware of the meeting plan.

5. *Has the right amount of time been allocated?* To keep from trying to put the proverbial "ten-pound sack" into a "five-pound bag," allow sufficient input and processing time to accomplish desired outcomes. To ensure that the schedule is neither too short nor too long, simply build a plan for the session and assign times for each segment. Not only will this protect people's time from being wasted; it will also guarantee that the investments they make will have a quality outcome. This may mean adding another day, but it is worth it.

6. *Is there an agenda and has it been published with sufficient lead time so that participants will know what to expect?* An agenda is nothing more than the meeting plan, including start and stop times, the meeting's purpose, and the desired outcomes. A well-crafted agenda, published in advance, eliminates confusion, minimizes surprises, and helps participants arrive better prepared to contribute. (A team may want to revise their answers to questions 1 through 5 and reset the agenda.)

7. *How will the team deal with the agenda items?* There needs to be a method for processing the team's work that everyone understands and agrees with. Some things to consider are the use of preliminary reading or data gathering. Will questions be allowed during presentations or will separate discussion periods be provided? Will subgroups be required and if so, how will they be formed? This effort can be tedious, but the more time a team spends up-front agreeing on their work processes, the more efficient and productive they will be during their deliberations.

8. *Who does what?* What roles will team members play during the meeting to facilitate the outcome? Productive team

meetings make use of four key roles that are assigned to team members:

- *Facilitator:* This is the person designated to direct the session by leading members through the activities required to achieve their outcomes. The facilitator ensures that all members participate; summarizes discussions, decisions, and consensus; and reviews the outcomes. (Most often, this responsibility is retained by the team's manager, although it can be assumed by any member the team agrees upon.)
- *Timekeeper:* One team member should be assigned the task of monitoring agreed-upon time frames and giving updates to the group on time usage. When this happens the team can reevaluate their schedule and avoid "crunching" the process toward the end of the meeting.
- *Minute-taker:* This person's job is to capture and distribute proceedings of the session, which at a minimum must include *who* has agreed to do *what,* by *when.*
- *Scribe:* Another participant records key ideas and issues verbatim on flip charts and posts them on the meeting room walls for the whole team to refer to.

In addition to these roles, it's important that all participants accept responsibility for maintaining focus on the agreed-upon processes, as well as for disciplining one another's use of task and process behaviors in a mutual and responsive manner. The four key roles can rotate among members from session to session.

9. *How will decisions be made during the meeting?* This is a key process decision the group must buy into. Many successful teams today regularly utilize statistical tools in their decision making, but they also need to agree on their methods of selecting decisions, such as majority voting and weighted voting. Regardless of the method of decision making a team chooses, it is a wise meeting manager who presses for consensus from his team.

10. *Who will make the final decision?* Whether the purpose of the session is gathering data, solving problems, or developing

recommendations, everyone should know the purpose and who makes the final decision. Holding an effective meeting doesn't mean that the participants have to be the decision makers, but they do have to know that their time and talents have been wisely invested. Nothing can be worse for morale, or future gatherings, than believing you are involved in a group decision only to discover that you have been overruled by someone higher up.

Interpersonal Behaviors

How people actually react during a meeting has a profound effect upon the outcome. There has been much written on effective behaviors in group settings; Tom A. Kayser's book, *Mining Group Gold* (1990), is perhaps the best of the recent works. Rather than duplicate what is available elsewhere, we will limit ourselves to three categories of behaviors that influence a group's effectiveness. All of these behaviors are usually present to one degree or another in meetings. How team members use them can have a profound effect on the outcome of their deliberations.

Group Task Behaviors. This category contains behaviors that advance ideas, concepts, suggestions, and courses of action; evaluate another's contributions; help get information out; and facilitate open communication. Initiating behaviors tend to create enthusiasm and are oriented to action. They include:

- *Proposing:* Putting forth an idea, suggestion, or proposal that is new and actionable.
- *Building:* Extending or developing someone else's proposal.
- *Agreeing:* Directly declaring agreement or support for other people, their concepts, or their opinions.
- *Disagreeing:* Directly disagreeing or raising obstacles and objections about issues, rather than the person. (This is not the same as attacking a person by using value judgments with emotional overtones.)

Group Maintenance Behaviors. This includes behaviors that bring about the exchange of information, facts, opinions, and other clarifications. These behaviors tend to increase mutual understanding and foster a deeper analysis of issues. They include:

- *Giving information:* Offering facts, opinions, data, or clarification to others in the meeting
- *Seeking information:* Requesting facts, opinions, data, or clarification from others
- *Summarizing:* Condensing previous information; always a statement that doesn't require a response
- *Testing understanding:* Checking to be sure that the information is understood; always a question that requires a response

Gatekeeping Processes. Unlike the other behaviors, gatekeeping behaviors do not possess content in themselves. They occur in conjunction with other behaviors and have one element in common: they both control the participation of others. They consist of:

- *Gate opening:* Direct attempts to involve another individual in the meeting or to increase the individual's opportunity to contribute to the discussion
- *Gate closing:* Excluding another individual from the discussion or reducing the individual's opportunity to contribute to the discussion

With varying degrees of application these are the tools and processes we observed the Baldrige winners and similar quality organizations use. The content of this chapter should be considered the minimum knowledge required to implement and sustain TQManagement. Without a solid footing in these tools and processes, employees will be unable to effectively evaluate their work process, join with others in teams, and find and eliminate the variabilities that hinder quality improvements. These tools and processes give employees the knowledge and skills that let them perform Total Quality work. Once you have decided what learning is essential for the effort, the next step is transferring this knowledge to the employees of the TQManagement organization.

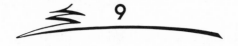

9

Strategy No. 3:
Implement Long-Term
Educational Programs

*In time of drastic change, it is the learners who inherit the
future. The learned find themselves equipped to live in a world
that no longer exists.*

— Eric Hoffer

Total Quality is a powerful strategy for improving productivity
and quality. However, it requires the complex and often painful
challenge of change, and changing management and work practices is not easy—traditional patterns of behavior have been
learned too well. They must be replaced with new learning that
gives everyone in the organization the tools and processes of
quality. This is why educational programs make up one of the
five pillars of a TQManagement implementation strategy.

There is little doubt that most Americans work hard, that
they want to work and take pride in doing high-quality work, and
that they are highly innovative. Nor do we doubt any more that it
is management's responsibility to create the kind of work environment where employees can bring their energy and talent to
bear on their work problems. In the early days of quality, organizations that had success creating work environments based on
employee involvement and the quality of work life came to

realize that greater quality and productivity improvements could be reached by providing training in the tools and process of Total Quality. They also discovered that these educational programs had to be designed in such a way that they would work in conjunction with the other TQManagement building blocks.

Specifically, training had to be designed to provide all employees with the knowledge and skills needed to continually improve the quality of the products and services they delivered to both their internal and external customers. In this chapter we will discuss nine learning goals that form a framework for five objectives of an educational strategy. We then will review seven strategic guidelines for achieving the five objectives and will briefly describe the key elements that make up a core curriculum for Total Quality.

Traditionally, organizations train their employees when additional knowledge and skills are required for an employee's future performance, but for training to be effective in supporting the transition to TQManagement it must do more. As in traditional organizations, the knowledge and skill requirements must be known and learning programs must be designed and implemented that will facilitate the desired changes in behavior, but in addition, this must be done within the context of all the other management actions that support the organization's change strategy.

Nine Learning Goals

First, it is important to realize that the purpose is *both* education *and* training. Education is the presentation of concepts and information for the purpose of imparting knowledge. Training is more an interactive event, designed to make a person more proficient. It is one thing to *know*; it is something else again to be able to *do*. TQManagement requires both. In developing their organization's quality strategies, the Baldrige winners had several purposes in common, which we have restated as nine learning goals that support all the elements of TQManagement:

1. Training of all employees on the basics of quality
2. An educational plan that is an integral part of the TQManagement implementation strategy
3. Whenever possible, training conducted by natural work groups (a manager and her direct reports), so that work groups can learn and apply the appropriate skills together
4. Tailoring of the training plan to the level, function, and business area of work groups, for example, by recognizing existing employee involvement activities or functional needs
5. A curriculum that covers three major areas of Total Quality:

   - The principles of quality
   - The tools and processes required for Total Quality
   - The management actions and behaviors necessary to make Total Quality a reality in the organization

6. Training in content and design that is grounded in core concepts and processes, such as quality improvement and problem solving
7. Instructional methods and delivery approaches appropriate to the level and needs of those being trained (cost benefit analysis)
8. An educational plan that facilitates the transfer of the skills and knowledge of Total Quality to the actual environment of the work group, with feedback and evaluation mechanisms built in to ensure its effectiveness
9. Classroom training that is reinforced on the job by coaching and refresher courses

These nine goals form a framework from which an organization can draw to establish what it wishes to accomplish through training. As an example, Corning (Houghton, 1986) established a Quality Institute, a formal training program in quality concepts tailored to their specific needs. The first class included the half-dozen top executives who make up their management committee, demonstrating top management's commitment to the training. Corning built special classrooms and trained over a dozen instructors to teach the basic quality-awareness courses around the world. Every employee has attended the Corning Quality Institute. That was the first phase — focusing on knowing what needed to be done. The second phase followed up with training in statistics, problem-solving skills, and communication and group dynamics, involving employees at all levels directly in the transformation by organizing quality-improvement teams in every department. Everyone — both individuals and organizational units — had to develop specific quality-implementation goals and measure their progress against these goals. When new or remedial training is necessary it is the team's responsibility to seek it out. Although it is a simple, straightforward approach, Corning's two-phase process covers all the elements of the nine goals. The U.S. Naval Hospital in San Diego (1991) launched a Total Quality training effort in 1989 consisting of two days of briefing and orientation for senior managers and half-day departmental briefings. This is followed by eight hours of training for first-line managers, and three days of statistical training for all participants. Facilitators and team leaders receive an additional three days of training. This customized, comprehensive training program had been delivered to over 3,800 military and civilian personnel by early 1991.

Training Objectives

Most of the successful TQManagement organizations we studied have built their training strategies on five training objectives that relate to the nine learning goals and that are used as the primary measures, or standards, of training progress toward Total Quality:

1. *A structured and disciplined training process, cascaded through the organization from the top as the best way to demonstrate senior management's commitment and provide role models.* By starting training at the top an organization is able not only to show management's commitment to the process (just as Bill Conway advised the Ford executives visiting Nashua to do) but also to provide examples of what is expected once training is complete. At Globe Metallurgical (Leach, n.d.), managers first received a

series of videotaped lectures by Deming, then were trained in statistical process control techniques along with their direct reports. At Xerox (1990b), training was delivered in "family groups" consisting of a manager and his direct reports. The manager, assisted by a professional trainer, conducted the week-long problem-solving and quality-improvement training. The training began with the CEO and his staff and cascaded through the organization.

2. *A front-end kickoff session for all employees to orient them to the meaning of TQ Management, to create an awareness of the need for quality, and to describe the organization's Total Quality implementation plan.* Especially when a cascade process is used, it will be important to share with all employees what is happening, not only to stimulate their interest and remove concerns, but to let them know when they might participate in the training. In 1986 Motorola (Wiggenhorn, 1989) conducted a corporate-wide series of live video management seminars, called "Rise to the Challenge." These seminars were intended to heighten managers' awareness of global competition and graphically underscore Motorola's response. The series was then shown to employees throughout the company. This was followed up in 1987 with two more video presentations to all employees, "Understanding Six Sigma" and "Competitive Awareness." Xerox (1990b) provided a half-day briefing to all its employees to announce their effort, establish an appreciation of quality, and explain their training cascade process.

3. *A curriculum plan that includes both classroom training and hands-on practice in the use and inspection of quality processes, and familiarization and training in statistics and other tools and processes.* The object of training is to change the way people do their work; for many the application of statistical tools will be new, and reinforcement and on-the-job examples will be essential to learning. At Cadillac (1991), each plant and staff unit has a Training Priorities Committee to determine what skills and knowledge employees must have to accomplish their quality goals, and training programs are crafted to individual needs. In 1990, for example, skilled hourly personnel received a minimum of eighty hours of formal instruction in such areas as quality improvement, leadership skills, process modeling, statis-

tical methods, and health and safety. At Wallace Company (1991), to address the problems of insufficient training and inconsistency in process performance, standard operating procedures and job work instructions were devised by on-the-job teams. These teams were made up of people designated "best of class" from each branch in their particular positions.

4. *A curriculum that emphasizes teamwork, trust, openness, and collaborative skills.* A training plan that only delivers statistical tools will certainly fail. These tools cannot impact the job unless people who work together are able to optimize their use. But working together is a new experience for many American workers and they will need new tools and direction. At IBM Rochester (1991), the human resources strategy is designed to bring about a cultural shift from a product-driven quality focus to a market-driven focus based on three initiatives: formal education, on-the-job customer contact, and participation. Their investments in training are five times the normal average. They measure their effectiveness based on employee morale, productivity, buy-in, and participation. Their quality training is backed up by employee opinion surveys, suggestion plans, roundtables, and recognition programs.

5. *Early integration of all the quality processes into the organization's other training courses.* In addition to attending quality training, it is likely that employees — especially managers — will attend other company training that reinforces Total Quality principles and concepts. As an example, Globe (Leach, n.d.) has developed in-house training capabilities in a number of advanced techniques and utilizes outside programs such as Taguchi techniques. At Milliken (1990), for example, all newly hired management employees attend a Leadership Orientation Program that includes information on corporate philosophies and objectives and corporate support functions, plant visits, and skills training in industrial engineering, quality management, interpersonal management skills, and statistical process control.

These five objectives represent the requirements upon which sound, strategic educational guidelines can be based. Just as the nine goals (*the vision of the plan*) are the touchstones for planners in articulating the five objectives (*what is to be achieved through the training plan*), these desired end results form the basis for seven strategic guidelines, which describe what specific actions will be required to achieve the training objectives.

Seven Strategic Guidelines for Educational Programs

Guideline 1: Train All Employees in Total Quality

One of the hallmarks of TQManagement is the consistency with which processes and tools are applied within the organization. With consistency, everyone from the boardroom to the shop floor, from engineering to marketing, will speak the same language of quality improvement. Reaching this kind of consistency means that all of an organization's people, at a minimum, will need to be trained by a common set of core modules that supports the practice of quality improvement in their job. When an employee's work environment requires specialized technical skills that the majority do not need, relevant skill training should be provided for that employee alone. As an example, managers have to know the basic concepts, tools, and processes just like everyone else, but they also need to learn skills for managing the use of quality tools, as well as processes for inspecting work so that they can facilitate their employees' quality applications on the job.

A quality-training design has to take into consideration the diversity of employee backgrounds and experiences. Students will come from a variety of professions that range from auditors to systems analysts, engineers to production workers, technicians to sales representatives, and professionals to paraprofessionals. The courses must address both college and high school graduates, workers with no math skills and working statisticians, and the interested as well as the uninterested. Another issue to consider is the variety of work environments. Will production workers be released from their assignments for training, or will training occur during overtime? And what about second shifts? Will training be delivered in the evening or will second-shift employees be brought in early and paid overtime? Is there a field sales or service force to be trained and how dispersed are their offices? All of these things require careful thought when designing and developing a curriculum. Quality-training designers also need to (1) recognize the diversity of the work force and determine the extent to which it exists; (2) allocate class time to minimizing diversity in job differences, math skills, and backgrounds; (3) incorporate "real-life" examples to motivate diverse groups to want to learn and use the tools; and (4) take time to learn the problems of the organization in implementing Total Quality and build course designs that address those problems.

Levels of Employees. In considering a core modular design and the specialized modules that may be required, an organization's quality-education designers have to think about reaching all employees. To do so it helps to think about five levels of employees:

- *Executives and general managers:* Those senior managers who are accountable for directional strategy, profit, planning, and resources; usually direct reports to the CEO, corporate staffs, group heads, and general managers
- *Senior managers:* Managers of major operational and functional areas; usually direct reports to the organization's senior staff
- *Middle managers:* Managers of operational and functional areas below senior managers, but larger than a single work group
- *First-line managers:* Supervisors of basic work teams
- *Individual workers and specialists:* Employees responsible only for their individual outputs

Core Modules. At a minimum, a comprehensive quality curriculum needs to address five modules: (1) an orientation module, (2) a Total Quality start-up module to relate Total Quality to work groups, (3) a Total Quality knowledge- and skills-training module to teach the tools and processes, (4) an initial quality-improvement module to transition training to the job site, and (5) specialized technical skills modules as required. It is the quality office's responsibility to establish the specific learning objectives for the core modules based on the requirements defined by the organization's quality-implementation plan. The organization's operating units are responsible for supplementing the core modules with examples and case studies that satisfy their specific functional and business needs. The planning and design of the modules should take into account a high-priority process for scheduling Total Quality training to ensure that it reaches all employees in the most reasonable time possible. This is no small task for any organization. Nearly all of the Baldrige Award companies approached the training challenge in some kind of phased method. We have consolidated their inputs into our recommendation for a five-phase process:

1. Orientation module (one-half day)
2. Total Quality start-up module (one-half to one day)
3. Knowledge- and skills-training modules (three days)
4. Initial quality-improvement activities (up to two months)
5. Specialized technical-skills modules (as required)

    1. *Orientation.* The purpose of an orientation is to provide a basic awareness of the need and importance for a Total Quality process within the organization and to serve as a kickoff for TQManagement. A comprehensive orientation introduces TQManagement, the principles of quality, the rationale and definition of customer satisfaction, and the customer-supplier relationship as the basis of quality improvement. One advantage of an orientation module is that it establishes the link between Total Quality and other quality-of-work-life activities in the organization, such as employee involvement and work-planning teams. Orientations can last two to eight hours, depending on the scope of the organization's transition plan and how close a work group is to their actual training. To be effective an orientation is best cascaded throughout the organization within four months of the senior management team's training. The orientation is usually delivered by the work group's manager and often includes a videotaped message from the senior executive stressing management's commitment and support. In addition to

kicking off training, an orientation begins the organization's communication strategy in support of TQManagement.

2. *Total Quality start-up*. A Total Quality start-up initiates formal Total Quality training. The purpose is to establish a knowledge base to enable work group members to understand the implications of TQManagement for both themselves and the organization. Since the effectiveness of a group depends on the knowledge and skills of all the individuals and the way they work together, a Total Quality start-up provides a beginning point for the team to reevaluate both their process and their interpersonal behavior skills. A start-up module begins with an overview of Total Quality and the customer-supplier relationship; it then requires the team to diagnose their current status by revisiting, or developing, their mission statement (see "Team Start-Up" in Chapter Eight). On the basis of their mission the team then identifies their major work outputs (what they do as a team). Finally, in preparation for their activities and training in tools and processes, the team identifies the customers for their outputs. Most important, during this activity they are asked to evaluate their effectiveness in working as a team and to evaluate where they will need team-process help.

3. *Knowledge and skills training*. Commonly, across Total Quality organizations knowledge and skills training has two major components. First, employees are trained in a systematic process to identify and agree on internal and external customer requirements, to design work processes to meet those requirements, and to evaluate their process capabilities. (This includes problem-solving methods, basic statistical tools, and collaborative skills, such as those described in Chapter Eight.) Second, managers are provided with the skills to manage quality-improvement activities (including the management of fact-based performance measures) and are prepared for their roles as work group managers, coaches, trainers, and group facilitators. At a minimum, all of the Baldrige winners taught their employees statistics, problem solving, and a quality-improvement process. At Globe (Leach, n.d.) the training is intentionally kept on a fundamental level so that employees are able to maintain, read, and interpret Statistical Process Control

(SPC) control charts. At Wallace (Horton, 1990), the quality-awareness classes provide an introduction to both the statistical and human sides of quality, the latter covering problem solving and meeting and team-building skills. At Xerox and IBM Rochester, managers are taught skills for managing with quality tools and methods for guiding quality-improvement efforts to achieve customer and organizational goals.

4. *Initial quality-improvement activities.* Initial quality-improvement activities are on-the-job applications of the organization's quality-improvement process (as in the nine-step model or Six Steps to Six Sigma) or of the problem-solving process to one or more of the work group's units of work. This phase is usually constructed to reinforce the newly acquired knowledge and skills. The initial project phase usually doesn't last more than two months and is often completed much sooner (if a team is struggling after two months, some kind of remedial help is probably necessary). At Xerox (1983) the manager-members of a work group are not allowed to train their own work groups until their team has successfully completed a quality-improvement project. At Wallace (Horton, 1990) they use on-the-job teams to follow up training with analyses of their work processes that everyone can then follow. These teams define their mission, break into two groups that define the process separately, and then "merge" the two versions into a consensus definition for others to follow.

5. *Specialized technical skills.* Specialized technical skills are generally needed to provide advanced techniques. Design engineers, for example, need to know how to design products to customer specifications with greater speed and accuracy, and quality professionals need advanced statistical techniques, such as multiple regression, to assist work groups. (Some of these programs are discussed in Chapter Eight.) These programs include Taguchi Design Methods, Design for Manufacturability, Design for Assembly, and Quality Function Deployment.

Guideline 2: Customize the Training to the Organization

We noted earlier the need to consider the diversity of the work force in designing the training plan and modules. In addition, the nature of the organization itself, its mission, products, and work environment, will dictate what kind of curriculum is required. As an example, production workers are not likely to require the level of process detail that Engineering or Marketing may need. An eight-hour-a-day classroom delivery will not be operationally appropriate for all employees; more streamlined, bite-sized elements may be better for production and field personnel. And, of course, the investment must be considered. Training is not cheap and customization is one way of "getting the most bang for the buck."

Between 1988 and 1991, Wallace (1991) invested nearly $2,000,000 in training for 280 employees. Their list of training subjects is lengthy, including quality awareness, statistical process control (SPC), sales, customer service, coaching, leadership, SPC problem solving, communication and motivational skills, data collection skills, product knowledge, cycle-time reduction, failure mode and effects analysis, process capability, vendor certification, newsletter production, benchmarking, quality business planning, and information analysis. But in all cases, training is targeted to the appropriate population. For example, 100 percent of employees receive quality-awareness training, but only those for whom it is relevant receive detailed SPC training. At Federal Express (1991), every manager in the company has been trained in their lead course, "Total Quality Advantage," but not all employees—although that is their ultimate goal.

At Motorola (Wiggenhorn, 1989), all 240 officers of the corporation attend the "Senior Executive Program" with a fundamental focus on Total Customer Satisfaction. Motorola's middle managers attend a series of institutes on customer-focused marketing, Design for Manufacturability, cycle-time reduction, supply management, information systems, and the management of change. Their "Statistical Process Control" curriculum consists of nineteen modules organized into three cores. The first core provides skill-based training in methods of data collection and display, such as how to construct a scatter diagram. The second expands on the first and covers control charts, process capability, and measurement system analysis. These two cores are structured for factory operators and for engineers who design and supervise manufacturing processes. The third core is planned for design engineers and consists of courses such as "Design for Manufacturability" and "Product Design for Assembly." All nontechnical employees attend "Understanding Six Sigma."

Of course the issues of availability, cost, and convenience will weigh heavily in planning the curriculum. It is unlikely that a single vendor will be able to provide the full range of an organization's needs and even if one could be found, an organization's peculiar environmental issues will certainly require some customization. Houghton (1987, p. 20) noted that in the early quality days Corning had visited IBM and learned that they were sending their people to Phil Crosby's school, but that in subsequent visits IBM advised, "Don't do that. Set up your own school." That advice led to the Corning Quality Institute.

Roy Brant, Solectron vice president of corporate services, says, "What made Solectron a serious competitor and winner of the 1981 [Baldrige] award was driven by our intensive training program. The true measurement of a business's ability to achieve the award is its commitment to educating employees at all levels about its product and every element of the company's quality efforts." Solectron trained 1,230 of its 2,100 employees in statistical process control and surface-mount technology using funds made available by the California Employment Training Panel (1992, p. 2).

Guideline 3: Total Quality Should Be Implemented Top-Down

Many Total Quality companies implemented their training by a top-down method in order to systematically effect change throughout their organizations. (This is consistent with Deming's view that quality should be implemented from the top down.) In a top-down process every manager participates twice: first as a learner and second as a teacher. This kind of cascading process allows people at all levels to have the benefit of role models and examples above and beside them, who can then guide them in changing their behavior. In a top-down process each work group manager is accountable for developing the knowledge and skills of her subordinates and their subsequent application of quality improvement in the practical work environment.

Unfortunately, it has been the experience of most training programs that newly acquired skills are not always applied to the trainee's work activities. The major cause of this is lack of on-the-job reinforcement. Most often, newly trained employees are not recognized, and in some instances are even criticized, for attempting to apply recently learned skills to their jobs. By conducting quality training by work groups (managers and their direct reports), organizations have found that they can facilitate on-the-job reinforcement because it is not an individual who has the new skills, but the entire work group. No one sticks out as being different! And making the group manager responsible for a portion of the training, as did Xerox, Federal Express, and Corning, strengthens the process because managers then have a vested interest in reinforcing the application of the new skills in the work environment. This kind of proactive involvement also better prepares managers for the task of removing the barriers that prevent teams from improving the quality of their work.

In a top-down process a work group is usually defined as a manager and his direct reports. There are, of course, all types of work groups within any formal organization and the different types will affect the way in which the quality-improvement process is applied. Therefore, even though a functional group and a cross-functional team (such as a program team) may have different direct-line-reporting relationships, if the common work group is their team, they should be trained as a team. Figure 9.1 shows an example of this principle.

The kind of top-down approach that has become the most popular is a cascade process based on a "learn, use, teach, and inspect" model developed by Xerox (1983). In this method, manager 2 first *learns* the concepts and skills as a member of work group 1 (led by the manager of work group 1). Then manager 2, along with her peers, *uses* the quality tools and processes, applying them to one or more units of work for which

Figure 9.1. Training Cascade.

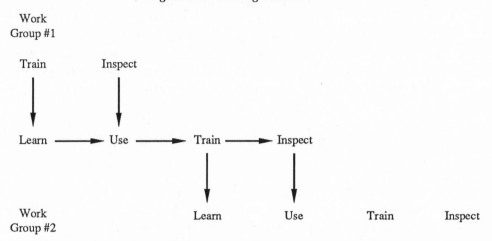

Work
Group #1

Work
Group #2

the group is responsible. During this time, manager 1 coaches the group and *inspects* their application of the processes.

When manager 2 has demonstrated an understanding of the tools and processes, and has proficiency in their application, manager 1 will designate manager 2 (and the rest of work group 1 as they demonstrate their individual understanding and proficiency) as being ready for Total Quality training. Manager 2 then *teaches* her own work group members, with the support of the unit quality officer and quality trainer. At a minimum the manager delivers the Total Quality start-up and initial quality-improvement activity phases, while the quality trainer teaches the knowledge and skills training. A good plan will allow able managers to take an active part in the skills training.

Finally, manager 2 *inspects* the application of the quality processes by her own group members. By inspection we are not referring to the traditional concept of evaluating results, but rather to Deming's notion of inspecting the steps used to accomplish the results (the "C" of PDCA). Since it is through effective application of the process that teams achieve improved results, the emphasis in inspection is on coaching, not judging. Inspection requires that the manager continually ask *why* in order to understand the actions, conclusions, and decisions of the team.

The process is then repeated with the subordinates and their own work groups, the decision of when to cascade training to the next level being based on the "learn-use-teach-inspect" approach. This cascade continues until training has reached the individual-contributor level.

Guideline 4: Assign the Quality Office the Leadership Role for Training

Using the resources of the organization's quality-implementation team and quality trainers, the quality office should have the leadership role in training because of their overall responsibility for TQManagement implementation. The quality office's training responsibilities cover four areas: (1) orientation of the organization's board of directors; (2) training of the CEO and his staff, as well as senior executives and general managers (first level); (3) training of quality specialists; and (4) developing the core modules for Total Quality training.

The purpose of an orientation for the board of directors is to provide them an understanding of the key elements and implications of the TQManagement strategy and implementation plan. Keeping the board advised and aware will go a long way to ensure senior management support and accountability.

It is critical for Total Quality that executives and general managers have the knowledge and skills to serve as positive role models and that they can manage the implementation in a consistent manner. They will provide an example for the organization by learning the skills associated with quality improvement, using them, teaching them, and inspecting the application of the processes in their areas of responsibility. Most TQManagement organizations ran training programs on four to five consecutive days for senior executives that integrated orientation, quality improvement and quality management, and skills and processes. This approach provides the necessary knowledge and skills without disrupting ongoing management activities. The members of the quality-implementation team, led by the organization's quality officer, form the initial core of quality specialists; they usually take responsibility for this training and for support of the senior management group's initial quality-improvement activities.

The organization's quality trainers, or consultants, design, pilot, and produce the core modules based on the requirements specified by the quality-implementation plan with guidance from the quality officer. Most Baldrige winners used a combination of internal and external consultants, and of existing internal and external materials. Research shows that with the possible exception of the specialized skill areas, there is no external package that can be taken in its entirety and used within Total Quality training. This particularly applies to the training needs of managers. Most organizations we studied drew on the marketplace, other TQManagement organizations, and internal resources in establishing their core modules.

The emphasis on teamwork and work groups in quality training implies a strong bias toward interactive group activities, rather than mass or individualized training approaches, in the final design. However, because certain of the basic skill components (such as statistics) lend themselves to an individualized format, a quality office is advised to research alternative delivery mechanisms such as interactive videodiscs or computer-aided instruction to support the core quality-training programs. Federal Express has been very successful in doing this.

Guideline 5: Integrating Total Quality into All Training

If quality is to be an organization's overriding business principle, it must be reflected in all of the organization's learnings. Total Quality principles, tools, and processes will therefore have to be integrated into all current and future training programs. As the training cascades throughout the organization's units, the quality message will need reinforcement in other training programs, including corporate-sponsored training as well as operating-unit training programs. Milliken's Leadership Orientation Program and Motorola's Middle Management Institute are examples of the kind of integration that is necessary. Xerox recently established a Management Institute to ensure consistency of messages and learning for all their managers; they located the institute in corporate headquarters so that senior management could participate in delivering the training.

Guideline 6: Establishing Unit Training Plans

Total Quality is an organization-wide goal with generic guidelines that apply to all operating units; implementation, however, is the sole responsibility of the operating units. In large organizations, operating units need to establish a training plan consistent with the objectives and guidelines specified in the organization's implementation plan. To ensure this consistency the quality office will need to periodically review their unit's operating plans, including the following elements:

- A detailed plan and schedule for training
- Staff and other resources required to support the plan
- The training activity's roles, relationships, and responsibilities within the unit to ensure that the plan is met
- A plan and schedule for amending functional training courses to reflect the quality policy

Guideline 7: Developing Advanced Quality Skills and Knowledge

Following the initial round of training and quality-improvement activity, nearly all organizations that have launched serious Total Quality efforts have found that in order to sustain their effort it is necessary to provide more advanced skill training in statistics and functional processes. The kinds of programs that are required are based on the organization's activities and their quality objectives. Cadillac's Training Priorities Committee is continually evaluating needs and recommending new programs. Federal Express relies heavily on "recurrency training" provided by a team of internal instructors. Motorola now offers "Structured Methods," a course to teach software engineers how to translate customer requirements into systems architecture, as well as classes in concurrent engineering and Quality Function Deployment (QFD). At Globe employees now receive QFD training as well as the Statistical Methods for Engineering Design and Just-In-Time methods of Shigeo Shingo.

A review of the Baldrige winners and other organizations committed to TQManagement indicates a wide array of Total Quality learning programs. They range from core programs in basic math and statistics to classes in measuring quality and benchmarking. These organizations support their staff's efforts to continue the pursuit of TQManagement with programs in topics such as creative problem solving, manager as facilitator, quality engineering design, reliability methods, manufacturability, engineering statistics, statistical quality control, value analysis, QFD, engineering root cause analysis, and many more.

Quality Begins and Ends with Training

Training is not an inexpensive investment, but it is an essential one if TQManagement is to be achieved. For the Baldrige Award–winning organizations training doesn't stop at the front door. Nearly all of the Total Quality organizations we visited now offer quality training to their suppliers and interested customers. Most have learned the value of doing this from direct experience. In fact, Milliken entered the "race without a finish line" at the urging of their customer, General Motors; Globe Metallurgical (Leach, n.d.) began Total Quality to meet the supplier certification requirements of Ford Motor Company; and it was Celanese Corporation's decision to limit its supplier base to companies that demonstrated reliable quality that sparked Wallace Company's (1991) venture into Total Quality.

Someone said, "Quality begins with training, and quality ends with training." This is true — it is a continual challenge to keep on top of quality technology and maintain a work force that has the latest knowledge and skills. But training is an investment that provides significant returns, and it is a key pillar in any TQManagement strategy.

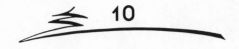

10

Strategy No. 4: Create Meaningful Recognition and Reward Systems

We need to adopt that famous Noah principle: No more prizes for predicting rain. Prizes only for building arks.
— Louis V. Gerstner

One of our greatest sources of satisfaction in work, regardless of what our responsibilities may involve, is to be told on a regular basis that our work is appreciated. When times are rough, a word of encouragement is often the incentive we need to keep trying. When we are doing well, recognition of our efforts can inspire us to even higher levels of achievement. William Glaser (1972, p. 24) said, "What one chooses that he believes is worthwhile must, sooner or later, be recognized by others or he will not gain a successful identity."

Recognizing people for their accomplishments has long been an American management principle. But the way organizations practice this principle is not always as effective as it might be. Deming (1986) has been the most critical in the context of quality. Of the third of his "seven deadly diseases"— "evaluation of performance, merit rating, or annual review"— he says: "It nourishes short-term performance, annihilates long-term planning, builds fear, demolishes teamwork, nourishes rivalry and politics. It leaves people bitter, crushed, bruised, battered, desolate, despondent, dejected, feeling inferior, some even depressed, unfit for work for weeks after receipt of rating, unable to comprehend why they are inferior. It is unfair, as it ascribes to the people in the group differences that may be caused totally by the system that they work in."

The concern is that performance evaluations encourage short-term thinking at the expense of long-term performance and improvements by introducing variability to the system. In a competitive environment that is becoming increasingly reliant upon teamwork and collaboration, linking performance evaluation to pay delivery may in fact be at odds with continuous-improvement goals. Rather than fostering interdependence, supervisory performance reviews encourage people to "look out for themselves." In Europe and Japan there is virtually no pay for performance systems, so organizations must find other ways to motivate employees. This explains their heavy reliance upon participation, involvement, and communication.

Our purpose here is not to resolve the issue of pay-for-performance systems, but it is important to point out that it is an important issue for Total Quality organizations to resolve. One strategy some quality organizations have started to use consists of team rewards and gainsharing. We will briefly discuss gainsharing at the end of this chapter, but for now we will limit ourselves to the use of recognition-and-reward strategies that support Total Quality.

Recognizing and rewarding people, more than any other management act, profoundly affects employee motivation and job satisfaction. Unfortunately, managers sometimes overlook the need to express appreciation on a day-to-day basis. There is also some uncertainty about how or when an employee's contributions should be recognized. Sometimes managers lose sight of the purpose and provide monetary rewards while forgetting to say "thank you." Rewards for individuals should never be abandoned when we feel that there may not be unanimous agreement for our actions. Recognizing and rewarding people is a vital pillar for TQManagement organizations because successful implementation requires management to communicate and reinforce the kinds of contributions and behaviors that are essential to Total Quality.

In this chapter we will review the definitions of *recognition* and *reward,* relate their significance to TQManagement, and present seven principles that quality organizations should consider when deciding on the objectives for their implementation plans. We will also describe the four objectives that Total Quality implementation plans need to establish and will recommend six strategic guidelines an organization can use in developing a pillar of appropriate strategies that will accomplish the objectives for recognition and reward.

Appropriate recognition and reward are critical to the healthy functioning of any organization. They are especially critical for change efforts and for maintaining an environment supportive of an organization's quality goals. It should come as no surprise, then, that the TQManagement strategies of successful Total Quality organizations include recognition and reward as one of their major change agents.

Recognition and reward are more than just management tools. They are also behaviors that must adapt to be compatible with the attitudes and strategies of Total Quality. An organization's managers play the key role in changing these processes, by determining the way recognition and reward are perceived, administered, and received.

Definitions of Recognition and Reward

We begin by clearly understanding what is meant by *recognition* and *reward.* Although these two terms are often thought to be synonymous, they are quite different. We start with *recognition* because it is at the core of any effective reward strategy (Mann, 1985).

Recognition is the act of acknowledging, approving, or appreciating an activity or service. It's helpful to think of recognition in terms of its derivation—*re* means "again" and *cognize* means "to think"; therefore, *recognition* means "to think again." An effective recognition strategy causes people to think again about the value and unique contribution each person brings to the pursuit of Total Quality. Recognition is an ongoing activity that doesn't focus only on one particular achievement, and that is not given only at award ceremonies. It is directed at an individual's self-esteem and social needs. It is an intangible acknowledgment of a person's or team's accomplishments—the sincere "thank you," the feeling of involvement when an employee is asked for input, the realization and demonstration of appreciation for each person's unique contributions to the business. In short, recognition is an ongoing appreciation and concern for people and as such it is central to reward-giving behavior. The forms of acknowledgment most commonly used in recognition are praise, personal "thank you's," letters, mementos, and special lunches or dinners.

Reward is the direct delivery of money or something of financial value. In contrast with recognition, rewards should punctuate appropriate achievements and serve as manifestations of ongoing recognition. While recognition is an intangible expression of worth, rewards are concrete expressions of appreciation that are meaningful to the receiver. Recognition is always powerful, but reward without recognition is weak. Unfortunately, too often we express appreciation with a plaque or cash award without demonstrating a sincere appreciation of an employee's contributions. When rewards displace recognition, they are a waste of an opportunity and resource. Typical rewards are pay, promotional increases, bonuses, benefits, company cars, profit sharing, and trips.

Seven Principles for Recognition and Reward

People's actions and behaviors determine the form Total Quality takes. As an organization progresses toward Total Quality, the existing recognition-and-reward systems will have to be reviewed to ensure support for the quality strategy and new systems that are developed. The following seven principles can be used to evaluate existing and proposed systems and to establish the appropriate recognition-and-reward objectives for an implementation plan.

1. *Place emphasis on success rather than failure.* Too often we

miss the positives by busily searching for the negatives. Managers should look for every opportunity to reinforce positive actions in a warm and personal way, especially during quality start-up when stumbling is certain to occur. Then the smallest of successes should be applauded. Any improvement, however small, is movement in the right direction.

2. *Deliver recognition in an open and publicized way.* It is important for others to be aware of accomplishments. If recognition and reward are not made in public, they lose much of their impact and defeat their purpose. Certainly, in a culturally diverse workplace, consideration of an individual's preference should have first priority, but teams are made by celebrating together.

3. *Deliver recognition in a personal and honest manner that is appropriate to the employee.* Avoid recognition that is too slick or overproduced. The reward or recognition should match the accomplishment, particularly during start-up. If the recognition goes well beyond what is justified it will be seen as manipulation and will degrade the value of future recognition activities.

4. *Tailor recognition and reward to the unique needs of the people involved.* Having a variety of recognition-and-reward options allows managers to appropriately acknowledge their people at different times in different ways. The old cliché, "Different strokes for different folks," works here. As an example, inviting an employee out to dinner with the boss and her spouse may seem like a nice thing to do, but for some production workers, it may have the opposite effect.

5. *Pay attention to timing.* Recognition should be ongoing, and reward should follow an achievement closely in time. Long time delays weaken the impact of most rewards. The rule is: if it is praise, provide it immediately; if it is a monetary award, make the response quickly.

6. *Strive for a clear, unambiguous, and well-communicated "line of sight" between achievements and rewards.* People should understand why they and others receive rewards; therefore, communicate the recognition-and-reward criteria to everyone, so that people know what is expected of them. It is important to remember that the members of the team know who is doing what,

and how well; recognition of individual members of a team should be consistent with the team's own evaluations.

7. *Above all, recognize recognition; that is, recognize the people who recognize others for doing what is best for Total Quality.* Recognition-and-reward criteria must not only support the goal of Total Quality but also apply it to other corporate policies and objectives and reinforce them as well. It can be very effective for a management team to recognize the members of the team who have been properly recognizing their employees.

The umbrella objective of a recognition-and-reward strategy is to ensure that quality tools and processes are used, work systems are changed or developed to support quality improvement, and team behaviors are adopted in support of Total Quality. Quality's success depends on the day-to-day activities of all employees; recognizing and rewarding their behaviors in supporting the organization's goals plays a critical role in the success of TQManagement.

Four Objectives for Recognition and Reward

Total Quality takes time and will require considerable behavioral change to occur between launch and the time the organization reaches its desired state. An organization's recognition-and-reward systems can provide immeasurable support for that goal. But first, the organization's existing and new recognition-and-reward systems need to embody four objectives that are at the heart of the Baldrige winners' strategies:

1. The disciplined use of quality improvement and problem solving are recognized and rewarded because the desired business results come from successful implementation and continual use.
2. Teamwork and efforts to eliminate internal competition are encouraged by recognizing and rewarding successful practitioners.
3. Clear and specific quality-improvement objectives are included in performance appraisal and reward systems.

4.   Promotion criteria include the actions and activities that
     support Total Quality.

Cadillac's Business Plan (Cadillac, 1991) drives their People Strategy. Selection processes are developed to place or reallocate people based on the needs of the business. Efforts are
made to develop employees, involve them in decision making
about their work, communicate the company's goals, and create
an environment in which employees can work effectively. The
recognition-and-reward systems are designed to support these
objectives and behaviors and thus tie back to the Business Plan.

Federal Express (1991) includes in their People/Service/
Profit strategy "providing outstanding wages, benefits, and
profit sharing opportunities" and "Saying 'Thank you' and 'Well
done' often."

Without supportive recognition-and-reward systems the
transition to actions and behaviors that implement Total Quality concepts will be incrementally more difficult. In the organizations we studied, we identified six strategic guidelines to overcome this barrier to TQManagement.

Six Strategic Guidelines for Recognition and Reward

Guideline 1: Recognize Positive Actions and Behaviors

To ensure successful implementation of Total Quality, all employees need to be involved in the process. Recognizing people
for their positive actions and behavior will accomplish this goal.
This requires visible and supportive management behavior, particularly by recognizing groups and individuals for their involvement immediately following the relevant accomplishment,
whenever possible. If a specific achievement occurs over an
extended period of time, it helps to continue the recognition to
reinforce the change. This is best done in an open and publicized manner that will maintain momentum and reinforce
progress. Most people like to be told that they are winners!
Glaser (1972, p. 24) notes: "A person may labor alone as an artist

or scientist for years, but eventually what he provides must be recognized by others or he will not gain a successful identity."

Westinghouse's Commercial Nuclear Fuel Division (Westinghouse Corporation, 1989b) has built into their strategy a plan to utilize corporate reward programs to recognize employees' quality-improvement contributions. They are the Group Quality Achievement Award, the George Westinghouse Signature Award of Excellence, and the Westinghouse Marketing Award.

Milliken (1990) offers no financial incentives. They believe that doing good things should be part of the job, not something separate. Instead they offer myriad recognition events and awards. Among them are letters from the CEO, Hero Success Stories, photographs posted on the Recognition Board, gold stars on name tags, caps, T-shirts, movie tickets, plaques, and a quality lapel pin. Most of these are presented at an awards banquet, Quality Reviews, or special celebrations, such as a quarterly sharing rally where anybody can present anything.

At Wallace (1991), Quality Wins are reported in the company's newspaper, acknowledged in congratulatory letters from CEO John Wallace, and rewarded with dinners for the associates and their families.

To facilitate the transition from the current state to the future state, several TQM organizations developed a certification system to recognize the achievements of progressive levels of training and skilled use of the tools and processes. Certification is given upon the successful *use* of the training, *rather than on completion of the training itself.* Other actions that promote the use of quality improvement and problem solving include publicizing successful projects and accomplishments, establishing events to share skills and knowledge (see Chapter Eleven), and developing an environment in which people share in the pride of the organization's accomplishments.

The human resources department needs to be a partner in the recognition-and-reward effort. They can be engaged to develop new programs that include recognition certificates, memos, plaques, and free dinner certificates for participating in problem-solving teams, implementing solutions, or demonstrating other appropriate behavior that exemplifies the principles of Total Quality.

Guideline 2: Recognize Managers for Implementing Total Quality

Managers at all levels are instrumental in implementing quality improvement by learning, using, teaching, and inspecting the process. They are involved in using the principles, teaching them, and evaluating or inspecting the results and outcomes in their area of responsibility. It is important for their achievements to be fully recognized by senior management.

Senior managers must be alert to every opportunity to recognize managers who are participating in problem solving, demonstrating teamwork, providing service to their customers, and practicing the other principles of Total Quality. These senior managers need to be comfortable in delivering praise and recognition. It is easier if they themselves are role models who get to know their people and become helpers. They must "manage by walking around." Since managers are leading the training of their subordinates (with the assistance of professional trainers) during the implementation phase, senior management can ensure that proper recognition is provided for exceptional managers-teachers-coaches. Careful evaluation and inspection not only ensure correct implementation of the process but let senior management know when recognition is appropriate. As an added bonus, senior managers are given more visibility by observing classes and attending presentations.

Guideline 3: Develop Promotion Criteria That Reinforce Quality Behavior

The management resource planning and promotion criteria of most Baldrige winners have been amended to reinforce the behavior and actions that managers are expected to practice in support of the principles of Total Quality. This helps to ensure that significant emphasis is placed on the implementation of TQM, which is vital, because TQManagement depends on the development of a cadre of knowledgeable and skilled managers to carry it out.

A TQM organization's management resource-planning process should be modified to include key criteria for quality improvement; a significant assessment of performance against these criteria will determine a person's readiness for promotion to a higher grade. Over time this leads to the development of managers who actively assist in the cultural change required to make Total Quality principles become a way of life. New hires can be selected with these same criteria in mind.

A candidate for promotion should exhibit personal behavior that supports quality. Such a person will be skilled in the use of the required tools and processes and will be comfortable in the role of trainer, counselor, and group leader. The selection of such an individual for promotion is the most powerful and significant form of recognition and reward that a company can bestow! Again, Human Resources is a partner in establishing the revised criteria, which include specific elements related to the use and implementation of Total Quality, such as problem-solving ability, behavioral skills, use of statistical tools, and overall involvement in the transition to TQManagement.

Motorola, Xerox, and IBM all have made it perfectly clear that managers are as accountable for achieving quality-improvement goals as they are for any other business goal. This is part of their managers' job requirements, and as such, it partly determines career advancement.

Guideline 4: Recognize Quality in Bonus Plan Objectives

The Baldrige winners learned that it is important to recognize the critical importance of Total Quality by placing a significant weighting on its implementation, use, and inspection in the objectives of management bonus plans. Bonus incentive plans are predominantly based on meeting or exceeding key business objectives such as profit and return on assets. Since the thrust of Total Quality is to improve these results by implementing quality improvement, it is therefore necessary to have a significant

The Race Without a Finish Line

portion of bonus objectives amended to reflect process and
Total Quality.

Specific quality goals in Motorola's Annual Plan (Germain, 1989) are deployed to the organizational unit level, where
targets are set through the Participative Management Program
(PMP). All of Motorola's employees are involved in the PMP
process, and the bonuses they receive are tied to the accomplishment of specific improvements targeted by their own PMP
teams. Goal setting involves everyone. At the executive level
incentives are tied to the achievement of specific quality-improvement goals through the Motorola Executive Incentive
Plan.

Guideline 5: Separate Appraisals from Salary Reviews

Many organizations' merit pay systems require a prescribed
distribution of appraisal results, which leads to a stacked ranking of co-workers. This creates the feeling of being a number
rather than a person who has been objectively assessed in terms
of skills, achievement, and contribution to the business. It also
encourages competitiveness among individuals and does not
promote teamwork in achieving group results. The primary
focus of appraisal should be recognition of both the accomplishment of results and the use of quality improvement.

In discussing the eleventh of his fourteen points, Deming
urges the elimination of such practices as supervision by numbers, work standards, quotas, management by objectives, and
merit ratings. Among other reasons, Deming believes that using
performance evaluations to direct a system of monetary rewards
will have the opposite effect, because concern for monetary
rewards will contaminate the feedback and evaluation system.
Peter Scholtes (1987, p. 26) of Joiner Associates says, "Performance evaluation is an exercise in futility. It is an activity that
lulls us into a belief that we understand something, when all we
have accomplished is to create an oversimplified illusion about
something that is very complex. When we act as though our
evaluations are accurate, when we reward, punish, promote,
commend or retrain people based on our evaluation, we are

making adjustments to a system about which we know very little. Adjusting the unknown is called 'tampering.'" He adds, "We would never consider indulging in this kind of blind tampering with our prized possessions, our bodies or even our electronic gadgets."

Separating pay from appraisal allows managers to evaluate individual performance more constructively. In addition, the removal of competition within groups enables managers to coach and counsel for both individual improvement and contribution to group results.

Guideline 6: Create a Bonus Plan for All
to Benefit from Total Quality

As the quality-improvement process is implemented throughout the organization, significant financial benefits will result. In the early years, these benefits derive from cost savings as a result of striving for work improvement, reducing internal and external costs of failure, and reducing costs of exceeding requirements. These cost savings diminish over time, but financial benefits will then result from increasing market competitiveness because of improved products and services. Establishing a bonus plan for all employees to allow them to benefit from the long-term financial gains that result from Total Quality will ensure ongoing commitment.

Such plans are constructed and implemented in many ways. The format should be designed by the appropriate compensation, personnel, and financial experts of the corporation. The resulting plans need to be consistent with the long-term health of the corporation, tied to the objectives and accomplishments of the organization's operating groups, understood by the people affected by the plan, and administered in a way that is perceived to be fair and equitable to people within the unit.

Additionally, quality organizations are going to have to look at the equity of the relationship between executive pay and worker pay. In a time when management is espousing the importance and power of the average worker, it is disgraceful that U.S. top executives, on the average, make more than 100 times the pay of their organizations' lowest workers. When compared to Germany (23 times) and Japan (17 times), this is difficult to defend. Given the success of Operation Desert Storm, there is something to be said for staying close to the troops: General Colin Powell, chairman of the Joint Chiefs of Staff, earns about $100,000, less than 10 times the salary of a private. Some progress is being made to decrease the gap, however. Worthington Steel of Columbus, Ohio, has profit sharing for all workers that can double their base pay in an up year. Lincoln Electric of Cleveland has an employee-elected advisory board and doesn't hire executives from outside. It bases bonuses on productivity, and all employees share. Lincoln's chairman makes just 11 times a line workers' pay (Flanigan, 1992a).

Globe (Leach, n.d.) has provided its hourly employees the same benefit and pension package as the salaried employees and has initiated a profit-sharing plan for all employees that provides, on the average, over $5,000 in annual bonuses. Federal Express (1991) and Xerox (1990a) have profit-sharing plans, and Xerox recently added an Employee Stock Ownership Plan. Motorola (Germain, 1989) has a bonus plan for both executive and worker levels that is tied to the accomplishment of specific improvement goals and that can add 3 to 5 percent to everyone's paycheck.

Gainsharing

Many organizations are looking to support their quality efforts with the addition of *gainsharing* plans, which are financial incentive plans for organizations, plants, or teams. They differ from ordinary profit sharing in that they require cost-reduction or performance-improvement negotiations with management to establish specific objectives and to define how results are measured and how gains are to be shared. The oldest gainsharing plan is the Scanlon Plan; others are the Improshare Plan and the Rucker Plan (Lawler, 1991). Unlike a suggestion program, in a gainsharing plan employees share in the gain for as long as the organization receives a return.

Although we did not identify any specific gainsharing

programs at work among the Baldrige winners, it is a subject that is worth examining. As Total Quality organizations mature and their productivity gains from continuous improvement become more difficult to achieve, they will most likely have to explore new incentives to maintain worker commitment and enthusiasm.

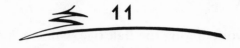

11

Strategy No. 5:
Encourage Complete and
Regular Communication

The first function of the executive is to develop and maintain a system of communication.
— Chester I. Barnard

Success in TQManagement is dependent on employees receiving consistent and credible messages in the broadest sense of the word. Messages that are formally communicated internally and to the public should be consistent with the organization's progress toward implementation of Total Quality. Every behavior, every action of the organization and its people — particularly senior management — needs to reinforce the basic principles of Total Quality. In this chapter we will review the significance of communication in the TQManagement strategy and outline nine strategic guidelines that we found common to the Baldrige winners.

Arnold Deutsch, an advertising executive, said: "Workers at every level are demanding more information and more kinds of information than ever before. No management team would attempt to operate an organization in today's market conditions and economic climate without a sophisticated capability to communicate" (Xerox, 1982, p. 8).

Virtually every survey taken on employee communication indicates that employees prefer, when possible, to receive information about their work and their company from their manager. They want their manager to be an authoritative source to answer their questions. But they also say, in overwhelming numbers, that managers are not performing that function well. Too many managers still seem to believe that the communication process is really not a process at all, but instead an extracurricular management activity to be handled when all of the other management tasks are done. That attitude can be a disaster for a Total Quality effort.

Management Actions to Establish Complete and Regular Communication

Tradition has established production quotas, sales figures, and other quantity-oriented bases as yardsticks of achievement, but the organization that uses such measures alone is sending conflicting messages about its quality goals. In the final analysis, actions are more important than words. Some examples of management actions that most forcefully communicate commitment to TQManagement include:

- Decision making and problem solving that follow the principles of Total Quality
- Giving recognition, rewards, and promotions to individuals who exemplify the behaviors of Total Quality
- Insistence that each individual have a clear definition of the customer, a clear understanding of the customer's requirements, agreement with the customer on the requirements and how they will be met, and identification of the means and resources necessary to meet those requirements
- Meetings—from the boardroom to the shop floor—that reflect Total Quality, including the use of quality-improvement and problem-solving processes
- Visible and consistent signs that quality overrides all other considerations in deciding how to behave as an organization and as individuals

Each reader could certainly add examples to this list that would speak louder than our words. But the point is that communication, no matter how carefully worded or creatively crafted, will not succeed if it is at odds with an organization's behavior. Motorola's Robert Galvin (Dobyns and Crawford-Mason, 1991, p. 35) says, "If the rest of the organization does not discern that the leader is all for a quality program, then there will be some degree of compromise."

Steps for Developing a Communication Strategy

Employees need to be continually informed of the overall TQM objectives of the corporation in general and their work group in particular and of progress toward those objectives. Communication must become a priority. Not communicating with employees is tantamount to a quarterback not calling a play in the huddle or a conductor not telling the orchestra what piece is to be played. The result is chaos. Following are some steps we identified in our dialogue with the Baldrige winners for developing a communication strategy in support of TQManagement that will help avoid chaos as the organization implements its Total Quality plan.

1. *Include quality objectives in the business plan in the same way that cost and schedule are included.* Each year Cadillac (1991) distributes to all employees a brochure detailing their Business Plan (which is also their quality plan) to make employees aware of the organization's major objectives. Using the Business Plan as a guide ensures that all employees are moving in the same direction with complementary efforts. That is why the business-planning process is also referred to as "aligning the arrows."

2. *Institute some form of employee feedback or satisfaction survey.* There must be good communication in all directions to ensure that people learn from what's happening locally and that policy decisions made at the top quickly reach people who are taking action locally. At Xerox (1990a) all employees complete an annual Satisfaction Survey that measures not only attitudes regarding corporate benefits, pay, and working conditions, but

also how managers support and practice the tools and behaviors of Total Quality.

3. *Adopt strategic guidelines as standards for communication on Total Quality, for the organization as a whole and for each operating unit.* At Westinghouse's Commercial Nuclear Fuel Division (Westinghouse Corporation, 1989b) the quality strategy is built on four imperatives: Management Leadership, Product/Process Leadership, Human Resource Excellence, and Customer Orientation. Communication is one of four "conditions of excellence" under Management Leadership and focuses on conveying the Total Quality message in workplace meetings, all employee meetings, employee roundtable meetings, and site newsletters and magazines.

4. *Require each unit to prepare an annual communication plan in support of the organization's implementation plan.* During implementation, Xerox's quality officers (Xerox Corporation, 1983) were required to review their unit's communication plans each year to ensure that quality was integrated into all media and that the messages conveyed the reality of the unit's progress. Today all operating units continue to develop annual plans and their progress against the plan is included in operations reviews.

All of an organization's efforts to pursue Total Quality send the strongest messages about their true intent. This includes the way people are trained, the way they are rewarded and recognized, the way managers set and measure standards, the decisions managers make and the way they make them, the way the organization treats customers, and the emphasis that is placed on quality. For an organization to achieve Total Quality, all these actions must communicate one thing: "We are a quality organization!"

Sending Strong Messages

It is especially important for managers to be sensitive to any actions and decisions that are contradictory to the principles of the organization's Total Quality effort. If a situation arises in which the perception is created that a manager does not support Total Quality, that manager must immediately take appropriate actions to communicate to his employees the reasons behind the decision and to demonstrate that the decision was in keeping with the organization's TQManagement goals. No matter how eloquent the words, if managers don't back them up with consistent behavior, employees will soon view quality as just another temporary fad—a "flavor of the month."

Houghton's (1987) favorite example is from Corning's State College, Pennsylvania, plant, which produces television bulbs. Some bulbs were out of spec, but one of Corning's customers said that he would take them because he was desperate. Although he knew they were out of spec, he planned to readjust his equipment and use them. But the plant manager wouldn't let the bulbs go out the door, because they didn't meet Corning's or the customer's requirements. Houghton notes that it took people in the plant about five seconds to understand that the plant manager was serious about quality.

Opening people's minds to new ideas usually produces conflict because old cultures, habits, ideas, and practices seldom shift without some irritation. It can be said that the organization in which there is no irritation or conflict is one that is not changing or growing. It is probably an organization in trouble. Our culture and values and our way of behaving in an organization are a function of ideas that have been expressed by words, spoken or written. Since executives usually do not do a lot of writing, what they say is taken as the substance of their ideas and values—and employees listen very closely to what managers say.

Sometimes we are inclined to believe that new ideas and practices will pass and life will change little. However, when substantive messages are repeated and reinforced often by significant people in the organization, employees and managers will respond. They react most strongly when the message expresses values they see as their own, or those that elevate their image of their organization. When messages appear that seem to be someone else's values, or show the organization in an "ordinary" light, the message is likely to be seen as just another in a long string of superficial efforts to increase productivity (as the boss in John Guaspari's *I Know It When I See It* learned when he decreed: "Try harder! Do better!"). Used as the slogan for achieving Total Quality, such messages reduce support rather than build it. For this reason, an organization's formal communication plays a powerful role.

Three Types of Communication

For purposes of considering the impact of a communication plan in a Total Quality organization, we see formal communication as embracing three distinct types:

1. Internal media, which includes such publications as the organization's newspaper; local publications for employees; slide presentations, video, film, newsletters, and speeches to employee groups; and the annual report
2. External media, including advertising, sales promotion pieces, trade show exhibits, and speeches to audiences outside the organization (employees see and hear these things too!)
3. Senior management presentations and plant tours that demonstrate management's interest and commitment — and that they "walk their talk"

Eight Objectives for Communication

Within the context of these categories, we observed eight major objectives for the use of these media that Baldrige winners incorporated in their communication plans:

1. Promoting and communicating the organization's quality policy to all employees
2. Explaining as explicitly as possible why the organization embarked on TQManagement and why successful implementation is key to long-term success
3. Explaining clearly, consistently, and continuously what Total Quality is and what it will accomplish through the stages of implementation, so that everyone understands the process to be a long-term one that must be implemented with discipline and patience

4. Promoting and encouraging the implementation of Total Quality
5. Portraying and reinforcing the value of continuous-quality improvement
6. Reinforcing understanding and encouraging the use and inspection of quality improvement by people at all levels
7. Tailoring communication to fit with the organization's TQManagement plan as it is implemented at different levels and in different units
8. Progressively influencing the following key constituencies (stakeholders) of the organization to equate the organization's name with quality:

   - Managers
   - Employees
   - Customers
   - Suppliers
   - Shareholders
   - The general public

Nine Strategic Guidelines for Full and Regular Communication

All of the organization's communication efforts, whether words or deeds, must say one thing: *This is a quality organization!* With that as the backdrop, an organization's Total Quality communication strategy that is designed to achieve the eight objectives should encompass nine strategic guidelines.

Guideline 1: Credibility Is Crucial and Must Be Earned

The culture of most organizations is inundated with short-term programs, crash projects, and campaigns. Total Quality should set itself apart from such short-term efforts and campaigns and convey an image that is deliberate and never-ending. Wherever possible this image should be communicated through the use of role models, real-world examples, and results as opposed to rhetoric, plans, and promises. Slogans, hoopla, and hyperbole must be strictly avoided. As an example, at Xerox, employees were prohibited from using the acronym LTQ to identify their quality process, Leadership Through Quality, in order to set it above the acronyms of previous productivity efforts.

On much the same theme, Wallace (1991) abandoned the internal use of the terms *employee* and *manager* in favor of *associate* and *leader*. "It's a symbolic change, but an important one," says CEO John Wallace. "We want to shift the focus away from control, and toward participation." At IBM Rochester (1991) the annual quality strategies have moved progressively from product reliability through customer and supplier partnerships to market-driven customer satisfaction to the current vision of "Customer, Quality, Products and Services, and People." But all exist under a simple banner: The quality journey continues...

Guideline 2: Managers Communicate Total Quality

The communication strategy needs to recognize that managers at all levels are powerful communication media. Training for managers in support of TQManagement needs to contain a segment on communication, including techniques for soliciting feedback, ensuring understanding, and facilitating two-way communication. This two-way communication should be aimed at gaining acceptance and building ownership of Total Quality. The more effectively managers communicate, the more people will feel they have a stake in the quality strategy and its goals.

In the book *A Better Idea: Redefining the Way Americans Work,* former Ford CEO Donald E. Peterson (Peterson and Hillkirk, 1991, pp. 43–44) stressed the importance of "walking around." He said, "When I visited one of Ford's 70 assembly plants I walked. . . . I would stop and talk with half a dozen people at a time. After we had exchanged the usual pleasantries, I would ask, 'How do you like it here? Having any problems? . . . Are you part of an employee involvement team?'" He described one encounter with a Ford employee: "I remember running into a giant of a man at our Buffalo stamping plant. He looked me in the eye and said, 'You know, I want to tell you one thing. I used to hate coming to work here. But lately I've been asked what I think, and that makes me feel like somebody. I never thought the company saw me as a human being.'"

Wallace (1991) uses a process called Performance Enhancement Program (PEP). The basis of PEP is a questionnaire that probes the extent to which various quality skills are used on the job, and how skilled the employees are at using them. The employees examine themselves and their jobs, and the manager, using the same questionnaire, rates the jobs and the employees. Their answers are compared to highlight areas of agreement and difference. Each employee then sets up a meeting with her manager—the employee has complete control over this meeting—structuring the conversation as she chooses. PEP facilitates an open, nonthreatening dialogue about the quality process while completely avoiding the judgmental trappings of a performance review.

Guideline 3: Show That Quality Is the First Consideration

The organization's communication must clearly and consistently demonstrate that quality is the overriding consideration for the way employees are expected to behave as part of an organization and as individuals. All communication media should reinforce the principles of Total Quality with consistent themes, including:

- Reinforcing the value of continuous quality improvement
- Encouraging the use and inspection of quality-improvement processes at all levels
- Emphasizing that the new environment will be characterized by teamwork, helpfulness, and respect for the individual
- Constantly striving for the improvement of work in the pursuit of quality
- Emphasizing that all employees have customers whether they are internal or external, and that in order to provide quality products, services, and work, it is important for everyone to identify those customers and their requirements

- Stressing that the cost of not conforming to customer requirements (for example, by failing to understand customer requirements, not doing things right the first time, or performing work that is neither needed nor desired by the customer) represents a major financial opportunity for improvement.

During TQManagement start-up, Total Quality organizations strive to keep advancing their messages, because they know that in the early days quality is something that can easily be forgotten. Houghton (1987, p. 22) says, "Communicating the total quality imperative means me yelling about it all the time." But Corning backs that up with a comprehensive plan that is designed to present to the entire company information about their objectives and progress, and to encourage two-way dialogue. This plan includes a daily "Headlines" sheet, quality success stories in their monthly newspaper, slide and videotape presentations on goals and progress, regular televised summaries of what's going on, and surveys of employees to discover the barriers to Total Quality.

Since 1983 Westinghouse's Commercial Nuclear Fuel Division has published an annual quality outline for all employees. The plan outlines CNFD's quality goals and accomplishments, each year with a different theme. Over the years the plan has highlighted such themes as Quality Improvement, Striving for Perfection, Quality Measures, Leadership Through Total Quality, Continuing the Commitment, and Quality Ownership.

Guideline 4: Select a Name for Your Total Quality Effort

After you've selected a name for your Total Quality effort, guard and protect it. It is your rallying cry and should not be taken lightly. Total Quality organizations invest effort, resources, and their reputation in their quality activity, and they must work to prevent it from being seen as just another "program" from management. We recommend the following:

- Avoid acronyms and logos—let the organization's efforts and accomplishments build the stature of your quality name and reputation.
- Register your quality name as a legal trademark.
- Use the term in external communication in an evolutionary fashion, as your behavior, products and services, and business results merit its use.

From the beginning Xerox's (1983) Total Quality efforts have been labeled Leadership Through Quality and the label has not changed. Six Sigma has become synonymous with Motorola. At Ford, Quality Is Job One. The Wallace (1991) "W" logo was revised to include a "Q" for quality. On the other hand Wallace avoids a display of banners, slogans, or mottos. Paul Vita said, "There isn't anything you need to say beyond quality. If we had to have a slogan, it might be 'quality will not be sacrificed.' But we're not big into banners—we're into action" (Gilbert, 1991, p. 5). Of course, all the Malcolm Baldrige winners now adorn their publications, letterheads, and memos with the National Quality Award Winner logo that goes with winning the Baldrige Award. That really says it all!

Guideline 5: Treat Management as the Most Significant Communicator

Management behavior is the single most important and effective means of communicating Total Quality. All the Baldrige winners take care to ensure that management behavior and actions reflect the principles of TQManagement before statements and promises are made. Use of the problem-solving processes, demonstration of teamwork among peers, and expressions of openness and trust in communicating with employees come before fancy newsletters and speeches.

For many Total Quality organizations this objective is partly met by their training cascade, which involves managers in establishing awareness and knowledge by having them participate in a posttraining quality-improvement activity before they stand in front of their own team to teach Total Quality.

Bowles and Hammond (1991) point out that before Roger Milliken and Fred Smith of Federal Express decided to pursue Total Quality, they were among the least accessible executives in the United States. And they note that until James McDonald and Robert Stempel (now CEO) took over at General Motors from Roger Smith, there was no true commitment to GM's quality effort.

Guideline 6: Tailor Communication to Progress

Total Quality evolves at different levels, in different places, and at different paces in organizations, so it is important not to let communication efforts get out in front of reality. Change invariably is slow, and communication in TQManagement organizations reflects actual progress, with the emphasis on reporting what *has* happened, not what *may* happen. One powerful reason why so many Baldrige Award–winning companies push communication planning and implementation down to the operating-unit level is to minimize the chance of communication outstripping reality.

About the time they won the Baldrige Award, Wallace Company (1991) launched an effort to facilitate more open lines of communication between employees and customers. Their Total Customer Involvement Program organizes meetings between employees and their logical customers. Wallace truck drivers, for example, meet with receiving clerks; accounts receivable people meet with their counterparts in payables. According to HR manager Paul Hollis, "It sharpens our focus on the customer. That lesson then carries over to team discussions related to the quality process" (Horton, 1990, p. 248).

Guideline 7: Communication Is a Two-Way Street

Each unit of the organization will want to use one or more means to facilitate upward communication that elicits employee ideas for improving quality, and to provide prompt feedback. In the Baldrige winners we studied, these communication efforts included suggestion systems (but be careful about conflict with team efforts), open-comment programs, executive roundtables, and management interviews, but also a system for measuring employee understanding and attitudes about Total Quality. This often meant establishing a new employee attitude survey or modifying existing surveys, but the investment was worth it.

At Federal Express (1991) they say, "'Do the right thing right the first time' is the motto for quality management. Quality changes the role of the manager from order-giver to helper and coach." One way they work at that is by using the management evaluation system called Survey/Feedback/Action (SFA). SFA consists of a survey of employees, analysis of each work group's results by the work group manager, and a discussion between the manager and the work group to develop an action plan for improvement. (This is described more fully in Chapter Thirteen.)

Guideline 8: Communicate the Plan to Everyone

People need to know where Total Quality is taking them. This is a new way of operating and care should be taken to explain very precisely how the organization will function when TQManagement becomes a way of life. Unit management of successful organizations should provide periodic updates of progress against the implementation plan, clearly report what has been learned, and share success stories, while taking care not to build unrealistic expectations.

Successful TQManagement organizations began their quality race by communicating their quality policy and implementation plan (most did it with an orientation or kickoff) and using a variety of techniques to keep employees up-to-date on progress against the plan. Wallace (1991) engaged all their associates (employees) in drafting their quality mission statement, and the company holds frequent quality-planning retreats with management to stay current and consistent about their overall goals for quality and progress. Following the retreats, they communicate to the associates through a bimonthly newsletter named *Quality Pathfinder,* meetings, and teleconferences.

Both Wallace and Milliken (1990) host "sharing days" where teams come together not only to be recognized for their accomplishments, but to learn from one another about applications and results of the tools and processes. Not only does this serve as a team learning venue but also as an opportunity to assess the organization's progress at the most practical levels. The idea of teams sharing with one another began with Xerox (1990a) in 1983 when they held their first Teamwork Day event in Webster, New York. The agenda consisted of a noontime event in the cafeteria where more than twenty teams set up booths to demonstrate their problem-solving and business-improvement activities. The five teams rated as "excellent" made presentations to an audience of managers and employees, including CEO David Kearns. That event has grown to a multicity, all-day Teamwork Day that involves upward of 600 teams displaying their projects and activities and competing for cash Excellent Team Awards. These events now attract audiences of 5,000 employees, managers, suppliers, and customers and have to be held in convention centers. Teamwork Day has become a focal quality day at Xerox (a progress measurement point in their race without a finish line!).

Guideline 9: Require Annual Unit Communication Plans

When Total Quality is an organization's basic business principle, the organization has to use every opportunity to reinforce its value. To ensure that this happens, the quality officer will want to review each operating unit's communication plans for supporting Total Quality. Virtually every communication vehicle can contain some implicit theme of support. For example, a new-product announcement needn't confine itself to a description of a piece of hardware. It can go beyond that to describe how the product was designed to meet customer requirements, how those requirements were identified, and how teamwork contributed to a successful product launch. The following are used by successful Total Quality organizations:

- Continuous quality improvement is the new way of life.
- Quality means meeting customer requirements.

- Continuous improvement drives market share and revenue growth; therefore, quality improvement widens the opportunities open to the organization and its people.
- Employee empowerment is the management style by which employees and managers alike participate in solving problems related to their work and work life.
- The pursuit of quality means constantly striving for the improvement of work processes and for doing things right the first time.
- The delivery of quality products, services, and work is the job of every employee.
- The new environment is characterized by teamwork, trust, openness, helpfulness — and respect for the individual.
- The cost of nonconformance to requirements is a staggering blow to the organization's bottom line and a major opportunity to improve financial performance.
- Total Quality is not a quick fix. It is long-term in nature and requires discipline and patience; it is a race without a finish line.
- The people who become recognized, rewarded, and promoted are those who exemplify the principles of Total Quality.
- Every employee has a customer in the work process, and that process eventually provides quality products and services to the external customer — the person who pays the bills.
- The long-term success of the organization requires that every individual practice the principles of Total Quality.
- Quality improvement, problem solving, statistical process control, and other Total Quality tools are effective and should be used by everyone.
- Customers today demand increasing levels of quality and timeliness. When it comes to meeting customers' requirements, everyone should always strive for improvement.
- In an environment that encourages prudent risk taking, some failure can be used as a valuable learning experience. Failures should be studied and analyzed — not punished — to enhance the probability of success in the future.

To succeed, Total Quality demands trust and openness. Trust is a firm reliance on the integrity, ability, and character of others. It requires confident belief and faith that people say what they mean and do what they say. It starts at the top of an organization and moves down, expanding as it goes; then it moves back up, across, and down, filling the organization with the atmosphere that creates teamwork and oneness of purpose. But trust can't live at only one level of an organization—it dies without support. It can only survive in partnership with openness. Openness is characterized by risk taking—the willingness to advocate what you believe is right. The fuel for trust and openness in an organization is open, complete, and regular communication—information, ideas, and feedback. Without communication, Total Quality is only a dream.

PART THREE

BREAKING OUT

OF THE PACK:

BUILDING ON

OTHERS' EXPERIENCE

In this section we look more closely at the organizations that are in the vanguard of the quality movement and then examine some of the management issues and problems this movement has brought into focus.

In Chapter Twelve we trace the history of the Baldrige Award, which has done so much to intensify American interest in quality. We then present the seven criteria of the Award, which thousands of companies have used to assess their own operations. We try to put the Award into perspective by discussing its impact on management thinking and practice. In a similar way we discuss the President's Award, which has made an impact on many agencies of the federal government.

In Chapter Thirteen we look at the twelve companies that won the Baldrige Award during the first four years of its existence. They differ greatly in size and products, but they share a common achievement in quality. We present a thumbnail sketch of each company and some of the strategies and practices they have found to be especially useful. Although we present learnings and examples from these companies throughout the book, this chapter gives us the chance to describe some of their distinctive practices more fully.

Chapter Fourteen presents an overall assessment of the quality movement, identifying some of the factors that account for its amazing growth in popularity as well as some of the developments that suggest a cautious approach to adopting it. We also examine the latest tools and processes that advanced practitioners of TQM are adopting. We believe that a critical examination of TQM—and its continuous improvement—is also "without a finish line."

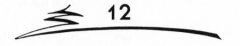

12

Auditing the Process:
The Baldrige and
President's Awards

Success produces success.

—Sébastien R. N. Chamfort

Like most movements, the quality movement has its symbols and ceremonies to recognize those who exemplify its ideals. Japan demonstrated the value of such recognition by creating the Deming Prize, named for W. Edwards Deming, the highest recognition a Japanese company can receive for excellence. (One American company—Florida Power and Light—was awarded this prize in 1989.) In the United States, various companies have developed their own symbols of excellence. In Westinghouse it's the George Washington Total Quality Award. In Motorola it's called the President's Award. Some organizations recognize suppliers who consistently provide quality goods and services. NASA, for example, gives an annual Excellence Award for Quality and Productivity to "organizations that continually demonstrate ways to sustain and improve the quality of their products and services."

Two national awards in the United States have given a powerful stimulus to the quest for organizational quality—the Malcolm Baldrige National Quality Award and the President's

Award for Quality and Productivity Improvement. These two awards have done much to focus attention on the key dimensions of a quality organization, to capture the imagination of thousands of corporate and governmental executives, and to develop a common language for sharing ideas and experience. In this chapter we discuss the background of these two awards, the aspects of organizational life on which they focus, and some evidence of their impact on Total Quality thinking in the few short years of their existence.

The Malcolm Baldrige National Quality Award

We would agree with David A. Garvin's (1991, p. 80) assessment that "more than any other initiative, public or private, it [the Baldrige Award] has reshaped managers' thinking and behavior." In this chapter we trace the fascinating history of this award, discuss its criteria and examination process, and describe its impact on the way managers think about their jobs and their organizations.

The Beginnings

The idea of a national award for quality was imported from Japan. That nation's Deming Prize proved to be a powerful stimulus for Japanese industries. The importer was Rear Admiral Frank C. Collins, Jr. (1989), in the early 1980s. Admiral Collins was executive director of quality assurance for the Defense Logistics Agency, which had a central role in authorizing payment for some $50 billion in defense materials annually. He was deeply impressed with the kind of management practices he saw during his trips to Japan, and he came to appreciate the importance of the Deming Prize when a Japanese company took a half-page ad in the *Wall Street Journal* featuring the medal and the legend: "The most important name in Quality Control in Japan is American." The company was still bragging about an award it had won twenty-three years earlier!

Would this kind of award succeed in America? Collins first presented his idea in 1982 to the National Academy of

Sciences, reasoning that it would be a prestigious, nonpolitical sponsor. After some initial enthusiasm, the idea died. He next approached Bruce Merrifield, assistant secretary of commerce. Again there was initial interest, but the President's Council of Economic Advisers was cool to the idea.

The next opportunity to present the idea of a national quality award came during the White House Conference on Productivity in September 1983. The purpose of this conference was to look into the decline of American productivity and to find ways of encouraging American industry to meet the growing threat of foreign competition. All of the recommendations of the National Productivity Advisory Committee went forward to the President's Council of Economic Advisers except for the one requesting creation of productivity medal. The advisers tabled the resolution because no thought had been given to criteria or to how the venture would be administered and funded. Conference participants recommended that the establishment of "a National Medal for *Productivity* [emphasis added] Achievement be awarded annually by the President of the United States for high levels of verifiable productivity achievement by organizations rather than individuals." They also called for the establishment of a commission to develop criteria and select winners for such an award. The conference report, *Productivity Growth: A Better Life for America,* published in April 1984, contained eighty-two recommendations for governmental action and sixty-six private sector recommendations. There were seven specific quality recommendations and many others related to quality (such as a recommendation to increase employee involvement).

A key figure in both the White House Conference on Productivity and the National Productivity Advisory Committee was C. Jackson Grayson. A former dean of two business schools—Tulane and Southern Methodist University—Grayson was also at home in the Washington political arena. (He had served with distinction as the administrator of price controls during the Nixon Administration.) He also founded and directed the American Productivity Center (APC) in Houston, Texas, which was later to become the American Productivity and

Quality Center (APQC). Grayson chaired the Private Sector Initiatives Panel for the White House Conference. He and Admiral Collins got to know one another and discovered their common interest in the issue of quality as a touchstone for improved competitiveness.

In the fall of 1984 Grayson and Collins met in Washington. Collins had retired from the navy and was now the vice president for quality for the Aviation Corporation (AVCO). Grayson proposed that they join forces to create a National Quality-Productivity Award. Grayson selected Marty Russell, staff vice president for national affairs for the APC, to begin assessing corporate interest in the idea and moving it forward. There proved to be sufficient interest among business executives to convene an "organizing group," in September 1985, in Collins's AVCO office in Washington. The group was composed of eleven men and two women—Collins and Ed Graham (AVCO), William Ruch (Arizona State University), Debra Owen (American Society for Quality Control), Pat Townsend (Paul Revere Insurance), William Crosby and David Kennedy (American Airlines), Ray Smock (Ford Motor Company), Anthony Diamond (NASA), Charles Mercer (McDonnell Douglas Electronics), John Kendrick (George Washington University), and Grayson and Russell (APC). In their first meeting the group made two important decisions: (1) to press for a Quality Award, rather than a Quality-Productivity Award, and (2) to develop criteria that would fit both service and manufacturing companies. The fledgling group agreed to meet twice a month at the AVCO offices in Washington to develop criteria and establish policies and an organization for administering the award.

The assumption from the very beginning was that the award should be developed by the private sector. The group agreed that it should be prestigious enough to be given by the president of the United States, but that the selection and administration process should be kept out of political and bureaucratic hands. The membership of the group shifted somewhat, with ten or twelve participating every month in one-day or one-and-a-half-day meetings. The core group included Collins, Russell, Graham, Townsend, Owen, Smock, and Diamond from the original group, together with Charles Baila (Florida Power and Light), Joe Frolich (Campbell Soup Company), Richard Stimson and Eli Lessor (Department of Defense), and Joe Cahalan (Xerox). For a time the group had no name, simply referring to itself as Marty's Group, since she served as the executive secretary. Eventually it became known as the President's Quality Award Committee. Collins served as chair and regularly hosted the luncheons. A spirit of camaraderie developed during the approximately fifty meetings held over a period of two years. Surprisingly few conflicts emerged over criteria or procedures for handling the award.

Meanwhile, in 1986, the Congressional Subcommittee on Science and Technology was discussing a quality award bill, in some cases using material developed by the President's Quality Award Committee. D. L. Baila, the Washington-based representative of Florida Power and Light, served as the liaison between the two groups. A real shock hit Collins and his group when John L. Hansel, board chairman of the American Society for Quality Control (ASQC), testified before the subcommittee that "the last thing American industry needs is an internal competition for a national quality award, especially since the award implies winners and losers. We need to carefully and fully understand the proper context for a national award" (Collins, 1989, p. 42). He argued that the ASQC would support and participate in the award process only if it provided for "a substantial technical assistance support program to provide guidelines, training and sharing of effective strategies with all industry and government." Following this testimony, Debra Owen, ASQC's representative, dropped out of the Collins group. The loss of support of the most important national organization devoted to quality was a shocking blow!

The irony was that the Collins group had also felt Hansel's concern about "winners and losers" and the importance of sharing strategies among companies, but they felt that they had worked out provisions to deal with these concerns. The group was depressed and the task of trying to interest additional CEOs became more difficult, even though Dana Cound, the president of ASQC, expressed the hope that ASQC and the President's

Quality Award Committee could "continue to explore areas of mutual cooperation" (Collins, 1989, p. 43).

The congressional activity spurred Collins and his colleagues to work more intensely to complete their plans for a completely privately administered award, while at the same time keeping open a "fallback" position from which they could work with any legislation that might be enacted. After developing the criteria and selection process, the committee faced the task of developing a funding procedure. They finally agreed to establish a $3 million foundation to fund both the administrative process and the award themselves.

One of the critical moments in the life of the committee was deciding how to collect $3 million from private sector companies. In 1987, Sanforth N. McDonnell, chairman of McDonnell Douglas, stepped forward and made the first commitment of $300,000 and offered to solicit other CEOs. His close colleague in this effort was John Hudiburg, chairman and CEO of Florida Power and Light.

The Legislation

Everything changed in August 1987, when Malcolm Baldrige, the secretary of commerce, was thrown from a horse in a California rodeo. His shocking death was a stimulus for quick congressional action. The National Quality Improvement Act of 1987, which had passed the House on June 8, was renamed to honor the former secretary, and on August 20 the U.S. Congress passed the Malcolm Baldrige National Quality Improvement Act of 1987 (Public Law 100-107). Its stated purpose was: "To provide for the establishment and conduct of a national quality improvement program under which (1) awards are given to selected companies and other organizations in the United States that practice effective quality management and as a result make significant improvements in the quality of their goods and services, and (2) information is disseminated about the successful strategies and programs."

Awards were to be given in three categories of companies: manufacturing, service, and small business. No more than two were to be given in each category in a single year. The act also provided that "the award shall be evidenced by a medal bearing the inscription: 'Malcolm Baldrige National Quality Award' and 'The Quest for Excellence'" and that the President or the Secretary of Commerce should present the award "with such ceremonies as the President or Secretary may deem proper." The award was to be administered by the National Bureau of Standards (now the National Institute of Standards and Technology or NIST) through contracting with "one or more broad-based nonprofit entities which are leaders in the field of quality management and have a history of service to society." The "nonprofit entity" selected was a consortium made up of the American Productivity Institute and the ASQC. The reasoning was clear: Grayson's APC had spearheaded the two-year effort to define criteria, establish procedures, and raise the necessary funds. The ASQC was the largest national professional organization in the country devoted to quality. Douglas E. Kings of Xerox chaired the consortium.

The Administration

Curt W. Reimann, deputy director of the National Measurements Laboratory, was selected to be the director of the Baldrige Award Program. On September 25, 1987, he convened a team that included seven members of the original group that had worked to develop criteria and procedures, together with staff members of the National Bureau of Standards. At this first meeting the group was informed that because President Reagan wanted to present the first award during his term in office, an all-out effort had to be made to get the administrative machinery in place rapidly. This meant publicizing the award, developing application forms, recruiting and training examiners, coordinating the examination process, creating the medal, and organizing the presentation ceremony in fifteen months!

     The two years of work by the President's Quality Award Committee began to pay off. Reimann had a knowledgeable team from the APC and ASQC ready to get the process off to a quick and well-designed start. Sixty-six companies applied for the award in 1988. Of these, thirteen passed the initial screening and received site visits by examiners, and ultimately three — Motorola, Globe Metallurgical, and the Commercial Nuclear Fuel Division of Westinghouse Electric — were selected as the nation's first winners of the Malcolm Baldrige National Quality Award.

The Baldrige Award itself is composed of two solid-crystal prismatic forms, made by Steuben Glass Medal, standing fourteen inches high and weighing about twenty-five pounds. The crystal is held in a base of black, anodized aluminum with the winner's name engraved on the base. A solid-bronze, 22-karat, gold-plated, die-struck medallion is embedded in the front section of the crystal. The medal bears the inscriptions: "Malcolm Baldrige National Quality Award" and "The Quest for Excellence" on one side and the presidential seal on the other side.

The first Baldrige Awards ceremony took place in the East Room of the White House on November 14, 1988. The winning companies were represented by their CEOs and the people who had worked most closely on their application efforts. The president presented each CEO with a red leather binder containing a picture and description of the award (while the delicate crystal award sat safely in a central place on a table). Only a few of those who witnessed the simple ceremony knew how many thousands of hours of creativity, effort, and commitment were required to make this ceremony a reality. None of those present could have predicted what an impact this simple, elegant award would have on the thinking of managers across the country!

Basic Eligibility

Public Law 100-107 establishes three eligibility categories for the Baldrige Award: manufacturing, service, and small business. Any for-profit business located in the United States or its territories may apply. Eligibility is intended to be as open as possible to all United States companies. Minor eligibility restrictions and conditions ensure fairness and consistency of definition. For example, publicly or privately owned companies, domestic or foreign-owned companies, joint ventures, incorporated firms, sole proprietorships, partnerships, and holding companies may apply. Not eligible are local, state, and national governmental agencies; not-for-profit organizations; trade associations; and professional societies.

Manufacturing. This includes companies or subsidiaries that produce and sell manufactured products or manufacturing processes, and those companies that produce agricultural, mining, or construction products.

Service. These are companies or subsidiaries that sell services (proper classification of companies that perform both manufacturing and service is determined by the larger percentage of sales).

Small Business. These are complete businesses with not more than 500 full-time employees. Business activities may include manufacturing and/or service. A small business must be able to document that it functions independently of any other businesses that are equity owners.

The Categories

A company applying for the award must review a thirty-two-page list of award criteria and submit a comprehensive application with a four-page overview. The award criteria consist of seven categories with a total of twenty-eight examination items (down from thirty-two in 1991). Each item focuses on a major element of an effective quality system and has an assigned point value; there are a total of 1,000 points possible. Within each item are a set of Areas to Address that serve to illustrate and clarify the intent of the items and place limits on the type and amount of information that has to be provided. The number of areas to address has been reduced to eighty-nine from ninety-nine. Although the overall total point value remains the same (1,000), adjustments were made in 1992 to provide a better overall balance among items and to place more emphasis on results.

The changes in criteria were adopted to strengthen certain key themes:

- Cycle-time reduction
- Productivity
- Overall company performance
- Work process and organizational simplification and waste reduction
- The relationship between quality and other business management considerations: business planning, financial results, overall company effectiveness, innovation, and future orientation
- Alignment of requirements in plans
- Design quality and prevention
- Data aggregation, analysis, and use
- Work force deployment
- Quality system integration

The seven categories and their point values are as follows:

1. *Leadership (3 items, 90 points).* Senior management's success in creating and sustaining a quality culture. This involves evidence of the continuing role senior management plays in fostering quality values, how quality values influence day-to-day management, and how the company functions as a good corporate citizen.

2. *Information and Analysis (3 items, 80 points).* The effectiveness of the company's collection and analysis of information for quality improvement and planning. This includes how it evaluates quality, how it uses competitive comparisons and benchmarks, and how data and information are analyzed to support the company's overall quality objectives.

3. *Strategic Quality Planning (2 items, 60 points).* The effectiveness of the integration of quality requirements in the company's business plan. This involves both the planning process and the quality goals and plans.

4. *Human Resources Development and Management (5 items, 150 points).* The success of the company's effort to utilize the full potential of the work force for quality. This involves an examina-

tion of the overall human resource management system, employee involvement, quality education and training, employee recognition and performance measurement, and attention to all the factors that affect employee well-being and morale.

5. *Management of Process Quality (5 items, 140 points).* The effectiveness of the company's systems for assuring quality control in all operations. This involves looking at how products and services are designed and introduced, how processes are controlled, how quality is assessed and documented, how the business processes and support services support quality, and how the quality of supplies is assured.

6. *Quality and Operational Results (4 items, 180 points).* The company's results in quality achievement and quality improvement. This involves examining both trends and levels in quality improvement of products and services, business services, and suppliers' quality.

7. *Customer Focus and Satisfaction (6 items, 300 points).* The effectiveness of the company's systems to determine customer requirements and demonstrate success in meeting them. This involves looking at how the company determines customer requirements and expectations, how it manages customer relationships, its customer-service standards, its commitment to customers, how it uses complaints to improve quality, how it determines customer satisfaction, the trends in its customer-satisfaction ratings, and how it compares with other companies offering similar products or services.

The changes in the category weights during the first five years of the award are shown in Table 12.1. The biggest change has occurred in the emphasis given to Leadership (reduced from 15 to 9 percent) and Quality Assurance and Operational Results (increased from 10 to 18 percent). To assess this latter category, examiners will also look at the current quality and performance levels of the applicants' competitors.

The Review Process

Every effort is made to make the evaluation process fair and useful to the companies that choose to enter. A board of exam-

Table 12.1. Changes in Category Weights from 1988 to 1992,
by Examination Category.

Category	1988	1992
Leadership	150	90
Information and analysis	75	80
Strategic quality planning	75	60
Human resource utilization	150	150
Quality assurance of products and services	150	140
Quality and operation results	100	180
Customer satisfaction	300	300
Total	1,000	1,000

iners evaluates Award applications, prepares feedback reports, and makes Award recommendations to the director of NIST. The board consists of quality experts who come primarily from the private sector. Members are selected by NIST through a competitive application process. (In 1991 more than 1,300 applied for the voluntary prestigious Baldrige examiner position; only 227 were selected.) For 1992 the board will consist of more than 250 members. All members of the board take part in an examiner preparation course. Examiners receive no fee for their services.

All applications are reviewed and evaluated by members of the board of examiners. When board members are assigned to review applications, their business and quality expertise is matched to the business of the applicant. Accordingly, applications from manufacturing companies are assigned primarily to board members with manufacturing expertise. Strict rules regarding real and potential conflicts of interest are followed in assigning board members to review applications.

Company applications for the Baldrige Award enter a four-stage review process:

1. *Scoring of the written application.* This is done by a team of examiners who give their individual scores to a senior examiner, whose primary responsibility is to develop a consensus score. A company receiving a low score at this point is provided with feedback.

2. *Consensus review.* Applications passing the initial screening are submitted to a panel of nine judges on the board of examiners. These judges decide which companies warrant a site visit.

3. *Site visits.* Site visits allow companies the opportunity to expand insights and information beyond those in the application. It also gives examiners the chance to verify information, interview employees, and inspect facilities. The team consists of four to six people: two or more examiners, one senior examiner, and an observer from NIST. The visit usually lasts three to five days.

4. *Final selection.* The final decision is made by the nine judges. Once the decision has been made, Reimann phones all of the finalists who were not chosen. When this has been done, the secretary of commerce phones the winners.

The Impact of the Baldrige Award

The cost of the Baldrige Award is very high — for the companies that prepare the comprehensive application, the examiners and judges who give days of their time, and the industry-supported foundation that funds the administrative expenses. Is it worth it? The answer after four years is a resounding "Yes!" — but with a few caveats and concerns that make the principle of continuous improvement appropriate for even this most distinguished enterprise!

Let's begin by looking at the positive results of the Baldrige Award:

1. *The Award has focused attention on quality.* Jerry Jazinowski, the president of the National Association of Manufacturers, wrote in a November 18, 1991, issue of *Industry Week* that whereas ten years ago CEOs talked about their strategic goals of cutting costs and becoming "leaner and meaner," they are now talking more about the pursuit of quality as the key to achieving success in world markets. The executives we have talked to have given the Baldrige Award credit for contributing to this significant change of priorities.

2. *The Award has provided guidelines for organizational assess-*

ment. The seven criteria presented in the Baldrige application have been widely used by companies to examine their own operation, even when they do not apply for the Award. It is notable that IBM Rochester went through the entire process of filling out a Baldrige application in 1991 even though as a 1990 winner, they were ineligible to compete. They found this to be an excellent way to identify what they call "holes" in their operation—places where there is room for significant improvement. Xerox, Cadillac, Motorola, and other winners report using the Baldrige criteria the same way.

3. *The Award has stimulated quality management education.* Every Baldrige winner is expected to, and does, become a role model for other companies. By staging day-long Showcase Seminars and Quality Forums, these exemplary companies share their hard-won experience with executives from other companies—even competitors! Executives and managers from Baldrige winners are in great demand as speakers at management conferences and seminars. Everyone wants to hear how the winner does it! For some reason, learning from a Baldrige winner does not seem to be a demeaning experience, and it's acceptable to copy what someone else has done successfully. In our survey at the end of 1991, we learned that more than 50,000 executives had attended day-long "showcase" seminars, and more than a half-million had been in various audiences addressed by Baldrige-winning executives. The cost to the winning companies for this sharing during the 1989–1991 period amounted to close to $10 million.

In return for this contribution, however, Baldrige winners reported that their major gain was access to top executives in a new array of organizations. They also said that the publicity and excitement generated among their own employees was well worth the investment, along with the satisfaction that comes from sharing useful ideas.

One result of this sharing has been the discovery that the advantage of holding proprietary secrets is not nearly as valuable as the goodwill that comes from sharing them. The "not invented here" syndrome has been replaced with an open admission that "we stole ideas shamelessly from Motorola and Xerox."

4. *The Award has provided a common vocabulary and philosophy.* Curt Reimann believes that this may be one of the best contributions of the Award to date. One of his major goals from the beginning (as a veteran of the Office of Standards and Measurements) has been to establish a framework for quality that facilitates communication between managers in widely different fields. Terms such as *empowerment, benchmarking, Pareto charts, internal customers, cycle time,* and *teams* have meanings that managers from different organizations and disciplines can discuss easily, knowing that they're talking about the same thing. This has accelerated the sharing and learning that is required to build a quality culture.

5. *The Award has brought excitement to the management arena.* The Baldrige Award has been described as the Super Bowl or Academy Award of organizational life. In just four years, it has become the most important catalyst for transforming American business. Winners are deluged with requests and invitations. Parties and press conferences punctuate the daily life of employees. Visitors come from distant places and ask interesting questions. There is something fascinating about watching a well-run quality organization in action! And there is something energizing about trying to be the best in your field. The Award provides an occasion to make these things happen.

6. *The Baldrige winners have extended their influence for quality beyond their companies and industries.* One of the unexpected outcomes of the Award process has been the involvement of winning companies with community problems. In Memphis, Tennessee, for example, the executives of Federal Express are involved in efforts to improve the quality of education. IBM, through its managers and employees, plays a very influential role in dealing with the problems of Rochester, Minnesota. The same kind of systematic diagnostic thinking that can increase the quality of a company's productive process is equally useful in dealing with a community's need for better education and better law-enforcement.

With all these contributions there are, however, some reasons to keep a careful watch on the Baldrige Award and its concomitant activities:

1. *Winning the Award may become an end in itself.* Americans like to be number one. When winning becomes the focus, the temptation is to look for shortcuts or superficial results without building quality strength. We do not know of any specific situations, but there is always the possibility that some CEO will say to his staff, "Let's win one of those awards," without understanding what kind of commitment to change is essential on his part to build a quality culture. Nadler worries that "with the growing visibility of Baldrige, there's a growing misunderstanding. The goal of winning may replace the goal of achieving real quality" (1992).

2. *The application process can become too expensive for a small company to undertake.* This concern stems from a recognition that big companies can free staff to do the research and writing of an application and therefore can present their materials in an elegant fashion, whereas a smaller company must depend on their personnel to do this over and above the call of duty. Much of the writing of the Zytec application, for example, was done by the president's secretary in overtime hours. (It might be noted, however, that Globe Metallurgical's application was written largely over one weekend, and they won the Award in 1988.)

3. *The Award ignores some very important aspects of company success.* The application does not deal with such critical factors as financial performance, innovation, and long-term planning. These are elements that most American CEOs have focused on most consistently because shareholders hold them accountable on these dimensions. The Baldrige Award is based on the assumption that if a quality process is in place and quality products are produced, the other matters will take care of themselves. Jerry Bowles, publisher of the *Quality Executive,* and Joshua Hammond, president of the American Quality Foundation, wrote: "The [Baldrige] process is limited, and it ignores 'forward quality'—developing new products, services and markets. Companies focusing on technical quality but ignoring this are buying a one-way ticket on the extinction express" (Garvin, 1991). Reimann insists, however, that the modification of criteria during the past four years has been in the direction of integrating

more of the elements that contribute to company success, including measures of productivity and effectiveness.

4. *Some individual consultants exploit the interest in the Award.* Baldrige examiners and judges are highly regarded. Some companies feel that if they can engage the consulting services of a Baldrige examiner they will enhance their chances for winning the Award. Some are even said to offer extravagant bonuses to consultants who can help them win the Award.

5. *Winning companies may be tempted to overadvertise their success.* Winners are explicitly permitted to advertise the fact that they have won the Baldrige Award. This must be monitored carefully, however, because if the Award becomes too valuable an asset, the focus can easily shift to an emphasis on winning, rather than on using the Baldrige system as a vehicle for examining one's processes and learning to improve quality.

Despite the negatives, however, the Baldrige National Quality Award is widely viewed as a phenomenal success. It gained prominence much more quickly than Frank Collins, Jack Grayson, Marty Russell, and their ten colleagues imagined when they met on that September day in 1985. It has become a rallying point and symbol for the growing group of American managers who are interested in focusing more of their own and their colleagues' attention on quality.

The President's Award for Quality and Productivity Improvement

Background

The federal government is the largest consumer and producer of goods and services in the United States. Although some would argue that "quality in government" is an oxymoron, serious efforts to bring a quality point of view to governmental agencies have been proceeding in an earnest way since the early 1980s. The establishment of the Federal Quality Institute (FQI) in 1988 was a clear signal that Total Quality Management in the federal government was to be taken seriously.

The FQI began administering the Federal Quality Improvement Prototype Award in 1988 and created the President's Award for Quality and Productivity Improvement in 1989. This Award is given annually to "an agency or major component of an agency that has implemented TQM in an exemplary manner, and is providing high quality service to its customers." An agency becomes eligible to apply for the Award if one or more Quality Improvement Prototypes have been selected from it. The 1989 Award was given to the Naval Air Systems Command, the 1991 Award went to the Air Logistics Command, and the 1992 Award was given to the Ogden (Utah) Service Center of the Internal Revenue Service.

The Criteria

The President's Award focuses on eight categories of organizational behavior. They compare roughly with the seven Baldrige categories, but are specifically tailored to a public agency. The categories and weights are as follows:

1. *Top Management Leadership and Support (20 Points)*. How all levels of senior management create and sustain a clear and visible quality value system along with a supporting management system to guide all activities of the organization.
2. *Strategic Planning (15 Points)*. The extent to which quality considerations are taken into account in the planning process.
3. *Focus on the Customer (40 Points)*. The organization's overall customer service systems, knowledge of the customer, responsiveness, and ability to meet requirements and expectations.
4. *Employee Training and Recognition (15 Points)*. The organization's efforts to develop and utilize the full potential of the work force for quality improvement and personal and organizational growth, as well as its efforts to use rewards and incentives to recognize employees who improve quality and productivity.
5. *Employee Empowerment and Teamwork (15 Points)*. The effectiveness and thoroughness of employee involvement in TQM.
6. *Measurements and Analysis (15 Points)*. The scope, validity, use,

and management of the data and information that underlie the organization's TQM system and how the data are used to improve processes, products, and services.

7. *Quality Assurance (30 Points).* The systematic approaches used by the organization for total quality of products and services, and the integration of quality control with continuous quality improvement.

8. *Quality and Productivity Improvement Results (50 Points).* The measurable and verifiable results of the organization's TQM practices.

Administration of the Award

The Award cycle begins each year when the FQI distributes the Quality Improvement Prototype application package to federal organizations. The application package for the President's Award is mailed to eligible federal agencies each November after the prototypes for that year have been selected. A panel of examiners selects the winning agency. The 80 to 100 percent range describes a world-class organization; the 40 to 60 percent range indicates an organization with a sound, well-implemented program.

The Impact of the President's Quality and Productivity Improvement Program

Between 1988 and 1991 154 agencies applied to be designated as a Quality Improvement Prototype and 20 have been accepted. The winning applications serve as case studies that, according to Tina Sung of the FQI, are widely read throughout the federal agencies. Like the Baldrige winners, prototype recipients are inundated with requests for videotapes and presentations by executives. All agencies that apply are given feedback similar to that of the Baldrige applicants.

The Role of Awards in the Quality Management Arena

Giving highly visible recognition to some and not to others is always a delicate process. John Hansel's concern about creating losers whenever you create winners is justifiable. Those who manage the award process have a responsibility to monitor it in such a way that those who do not win do not feel like losers; instead, they should feel as if they have gained from a systematic review of their own processes with the help of outside experts.

The metaphor of a marathon race gives some useful guidance here. The thousands of people who run in a marathon all gain because of what happened to them as they conditioned themselves for the race. They tend to encourage and support one another even as they compete. Only one person wins, but all who complete the race feel a sense of accomplishment. And all are healthier because they prepared themselves and participated.

Thus far it seems that both the Baldrige Award and the President's Award have succeeded in maintaining a balance in which participating is advantageous even if someone else carries off the trophy.

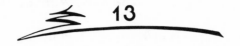

13

Sharing the Experience: Comments and Reflections from the Award Winners

Winning isn't everything, but wanting to win is.
— Vince Lombardi

The race for quality never ends, so there is no undisputed winner. There are leaders, however — organizations that are recognized as being exceptionally well managed in every respect, producing goods and services that delight their customers. America's most prominent vehicle for recognizing quality companies is the Malcolm Baldrige National Quality Award, which we discussed in the previous chapter. The companies selected for this recognition have been carefully scrutinized by well-trained Baldrige examiners and have been judged to be leaders in the quest for excellence. They are worth learning from, and our survey at the end of 1991 showed that more than a half-million American executives and managers have done exactly that by listening to speeches and attending seminars presented by the managers of these twelve companies.

In our study of the Baldrige winners we read their materials, interviewed some of their executives and managers, and attended some of their seminars to get a feel for events that had provided special insights or energy to help them pursue their quest for quality so successfully. We included some of these examples throughout the previous chapters. In this chapter we will do two things: (1) present a brief sketch of each of these quality companies and (2) report on some of the experiences and events that contributed to their success but did not fit easily into the previous chapters of this book. These stories gave us a special insight into what it takes to create and sustain a Total Quality effort in an organization. So join us in a quick tour of some of America's most successful companies.

1988 Winners

During the first year of the Baldrige Award, some 12,000 companies asked for copies of the application form, but only 66 actually applied for consideration. Of these, 13 qualified for site visits and ultimately 3 were selected as winners: Globe Metallurgical of Cleveland; Motorola, Inc.; and Westinghouse's Commercial Nuclear Fuel Division. On November 14, 1988, President Reagan presented the first Baldrige Awards in the East Room of the White House—the only time this venue (with very limited seating capacity) has been used for the prestigious event.

Globe Metallurgical, Inc., Cleveland, Ohio (Small Business)

Globe is a small company that set out in 1985 to become the lowest-cost, highest-quality producer of ferroalloys and silicon metal in the United States. While many U.S. makers of iron-based metals were closing plants, this Ohio-based firm initiated a quality-improvement program that has made their products the standards of excellence in the metals industry. They employ 210 people in their plants in Beverly, Ohio, and Selma, Alabama, and produce some 100,000 tons of alloys each year for more than 300 customers. Their annual sales totaled less than $100 million in 1987, and they achieved a 30 percent increase in 1988, the year they won the Baldrige Award.

    Globe trained their managerial staff in statistical process control in 1985 and launched their Quality, Efficiency, and Cost (QEC) program. With workers involved in weekly quality circles

and a QEC committee in each plant, there is a constant reviewing of causes of out-of-control conditions, corrective measures,
and proposals. Globe attempts to monitor and quantify every
factor that influences product quality, making extensive use of
computer-controlled systems that continually advise workers on
whether target values for important processing variables are
being met.

The result of this rigorous monitoring and correcting has
significantly reduced energy consumption (a major cost for
Globe) and realized improvements in manpower efficiency of
over 50 percent in some areas. Customer complaints have decreased by 91 percent, from 44 in 1985, when 49,000 pounds of
product were returned for replacement, to 4 in 1987, when no
product was returned.

It is interesting to note that Globe was purchased by a
group of managers from Moore McCormack Resources in 1987.
One of the purchasers, company president Ken Leach, received
a copy of the Baldrige application only a few days before the
deadline. He completed the application over the weekend!

Motorola, Inc., Schaumburg, Illinois (Manufacturing)

Motorola is a sixty-three-year-old company employing nearly
103,000 workers at fifty-three major facilities worldwide, with
headquarters in Schaumburg, Illinois (a suburb of Chicago).
They produce a wide variety of products, but are especially
known for their communication systems, primarily two-way radios and pagers, which account for 36 percent of their sales.
They also produce semiconductors, cellular telephones and
equipment for defense and aerospace, data communications,
information processing, and automotive and industrial uses.
Sales in 1991 totaled $10.8 billion.

Motorola was one of the first American companies to
make a vigorous response to the rapid rise of Japanese products
in world markets for electronics. The triggering event for
Motorola's quest for quality occurred in April 1979 in a Chicago
hotel. In the middle of a three-day meeting of Motorola's officers,
the chairman, Robert Galvin, asked for comments, and the

national sales manager for the communications sector (the largest division of the company) rose to say, "My customers tell me that our quality stinks." At the time of his remark, Motorola was a highly regarded, successful company with a major share of market in every business they were in and with a reputation for superior reliability, so most of his colleagues dismissed the comment. On closer examination, however, it turned out that the company's products were showing "early-life failure." Later analysis indicated that this was directly related to a high-defect rate in the manufacturing process caused by insufficient design margins and lack of process control. In 1979 this was regarded as a "normal" situation in the U.S. electronics industry.

One outcome of the Chicago meeting was Galvin's decision to appoint Jack Germain, a senior manager, as the company's first corporate director of quality. After about a year in this position, Germain recommended to the Senior Management Committee that a quality goal be set. They agreed and the first goal, announced in January 1981, was set at a tenfold improvement in five years. This goal was reached, with many of their products clearly the best in the class. Some parts of the organization reached the goal in as little as two and a half years!

However, this "success" led to a key insight! *The goal was not aggressive enough!* The purpose of an aggressive goal is to force the organization to change the way they run the business. You can improve 10 to 15 percent a year without changing the organization by just working a bit harder. A more aggressive goal, however, forces you to reassess your whole production process.

A second insight came when Motorola got a contract with the Pennsylvania State Police to design, manufacture, install, and maintain their statewide communications system. These thousands of products provided excellent failure data. By tracing failures back to the production process on a systematic basis, the quality experts discovered that the more a product needed fixing during production, the more likely it was to fail in the field, and that this was the fundamental cause of early-life failures. This led to a focus on *defect prevention* as the most reliable approach to quality. In late 1984, George Fisher, the assistant manager in the communications sector (now chairman), issued a letter stating that both products and services were henceforth to be measured in terms of defects per unit of work.

The third insight came during a 1986 benchmarking trip to Japan. The Motorola executives visited various (noncompeting) electronics firms and discovered that they were operating at a defect rate that was as much as a *thousand times lower* than Motorola's! (The defect rate is computed by dividing the number of defects per unit of product by the number of "opportunities" for defects to occur. Each additional component or process adds another opportunity for failure.) This rationale for assessing quality led to the development of the now-famous and widely used Six Sigma standard, which was to be achieved by 1992. Each Sigma represents one standard deviation from the norm; Six Sigma represents an almost complete inclusion of any sample. In practical terms, this means only 3.4 deviations (errors) in a million opportunities—99.9997 percent perfect! Most companies are content to operate at a Four Sigma level, tolerating a 99.4 percent rate (Figure 13.1).

To dramatize the folly of settling for less than perfection, Motorola executives like to note that a 99.9 percent error-free performance would permit:

- Twenty thousand wrong drug prescriptions per year
- Unsafe drinking water one hour per month
- No electricity, water, or heat for 8.6 hours per year
- Two short or long landings at major airports each day
- Five hundred incorrect surgical operations per week
- Two thousand lost articles of mail per hour

To achieve their goal Motorola has invested heavily in training (2.9 percent of payroll). All employees worldwide are expected to participate in forty hours of training, according to Bill Wiggenhorn, director of Motorola University. "The target is that a minimum of 2 percent of employees' annual time be spent in formal training classes, on-the-job training, and application training assistance." At the heart of the training is a course titled "Utilizing the Six Steps to Six Sigma."

At one time achieving near perfection seemed like the

Figure 13.1. Four Sigma and Six Sigma Charts.

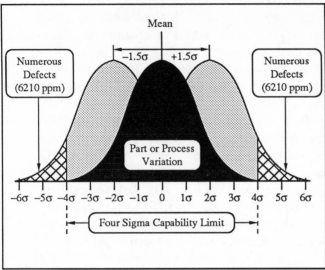

Four sigma capability causes defects to occur at a 6210-ppm rate with mean shifts of ±1.5 sigma. We have chosen mean shifts of ±1.5 sigma after much empirical study.

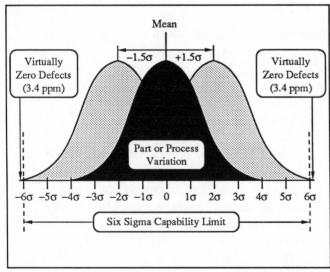

Six sigma capability causes defects to occur at a 3.4-ppm rate with mean shifts of ±1.5 sigma. *The defect rate begins to approach zero.*

Source: © Motorola, Inc. Used by permission.

height of unreality, according to Paul Noakes, Motorola's vice president for external quality, but since embarking upon the Six Sigma program Motorola personnel are consistently amazed at their own competence. Some groups of employees have gone for several months without producing a single defective product! Noakes attributes the continual improvement to "very tough" goals, regular reviews of data, involving all employees in the process, systematic inspection of the process, and an incentive system that supports the whole effort.

Two additional learnings emerged from the Motorola experience. One was that the fastest way to improve quality is to focus on reducing "cycle time"— the time it takes to fill an order, complete any process, or get a new product to market. They found that when they focused on cycle time, defects were reduced at a much faster rate than when they focused on defect reduction alone. Another learning was that workers do not have to be busy every minute. The concern for the "high cost of labor" has led many companies to keep a high inventory of parts so that workers will never run out of supplies. Motorola discovered that when workers have time to think on the job they come up with some very useful ideas for improving work processes.

What has been the return for Motorola? Since the end of 1986—when they began the Six Sigma thrust—Motorola's cost of quality has declined by over 7 percent of sales and the cumulative savings in cost avoidance has been $2.2 billion. Motorola's sales have grown 92 percent since 1986, and sales dollars per employee are up 78 percent, a compounded improvement rate of 12 percent, but without raising prices!

What does a vice president for quality learn from several years of working in this kind of system? Noakes says, "In the past we made the mistake of setting our sights too low."

Westinghouse Commercial Nuclear Fuel Division, Pittsburgh, Pennsylvania (Manufacturing)

The Westinghouse Nuclear Fuel Division employs over two thousand people at four sites, with headquarters in Monroeville, Pennsylvania. It produces the bundles of uranium-filled rods that fuel nuclear power plants. Prior to the 1980s CNFD's quality goals were geared toward satisfying regulatory requirements. Then, motivated by stiff competition and demanding customer requirements, they raised their sights and decided to become recognized as the world's highest-quality supplier of commercial fuel. The result is that CNFD is now certain that 99.9995 percent of the thousands of rods they supply will perform flawlessly.

A Quality Council, made up of the general manager, his staff, and quality assurance managers, directs the quality-improvement process. Supporting, measurable goals are developed in each of the departments and then for each worker. Progress is monitored through an extensive data collection and trend-analysis process. Workers address quality-improvement opportunities and help devise initiatives through participation in project-oriented teams. Nearly 1,400 employees were members of 300 such teams in 1991.

CNFD maintains very close — almost daily — contact with their customers. Customer service plans are created for each client and are jointly reviewed each quarter. A customers' Fuel Users' Group meets twice a year to share information and discuss needs for new products. How does the work force sustain the continuing pressure to improve? As recently retired executive Chuck Vogel puts it, "I used to think it was like going up a spiral staircase. Every time you looked up there were more levels. Now I think it's more like climbing a funnel — getting wider all the time."

Although it was the Nuclear Fuel Division that won the Baldrige, all of Westinghouse Electric Corporation has had a quality program in place since the early 1980s (in fact, other Westinghouse divisions were NQA finalists in 1989, 1990, and 1991). The first step was to establish a Corporate Productivity Center in Pittsburgh. The mission of the Center was to develop and apply techniques and technology to help Westinghouse become more competitive in the world market. Then chairman Bob Kirby established a Productivity Seed Fund for medium- to high-risk productivity projects. Over $60 million was invested, and from 1980 to 1985, when U.S. productivity was growing at a rate under 3 percent a year, the investment was paying dividends as Westinghouse's productivity grew at a rate over twice that percentage — even greater than the average improvement rate of industrial Japan. From this experience came a key insight: *quality was the most important driver of productivity!* When quality improved, productivity improved almost as a by-product. The result was a renaming of the unit as the Productivity and Quality Center.

1989 Winners

By 1989 the Baldrige Award was gaining increased attention in the business world. More than 65,000 companies asked for applications, although only 40 actually applied for the Award. Of these, 10 warranted site visits and only 2 were selected: a textile manufacturer, Milliken & Company, and Xerox, the internationally known firm identified with photocopying. No service companies or small-business firms won. The awards were presented by President George Bush on November 2, 1989.

Milliken & Company, Spartansburg, South Carolina (Manufacturing)

Milliken is a privately owned company headquartered in Spartansburg, South Carolina, with forty-seven manufacturing facilities in the United States. This 124-year-old firm employs 14,300 workers (called associates). Its twenty-eight businesses produce more than forty-eight thousand different textile and chemical fabrics, ranging from apparel and automotive fabrics to specialty chemicals and floor coverings, for more than eighty-five hundred customers worldwide. Its annual sales exceed $1 billion.

Milliken's associates work primarily in self-managed teams in a very flat organizational structure. Production work teams can undertake training, schedule work, and establish individual performance objectives. Any Milliken associate can halt the production process if that person detects a quality or safety problem. From 1981 to 1989, Milliken reduced the number of management positions by seven hundred, freeing up a large portion of the work force for assignment as process-improvement specialists. There has been a 77 percent increase in the ratio of production associates to management associates.

The Milliken Quality Process involves sixteen hundred Corrective Action Teams that were formed to address specific manufacturing or other internal business challenges. Some two hundred Supplier Action Teams worked to improve Milliken's relations with its suppliers. In addition, nearly five hundred Customer Action Teams were formed to respond to the needs and aims of customers, including development of new products. The company spent about thirteen hundred dollars per associate on training in 1988. When benchmarking showed that Milliken was trailing some competitors in meeting delivery targets, they addressed the problem and improved their on-time delivery from 75 percent in 1984 to an industry best of 99 percent in 1988.

Xerox Corporation, Stamford, Connecticut (Manufacturing)

Xerox (which now calls itself the Document Company) is synonymous with the process of photocopying documents. At the time it won the Baldrige Award it employed 110,000 people worldwide, with 40 percent residing outside the United States. Organized into nine business divisions, corporate headquarters is in Stamford, Connecticut. Xerox introduced the first plain-paper copier in 1959, creating and dominating the photocopying industry for fifteen years. Foreign challengers began to make significant inroads beginning in the mid 1970s and Xerox's market share was seriously eroding by 1983.

Under the leadership of chairman and CEO David Kearns, the senior management team launched a Leadership Through Quality effort that made quality improvement, and, ultimately, customer satisfaction, the job of every employee. Beginning with Kearns himself and his senior executives, all employees received at least twenty-eight hours of training in problem-solving and quality-improvement techniques. Prior to winning the Baldrige Award, the company had invested more than four million man-hours and $125 million in educating employees about quality principles.

Team Xerox is the label given to the firm's group-centered approach to problem solving. More than 75 percent of the workers are members of one or more of the seven thousand quality-improvement teams. In 1988, teams in manufacturing and development were credited with saving $116 million by reducing scrap, tightening production schedules, and devising other measures to enhance efficiency and quality.

From the start of Leadership Through Quality until they won the Award (1984–1989), revenues from business products increased from $8.7 billion to $12.4 billion and income rose from $348 million to $388 million. The impact on return on assets was 10.2 percent to 12.4 percent. Revenues in 1991 were $17.8 billion and profit was $454 million.

1990 Winners

Interest in the Baldrige Award increased significantly by 1990. More than two hundred thousand companies requested application forms. Ninety-seven applied for the Award, nineteen applications were strong enough to warrant site visits by examiners, and ultimately four companies were selected to receive the Award. Three were household names—Cadillac, IBM, and Federal Express—and one was a little-known pipe distribution company in Texas, Wallace Company. Federal Express was the first service company to receive the award; all previous winners were manufacturers. President George Bush presented the awards in October 1990.

Cadillac Motor Car Company, Detroit, Michigan (Manufacturing)

Cadillac, founded in 1902, is the flagship division of General Motors. It competes for the luxury segments of the automobile market. Cadillac employs about ten thousand people at its Detroit-area headquarters, two Michigan-based manufacturing plants, and nine sales and service zone offices in the United

States. Cars are sold through a network of sixteen hundred franchised dealerships. During the 1980s Cadillac's reputation as being synonymous with the highest level of quality was called into question by foreign imports as well as by other domestic manufacturers, and they began to lose market share.

Cadillac's turnaround began in 1985. Top management determined that what was needed was nothing less than a change of culture, a constant focus on the customer, and a disciplined approach to planning. During the next four years, that change was brought about by focusing on four elements: (1) Simultaneous Engineering, (2) Supplier Partnerships, (3) the UAW-GM Quality Network, and (4) People Strategy. Unlike Federal Express and other quality organizations, they did not use an inverted pyramid to communicate levels of importance; instead they used the Simultaneous Engineering Pyramid, which featured the same hierarchy of importance (Figure 13.2).

The Simultaneous Engineering Steering Committee Executive Staff, a top-level management team, was formed to implement Simultaneous Engineering—an approach that put the responsibility for designing and manufacturing a new car into the hands of an interdisciplinary group of designers, engineers, and manufacturers. This group of executives met regularly for several months, but made little progress. According to Lou Farinola, then director of organization development, a breakthrough came when the group confronted its lack of progress and decided to turn the task over to a team of "champions" who could work full-time on the design project. The original group became the Executive Steering Committee to whom the various teams reported. This change, together with an extensive company-wide training program on quality, brought about a remarkable change of culture.

Cadillac's success in *creating a customer-oriented culture* is probably best illustrated by one experience of the Baldrige examiners. They approached a worker who was buffing bumpers and asked him, "Who is your customer?" The worker put down the bumper and asked the examiner, "Do you mean my *internal* customer or my *external* customer?" The examiner asked him to tell about both, to which the worker replied, "That fellow

Figure 13.2. Cadillac's Simultaneous Engineering Pyramid.

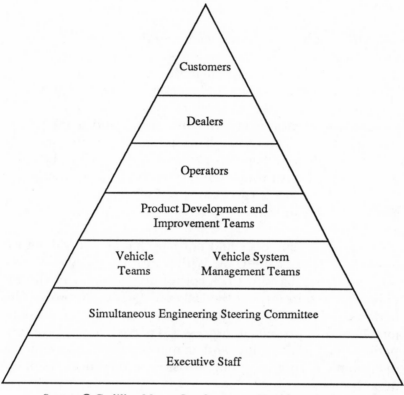

Source: © Cadillac Motor Car Company. Used by permission.

over there is my internal customer. I give him the bumper and he installs it. The external customer is the person who buys the car." When Farinola heard this story he knew that the cultural change had happened!

Cadillac also emphasized a *disciplined approach to planning,* with four objectives in mind:

- To involve every employee in the running of the business
- To continually reinforce the company's mission and long-term strategic objectives throughout the organization
- To align shorter-term business objectives with the goals and action plans developed by every plant and functional staff

- To institutionalize continuous improvement of products and services

Cadillac's mission statement describes its goals:

The Mission of the Cadillac Motor Car Company is to engineer, produce and market the world's finest automobiles known for uncompromised levels of distinctiveness, comfort, convenience and refined performance. Through its people, who are its strength, Cadillac will continuously improve the quality of its products and services to meet or exceed customer expectations and succeed as a profitable business.

Cadillac's success could not have happened without the full partnership of the UAW. With a history of UAW-GM relationships going back to 1973, corporate management and the union leadership formed the UAW-GM Quality Network. This network grew out of their joint recognition that a consistent, joint quality-improvement process was needed to improve competitiveness. Joint union and management quality councils operate the corporate, group, division, and plant levels of the organization.

Federal Express Corporation, Memphis, Tennessee (Service)

In 1973 Frederick W. Smith began operating the first air express operation. From the initial fleet of eight small aircraft, the company has grown to an aircraft fleet of more than 400 planes, 32,000 ground vehicles, and 85,000 employees and has an annual revenue of more than $7 billion. Each day employees at more than 1,000 sites process approximately 1.5 million packages to and from cities in 173 countries around the world. Each package is tracked in a central information system; sorted in a short time at facilities in Memphis, Indianapolis, Newark, Oakland, Los Angeles, Anchorage, and Brussels; and delivered by a highly decentralized network. Domestic overnight and second-day deliveries account for nearly four-fifths of the total, with the remainder being international deliveries. The company's share of the domestic market in 1989 was 43 percent.

The Federal Express management philosophy (and the basis of their success, according to chairman and CEO Fred Smith) is summarized in two triangles. The first depicts the "People-Service-Profit" sequence (Figure 13.3) that has been operational since the beginning of the organization.

A basic belief throughout Federal Express is that "customer satisfaction begins with employee satisfaction." The assumption is that employees who feel empowered and well treated will treat customers in a courteous, confident, and competent manner. This kind of service will result in customer satisfaction and profits will be a natural result. These profits, in turn, will return to the employees (as well as the stockholders) in the form of job security, various kinds of rewards, recognition, and opportunities for advancement.

In some organizations this triangle would be discounted as management propaganda, but in Federal Express it is a central part of the organizational culture. It is reinforced by policies and practices that ensure job security and employee empowerment, enabling employees to take risks in carrying out the company's Customer Satisfaction Policy:

- Take any step necessary to solve customer problems.
- Arrange the most expeditious delivery.
- Arrange a prompt refund or credit.

Figure 13.3. Federal Express Triangle Philosophy.

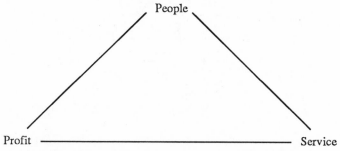

Source: © Federal Express Corporation. Used by permission.

A second triangle that expresses the Federal Express management philosophy is the inverted organizational chart (Figure 13.4).

From the beginning, Fred Smith has advocated the Servant Leader concept, which he explained to a Portland, Oregon, audience this way: "A courier's job is to work directly for the customer. . . our front-line manager's job is to make the courier's job easier. . . and her manager's job is to make the front-line manager's job easier and so on until you get to me. . . and my job is to do whatever it takes to help all of our people do their best." To make this system a reality rather than an idealistic intention, once a year every employee uses the Survey/Feedback/Action system to rate his boss (anonymously) on items such as the following:

- I feel free to tell my manager what I think.
- My manager lets me know what's expected of me.
- Favoritism is not a problem in my work group.
- My manager helps us find ways to do our jobs easier.
- My manager is willing to listen to my concerns.

Figure 13.4. Federal Express Structure.

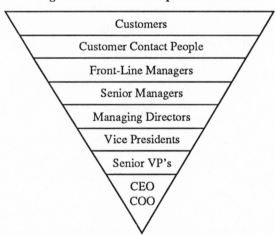

Source: © Federal Express Corporation. Used by permission.

- My manager asks for my ideas about things affecting our work.
- My manager lets me know when I've done a good job.
- My manager treats me with respect and dignity.
- My manager keeps me informed about things I need to know.
- My manager lets me do my job without interfering.
- My manager's boss gives us the support we need.

When the survey forms have been collected and tabulated, they are given to the manager and she meets with her staff as a group to report the results and what she intends to do to deal with any problems. To ensure that action results, one item on each survey form reads, "The concerns identified by my workgroup during last year's SFA feedback session have been satisfactorily addressed." Each employee also rates upper management on their performance in keeping the employees informed, their fairness, and their openness to ideas and suggestions. Since every manager's bonus and future are affected by the results of this annual survey, employee empowerment is taken very seriously!

How does a service organization quantify the quality of its performance? Federal Express began by developing a Hierarchy of Horrors and assigning weights to them. They considered how much irritation and inconvenience each error would create for the customer and assigned a weight of Failure Points. A Lost Package counts for 10, a Wrong Day Late counts for 5, and a Right Day Late counts for 1. The total score from twelve such errors provides a daily Service Quality Indicator (SQI), which is communicated to every Federal Express facility via the FedEx TV network. Surveys show that as the SQI goes down, customer satisfaction goes up. To accelerate the improvement process, an Action Team headed by a senior executive has been assigned to study each of the Failure Points to determine how they could be reduced or eliminated. By 1994 the goal is to reduce the SQI score to one-tenth of what it was in 1988, despite volume growth.

IBM Rochester, Minnesota (Manufacturing)

IBM Rochester manufactures intermediate computer systems, more than four hundred thousand of which had been installed worldwide at the time the company received the Baldrige Award. This plant also makes hard-disk drives, electromagnetic devices that store and receive information on magnetic disks. IBM Rochester employs 8,100 people who develop and manufacture their products. Their processes are also implemented in plants located in Japan, Mexico, the United Kingdom, and Italy.

Roy Bauer, Director for Quality, traces the beginnings of the quality effort back to 1981 with stimulation coming from IBM corporate headquarters. Initially there was considerable uncertainty, since the organization was already producing high-quality products (Bauer himself was among the skeptics). However, after he and several other key managers attended the Crosby Institute and studied zero defects, the quality movement began. Bauer remembers the engineers as being particularly skeptical. What changed their minds? Two things: (1) the commitment and pressure of the senior management team and (2) the results. "Without the results the resistance would have persisted," Bauer says. He makes the point that whatever is measured must be tied to the achievement of your goals. Otherwise, you may improve—but it doesn't really make a discernible difference.

The management of IBM Rochester focuses on six factors they consider critical for success:

- Improved definition of product and service requirements
- An enhanced product strategy
- A Six Sigma defect elimination strategy (learned from Motorola)
- Cycle-time reductions
- Improved education
- Increased employee involvement and ownership

To make progress in achieving these goals, IBM Rochester transformed their culture from one that was technology-driven to one that relies on market-driven processes that directly involve suppliers, business partners, and customers in delivering solutions. Most plans for achieving quality objectives originate with employees, with cross-functional teams identifying needs for equipment, staffing, education, and process development. Each of the six factors is "owned" by a senior manager, who assumes responsibility for plans and implementation. Progress toward improvement is closely monitored.

IBM Rochester invests heavily in education and training, allotting it the equivalent of 5 percent of its payroll. A Management System for Education offers skill planning, needs assessment, individual education plans, and on-line education road maps. In 1989, about a third of the work force moved into new positions, and 13 percent were promoted. Job flexibility and security, ample opportunity for advancement, and a well-developed recognition process are among factors contributing to rates of absenteeism and turnover that are well below national averages.

The Rochester quality process is viewed as a continuous one that begins, ends, and begins again with the customer. Of the approximately forty data sources used to guide improvement efforts, most provide information on customers' product or service requirements or customer relationship information. Customers and business partners representing over forty-five hundred businesses worldwide participate in developing new products as members of customer advisory councils.

The company has set as its goal for the 1990–1994 period achievement of "undisputed leadership in customer satisfaction." How does this consistent emphasis affect the people of IBM Rochester? Director for Quality Bauer puts it this way: "It's always fun when you're working on the positive side of the equation."

Wallace Company, Houston, Texas (Small Business)

Wallace is a family-owned distribution company, founded in 1942, primarily serving the chemical and petrochemical industries. Its ten offices, located in Texas, Louisiana, and Alabama, distribute pipe, valves, and fittings, as well as value-added specialty products such as actuated valves and plastic-lined pipe. Wallace distributes directly in the Gulf Coast area but serves international markets as well. The company employs 280 associates, all of whom have been trained in quality-improvement concepts and methods. In 1989, sales totaled $79 million.

The Wallace quality program was developed when the "oil bust" of the mid 1980s hit their customers hard. The price of oil dropped from forty-four dollars a barrel to twenty dollars. New construction projects were put on hold. Wallace's engineering and construction business dropped 30 percent almost overnight. The second point of pressure came from one of Wallace's key customers, Celanese Chemical, which began urging its suppliers to join the quality movement. After some initial floundering, Wallace engaged Sanders & Associates, a quality training and consulting firm, to do a needs assessment. Fear and distrust were more widely felt throughout the organization than executives had imagined. The results convinced them that the time was right to make some fundamental changes.

After top management became convinced that they had to change, things began to fall into place. Steps were taken to improve worker morale by installing new equipment in the warehouse, painting offices, and—most of all—responding to suggestions from associates. Intensive training began to take place (starting with the top management) using the Baldrige criteria as guidelines. Sixteen Quality Strategic Objectives were established, nine of them focused on customer satisfaction. The efforts began to pay off, with Wallace's market share increasing from 10.4 percent to 18 percent between 1987 and 1990. Its record of on-time deliveries jumped from 75 percent in 1987 to 92 percent in 1990. By July 1991, Wallace was committed to guarantee a 98 percent on-time delivery to select customers. As a result, sales volume rose 69 percent and, because of greater efficiency, operating profits through 1989 increased 7.4 times.

1991 Winners

From the 106 applicants, 19 companies received site visits and ultimately 3 relatively small electronics companies were selected as America's top quality enterprises: The Solectron Corporation of San Jose, California; Zytec Corporation of Redwood Falls, Minnesota; and Marlow Industries of Dallas, Texas. The awards were presented by Vice President Dan Quayle because the president was out of the country. Secretary of Commerce Robert Mosbacher said at the presentation ceremony, "This is the first time that all of the winners have been in the small to middle-sized category. I was pleased to see that because it emphasizes the point that we have been making that the jobs in this country are created by small to middle-sized companies."

Marlow Industries, Dallas, Texas (Small Business)

Marlow Industries, located in Dallas, Texas, processes raw materials into thermoelectric semiconductors, assembles semiconductor devices into TE coolers, and integrates the coolers into heat exchangers for commercial and defense applications. Started in 1973 as a five-person operation, Marlow now employs 160 people and has annual sales of $12 million. Exports account for 15 percent of annual sales.

Marlow's "top-to-bottom" approach to continuous improvement is directed by a TQM Quality Council, chaired by the CEO and including worker representatives. Monthly company-wide meetings are held to review company performance, recognize employees for quality contributions, review quality values, and make widespread acknowledgment of teams. In 1990, 88 percent of all personnel participated in "action teams," which focus on attaining corporate or departmental goals, or on "employee effectiveness teams," which concentrate on solving problems and preventing potential problems in specific work areas. Each team has a senior executive mentor, and all teams regularly make formal presentations before the Quality Council.

In dealing with their consolidated list of suppliers, Marlow cultivates long-term partnerships. Twelve of their twenty key suppliers are certified to "ship to stock" without inspection. Over the last ten years, Marlow has not lost a single major customer, and in 1990 their ten top customers rated the quality of Marlow thermoelectric coolers at 100 percent.

Solectron Corporation, San Jose, California (Manufacturing)

Solectron specializes in the assembly of complex circuit boards and subsystems for the makers of computers and other electronic products. They also provide system-level assembly services, such as assembly of personal computers and mainframe mass storage systems, as well as turnkey materials management, board design, and manufacturability consultation and testing. Their more than seventy customer firms include Sun Microsystems, Apple Computer, and IBM. Solectron employs twenty-two hundred people, two-thirds of whom are Asian immigrants. The company was founded in 1977 and in fiscal year 1990 had an annual revenue of more than $265 million.

One thing that has made a difference in Solectron's quality is their weekly survey of all of their customers. Each customer is asked to fill out a "report card" on four things: (1) the quality of the Solectron products, (2) whether the delivery was on time, (3) the ease of communicating with Solectron (promptness and courtesy of telephone response), and (4) whether the customer felt good doing business with Solectron. On each of these dimensions Solectron requested an A, B, C, or D grade. Initially each A was scored 100, B was worth 90, C received an 80, and D drew a lowly 70. At 7:30 each Thursday morning, the top management team — including the division managers — met to see if the score was 95 or better.

When the target was met week after week it was hard to see much chance for improvement. This changed dramatically three years ago when they simply lowered the weighting of the letter grades. A's remained 100, but B's now rated 80; C's were 0 and D's were counted −100. The target remained 95. A single C or D could ruin the weekly score! Each division manager receives his score on Tuesday, and if the score is less than 95, the manager must report what is being done to correct it the following week. The average project rejection rate has dropped by half since 1987 to 0.3 percent and the company is shooting for a Six Sigma (3.4 defects per million) by 1994.

Solectron provided training in statistical process control and surface-mount technology to its production, technical, and administrative employees. That training is producing results. Defect rates have fallen to within 233 parts per million. The on-time delivery rate has been 97.7 percent in the last two years and 95 to 97 out of every 100 circuit boards function correctly during their initial test, up from 88. Less than 0.2 percent of the circuit boards are returned by their customers compared to 2.0 percent two years ago.

Solectron applied for the Baldrige Award in 1989 and 1990. Each time they received valuable feedback from the Baldrige examiners. They tried to apply the suggestions and their scores improved each year. In commenting on what has impressed him most about the Solectron success, Richard Allen, the director of quality, says, "You've got to remember that you can't turn a ship in a day. Improvement is an evolutionary process—with resistance, chaos, and frustration. You have to take the long view to see the progress being made."

Zytec Corporation, Redwood Falls, Minnesota (Manufacturing)

Zytec is a small employee-owned company, with approximately eight hundred employees located at their headquarters in Eden Prairie, Minnesota, and their manufacturing facility in Redwood Falls. They design and manufacture electronic power supplies and repair power supplies and CRT monitors. Since the company began in 1984, Zytec has used the quality and reliability of their products and services as the key strategy to differentiate them from the competition. Sales per employee are approaching $100,000, as compared with an industry average of less than $80,000. Underlying these gains are a 50 percent improvement in manufacturing yields, a 26 percent reduction in manufacturing design cycle, and a 30 to 40 percent decrease in product costs since 1988—savings that are passed on to the customer.

At an annual two-day meeting, about one hundred fifty employees, representing all types of personnel, shifts, and departments, review and critique five-year plans prepared by six cross-functional teams. Zytec executives then finalize the long-term strategic plan and set broad corporate objectives to guide quality planning in the departments, where teams develop annual goals to support each corporate objective. To realize the full advantage of their employees, Zytec trains them in analytical and problem-solving methods—a major focus of the seventy-two hours of quality-related instruction received by most employees. One result of the attention paid to quality, involvement, and training has been that the mean time between failure of a Zytec power supply has increased to over one million hours and the on-time delivery has improved from 85 to 96 percent.

As we visited, interviewed, and read materials supplied by each of these twelve companies, we came away with a clear understanding of why they were chosen. They are all TQManagement organizations, led by executives who have a total commitment to quality of product and empowerment of people. Several of the companies applied more than once for the Baldrige Award because it provided an opportunity to examine their companies in a systematic, detailed way, and to get outsiders' critiques in addition. Having won the Award, most continue to use the Baldrige criteria to make an annual audit. In addition, they share their understanding by conducting seminars for interested executives from around the country, believing that even as they learned much from other Baldrige winners, they have an obligation to share with other executives interested in TQM. We found it exciting to see superbly run companies, with committed employees turning out world-class products and services, who are eager to share their hard-won knowledge with others—in some cases, even with competitors.

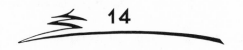

Striving for Quality: Rewards Without End

Even the woodpecker owes his success to the fact that he uses his head and keeps pecking away until he finally finishes the job he starts.

— Coleman Cox

How does the quality movement stand today and where is it headed? We think that the Quality and Productivity Management Association (QPMA) has put it into perspective with its description of the evolution of management style (Figure 14.1). The concepts underlying Total Quality Management have been around a long time. They have been practiced and tested in many individual organizations. It is only in the last decade that we have begun to see them as part of a pattern that promises to be the management methodology of the future.

When "Total" is part of any descriptive label, it is natural to think that this is the last word—that it embraces everything. TQManagement includes many concepts, many principles, and many techniques, but it does not include every dimension of the management process. It has been tested and proved effective in many organizations, but it is not a guaranteed formula for success. In this chapter we take a critical look at where TQM

Figure 14.1. Evolution of Management Style.

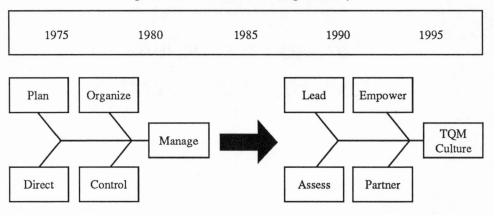

Traditional Management   *Management Style 2000*

Source: Ginnodo, 1991. Used by permission.

theory and experience stand after almost a decade of existence in the United States. The quality movement has brought into sharp focus some of the difficult questions and dilemmas a company will confront if it decides to change its culture to support a TQM effort. If we were to assess the status of the quality movement using the force field analysis model of Kurt Lewin (1951), we could readily identify four driving forces (supporting and advancing the practices of TQManagement) and four restraining forces (discouraging organizations from adopting those practices).

TQManagement's Driving Forces

The Visible Success of Many TQManaged Companies

The Baldrige Award winners conduct regular seminars for executives to describe their experience with TQM processes and how they have benefited. The U.S. General Accounting Office's (1991) study of these companies is one of the most widely requested reports ever printed by the agency. Major publications have featured articles about TQManaged firms that are generally laudatory. The language of TQManagement has established itself in boardrooms across America, and the executive of any company losing market share is under pressure to develop a customer-focused plan of action. Many would agree with Paul Noakes, Motorola's vice president for quality, that "if you don't get with it, you can't expect to stay in business very long."

The Creation of TQM Centers, Organizations, Networks, and Consortia

Some TQM resources, for example, the American Society for Quality Control and the Quality and Productivity Management Association, have been in existence for many years, but new groups are springing up to serve various specialized constituencies. The Federal Quality Institute is providing a steady stimulus to national governmental agencies. The Madison Area Quality Improvement Network is bringing together managers from state and city governments, educational institutions, and the private sector. Community Quality Councils are providing quality training and support to small-business and public sector organizations. A Public Sector Quality Improvement Network was formed to facilitate the exchange of problems and experience among career public servants. In addition, centers like the American Productivity and Quality Center (APQC) in Houston and a growing number of university centers are becoming stimulators of research and depositories of TQM experience.

Creation of an International Benchmark Clearing House

Initiated by the APQC, a group of representatives of about ninety American firms began meeting in early 1991 to design a process for exchanging information about best practices. This effort led to the creation of the International Benchmark Clearing House in February 1992. Participating members are assisted in finding benchmark partners through quarterly conferences, an electronic bulletin board, and the Clearing House's extensive data base on best practices in a variety of fields.

The Clearing House operates on the basis that benchmark partners have a mutual obligation to share information about management practices that have worked for them. The quid pro quo principle is relatively new in American businesses, which have usually regarded creative management practices as giving them a competitive edge. Influenced by some of the Baldrige winner's shared experience, however, most have come to discover that the mutual sharing of ideas is mutually enriching.

The Growing Experience and Appreciation of Teamwork

America has had a long tradition of valuing individual initiative and effort. Groups have often been viewed with suspicion because of time wasted in meetings ("Committees keep minutes and waste hours"). This is changing as group efforts pay off. The fifty years of experimentation and research in the field of group dynamics is proving its value as more managers and employees receive training in how to plan and conduct purposeful meetings. One indication is the shift in values of American managers between 1981 and 1991. A national survey of members of the American Management Association (Schmidt and Posner, 1992, p. 39) included an item that asked managers to finish the sentence: "I believe that the improvement of the quality of life in our country depends primarily on . . ." The difference in their answers between 1981 and 1991 is shown in Table 14.1.

This is a remarkable shift. Since TQManagement de-

Table 14.1. Shift in American Managers' Views from 1981 to 1991.

	Percentage	
Factor Considered to Improve Quality of Life	1981	1991
Technological advances	7	5
Return to basic values emphasizing individual initiative and responsibility	61	44
Strong, creative, and effective political leadership	12	8
Letting current social, political, and economic trends continue	1	1
Developing a value system emphasizing cooperation and improvement of the total human community	20	39

pends so heavily on team efforts, these beliefs are essential for the growth of the quality movement. One of the common explanations for Japanese success has been that theirs is a group-oriented culture, whereas the American culture is individually oriented. This trend toward increased appreciation of group-centered values is one that is consistent with the requirements of a TQM organization.

The Creation of the European Quality Award

This award, initiated in 1991, will be presented for the first time at the European Management Forum in Madrid in October 1992, to the company demonstrating "the highest standards in Total Quality Management." The trophy is held by the recipient for one year. The seven criteria for the award are: customer satisfaction, business results, impact on society, processes, leadership, policy and strategy, and use of resources. The creation of this award adds more impetus to the quest for quality in the global marketplace.

The Continued Pressure from International Competitors

When the American Quality Foundation and Ernst & Young (1991) conducted a study of the quality practices of more than 500 businesses in Canada, Germany, Japan, and the United States, their conclusion was: "Quality improvement is the fundamental business strategy of the 1990's. No business without it will survive in the global marketplace" (pp. 4–7). Some of their findings were:

- More than half of the businesses in all countries evaluate the business consequences of quality performance at least monthly.
- The use of quality performance as a criterion for compensating senior management is expected to rise dramatically in all countries.
- German and Japanese businesses place more importance

on incorporating customer research into the design of new products and services than do North American businesses.

- About 40 percent of the businesses in Canada, Japan, and the United States place primary (dominant) importance on customer satisfaction in strategic planning; approximately one-fifth (22 percent) of German businesses do so.
- Businesses in all countries, except Japan, expect to increase the involvement of employees in quality-related teams. (Japanese companies already have the highest rate of widespread participation of employees in regularly scheduled meetings about quality.)

New Partnerships Are Being Built Between Business and Education

In addition to the kind of linkages between local business firms and elementary and high schools that are happening across the country, a concerted effort is under way by executives of some of America's most prominent TQManaged firms to secure a more prominent place for TQM on college campuses. One action was the publication of "An Open Letter: TQM on Campus" in the *Harvard Business Review* (Robinson and others, 1991). A few excerpts from the letter reflect the urgency of this appeal, which was signed by six of the top CEOs in the country:

> We believe business and academia have a shared responsibility to learn, to teach, and to practice total quality management. If the United States expects to improve its global competitive performance, business and academic leaders must close ranks behind an agenda that stresses the importance and value of TQM. . . . Widespread adoption of TQM is moving too slowly to meet the challenge. . . . Our system of higher education is one of this country's most powerful competitive weapons. Working together, companies and institutions of higher education must accelerate the application of Total Quality Management on our campuses if

our education system and economy are to maintain
and enhance their global positions.

The letter was signed by James D. Robinson III of American Express, John F. Akers of IBM, Edwin L. Artzt of Procter & Gamble, Harold A. Poling of Ford, Robert W. Galvin of Motorola, and Paul A. Allaire of Xerox.

The driving forces described above indicate that the quality revolution has considerable momentum and can no longer be dismissed as just the latest in a long line of management schemes. On the other hand, several factors operate to discourage the spread of TQManagement in our country. These are significant and must be considered carefully.

Restraining Forces: Deterrents to TQManagement

Despite all the excitement generated by the Baldrige Award and the thousands of executives who are attending quality seminars, listening to enthusiastic and inspirational speeches, and reading a rapidly expanding library of TQM books, some are responding with caution and criticism. Following are some of the reasons.

The Failures of Some Companies Using TQM

There is always a market for new management approaches, especially among companies that feel bogged down or that are losing market share. Some executives are prepared to try something new before they have fully considered how it might fit their unique situation. With a total system like TQM, this kind of misjudgment can be very costly. The result has been a high failure rate among some companies that have tried it. We know of no definite study (it's easier to document successes than failures!), but some consultants report an 80 percent failure rate. For example, McKinsey's Pifer (1992) reports that "we are seeing a disturbingly large number of companies whose total quality management programs are failing to show signs of meaningful impact. . . . In a recent McKinsey survey of quality programs, more than half the companies interviewed expressed the view that their quality programs may have stalled or even failed." He cites four serious flaws in some failed TQM programs:

1. Insufficient linkage with the strategic priorities of the organization
2. Poor quality-related decisions that are not tied to market performance or financial results
3. Little sustainable impact — "going through the motions"
4. Employee confusion — "Why are we doing this, *really?*"

We heard about one new CEO who found his organization more preoccupied with the quality process itself — the procedures, measurements, training, and so on — than with good business decisions. A similar observation by James L. Broadhead, who became chairman and CEO of Florida Power and Light Company shortly after it won the coveted Deming Prize, led him to dismantle the "quality bureaucracy" that had developed when the company was working for the Prize. He found what he considered to be a lavish overuse of statistical tools, charts, and rigid problem-solving practices. In a May 15, 1990, letter to his employees, Broadhead noted "the frequently stated opinion that preoccupation with process has resulted in our losing sight of one of the major tenets of quality improvement, namely, respect for employees." (It might also be noted that the Deming Prize cost Florida Power and Light $400,000 in direct costs and $885,000 for Japanese consultants, and that the Florida Utilities Commission would not allow the utility to pass these costs on to customers.)

Robert Laza and Perry Wheaton (1990, pp. 17–21) have identified seven common pitfalls that may cause a TQM effort to fail:

1. Oversimplifying and underestimating the difficulty of bringing about cultural change
2. Failing to recognize that every company, every environment, is different

3. Lack of project management and/or the management of TQM implementation as a project
4. Conducting mass training before establishing support systems for TQM
5. Overemphasizing technical tools at the expense of leadership and management issues
6. Applying tools before needs are determined and direction is established
7. Failing to provide the structure to move the program to supplier or subcontractor organizations

A startling example is Wallace Company, which won the Baldrige Award in 1990. In late 1991 they filed for Chapter 11 bankruptcy protection. The reason? According to Gail Cooper, the consultant who was called in by the board of directors, the company executives got so caught up in the Baldrige Award and its aftermath that they neglected to see the growing problems of the organization. Cooper noted that "the limited management staffs of most small companies do not have the depth and breadth to be totally involved in the award process while paying attention to other vital areas of corporate strategy" (Cooper, 1992).

Untimely Crises and Dramatic Changes

TQManagement is a long-range strategy requiring high commitment and risk investment. If the market shifts suddenly in a way that threatens an organization's existence, naturally the long-term must give way to the urgent. In the turbulent 1990s (Peter Vaill's "white-water society"), there is a continual possibility of developments that may be perceived as such crises. Once a long-range strategy has been shelved, it is hard to get it back on-track and enlist the commitment necessary to move it forward.

Pressures from the Financial Community

Publicly held companies are particularly vulnerable to pressures from the financial community to produce quick results—

to make the next quarter's profit look better. While they may applaud a company's decision to launch a cultural change such as TQManagement, they may withhold their support until they see how it pays off. This short-range thinking on the part of investors has been a major deterrent to many long-term strategies in American business. In the public sector, similar pressures on elected officials for the immediate and dramatic payoff of any programmatic effort works against Total Quality. This is part of the price we pay for American impatience!

The Complexity of the Process

TQManagement is not a program that can be installed — or even explained — quickly and easily. Some aspects of it are readily understandable and seem familiar. The totality, however, including the changed roles of managers and workers and the need to learn precise measurement techniques, takes time to understand. The fact that the philosophy, goals, and procedures must permeate the entire organization is enough to discourage some executives from embarking on this change effort. A less drastic approach to improving quality and productivity is more appealing in the absence of any compelling pressure.

Questions Raised by TQManagement

Organizations are complex systems. Changes in one area impact other areas. To ensure that the TQManagement approach works, executives must confront and deal with a number of critical questions. We discuss some of these below.

1. *How can pay-for-performance be reconciled with a group reward system?* It is unlikely that everyone in an organization will buy into the TQManagement philosophy with equal enthusiasm. To some people a job is just a means to a paycheck — and the less effort expended to get it the better. If they are rewarded equally with colleagues who have carried a larger share of the team's responsibility, the inequity will be noticed and will not contribute to morale.

2. *How can a CEO deal with the financial community's interest*

in the short-term gains when it is clear that the up-front TQM costs will not pay off for two or three years? This has been a major problem for publicly held American companies whenever they have contemplated major capital investments or organizational changes. Stockholders—and institutional investors—press for quick returns, and executives who cannot deliver next quarter may be in trouble.

3. *Why should employees—particularly middle managers—become enthusiastic about organizational reforms that may eliminate their jobs?* When people are empowered by TQManagement methods, the need for supervisors is diminished. Entire layers of management may be eliminated. Organizations downsize or "right-size" to reduce costs and become more competitive. The threat of job loss can be the most powerful disincentive a worker can experience. For this reason, management must be open, clear, and trustworthy in their commitment to their employees.

4. *Will people be willing to persist in a long-term campaign of constant improvement?* TQManagement assumes that this is possible. Thus far the experience of the Baldrige winners is positive, but there is no guarantee that long-established habits of performing at a level that is "good enough" will not reassert themselves.

5. *How can you deal with the problem of multiple customers?* For some organizations, identifying the customer is easy—it's the person who purchases the product or service. This is the person who must be satisfied. But who is the customer for a school system? The students? The parents? The legislators who supply the funds? The future employers of the students? Hospitals must satisfy patients, doctors, insurance companies, and governmental agencies. Who gets priority attention when needs differ? What seems like a simple task in some situations can become very complex.

What Are the Next Steps?

As more and more companies master the tools of Total Quality Management and encounter competitors in the global marketplace practicing the same skills with the same positive results, how are the leaders gaining the upper hand? Where is Total Quality leading? Are new challenges and new practices emerging? These are the questions we ask; the answers present new horizons to consider. We will not attempt to explain fully the future of Total Quality, but only to highlight these new directions.

Policy Deployment

Policy deployment is rapidly replacing management by objectives (MBO) in most quality organizations. Policy deployment differs from MBO in that it is a three-phase process with a focus on quality improvement. The first two phases of the process, *establish policy* and *deploy policy,* comprise the Plan, Check, and Act steps of PDCA. In the *establish* phase, information from every area of the company about how to improve customer satisfaction is collected and analyzed, and this completes the Do step of the PDCA cycle. Senior management pulls all existing and potential new policies into an organizational perspective and appoints a senior executive to develop an improvement strategy for each policy or objective. Local management is engaged in functional evaluations and in developing problem statements, measurements, and proposed targets.

Functional management then completes an analysis and plans countermeasures for the proposed targets to confirm the initial plans. At this point budgeting is addressed so that projects impacting the organization's improvement are included in the normal budgeting process. Senior management then reviews the revised plans and issues the final policy deployment plan to guide the organization's efforts. Finally, local management develops and implements the plans to achieve the targets and thus completes the PDCA cycle.

In policy deployment both successes and failures offer something important. Whether or not goals are reached, an analysis at year's end should reveal opportunities for improving the process. And by incorporating the PDCA process in setting objectives, an organization can experience quality improvements across all aspects of their operations.

Senior Management Teams

Recently Xerox and Microsoft announced that they were eliminating the office of the president in their organizations and replacing that position with a senior management team. This trend is growing. Nadler (1992) recently reported that nearly two-thirds of large corporations have top-level management teams. Why is this happening? Speed! In an era when time-to-market is fast equaling productivity as a measure of success, many organizations are finding that they must accelerate their decision making while simultaneously pushing it to its lowest level possible in the organization.

Traditional vertical organizations and decision-making processes (marketing and manufacturing issues being raised up the chain of command) just take too long in a marketplace where new technologies are owned by many and the fastest one to the goal line wins. Total Quality has led to engaging "customer experts" early in the product-development cycle—in many cases maintaining "customer supplier teams" right through product testing and manufacturing. In a situation like this the process is accelerated, and extended senior decision making only causes delays. So more and more organizations are forcing collaborative decision making at the top by forming senior functional heads into a "general management team."

Nadler points out that in July 1991, AT&T chairman Robert Allen established a self-governing operating committee to serve as his COO. Allen isn't on the panel and the five executives will rotate the chair every six months. This is an extreme example. Most senior management teams consist of the CEO and the top five to ten senior executives. At Eastman Kodak's chemicals division, three senior vice presidents were replaced by self-directed management teams. One team focuses on manufacturing, another handles administration, and the third oversees research and development. The objective of all these teams is to get the product produced and delivered faster—and that means fewer layers between the policy level and the production level.

High-Performance Work Systems (HPWS)

With the success of employee-involvement and quality-
improvement processes, many TQManagement companies have
begun to blend autonomous work teams and open systems
planning into new work arrangements and processes. HPWS is
actually a set of job design principles (Delta Consulting Group,
1990).

- Work design that starts outside the organization based on
  the customer's requirements
- Empowered units designing whole pieces of work, with
  teams completing entire products or services based on max-
  imized interdependence
- Clear directions and goals, including mission, defined outputs, and negotiated measures
- Variability control at the source, where the team is given the
  tools, information, and capacity to control their own work
  process
- Accessibility to information—as opposed to data—about
  the customer, the output, the work process, and variances,
  allowing teams to create, receive, and transmit information
  rapidly among themselves and other work teams
- Shared jobs by cross-training, which provides increased autonomy, learning, and motivation
- Empowering human resource practices such as local selection, skill-based pay, peer feedback, team bonuses, and gainsharing plans
- A management structure and practice that supports autonomous units, with new approaches to planning, budgeting,
  information systems, and evaluation systems
- The capacity to reconfigure as required, using a "learning
  organization" where teams can learn from their experiences
  (including having the time for discussion and reflection) to
  gain insight and to be able to act on their learning

With time-to-market becoming an increasing measure of
success, HPWS would appear to be an essential step to maintain-

ing continuous improvement. Deming would certainly applaud this direction.

Learning Organizations

Quality requires risk taking, and the notion of continuous improvement suggests that workers can learn from their mistakes. As management develops the patience and ability to focus on incremental improvements and on PDCA as the means of learning more about work processes, workers are increasingly able to learn from their mistakes. Most breakthroughs in work activity are the result of gaining insights from personal experience. Many quality organizations are learning that if they can institutionalize this phenomenon they can anticipate significant improvements in work processes and technological development. Especially in an era of "intellectual property," where white-collar and blue-collar workers are fast being replaced by "gold-collar" workers (persons who possess strategic knowledge), it behooves an organization to facilitate the transmission of knowledge to as many workers as possible in the shortest time possible.

The subtitle of Peter Senge's book *The Fifth Discipline* (1991) is *The Art and Practice of the Learning Organization.* Senge argues that organizations that excel in the future will be the ones that "discover how to tap people's commitment and capacity to learn at *all* levels of the organization" (p. 4). Our studies have led us to agree with his analysis that five "component technologies" are gradually converging to make such organizations possible: (1) systems thinking, (2) personal mastery, (3) mental models, (4) building a shared vision, and (5) team learning.

The Bottom Line: It's a Race Without a Finish Line

Every Baldrige winner we've interviewed has had the same attitude: "We're not there yet, and we probably never will be. But we'll keep trying to do better." In the 1960s, 1970s, and early 1980s, American managers liked to say, "If it ain't broke, don't fix it." (President Reagan was still saying this in 1990!) Now this has changed to: "If it isn't perfect, improve it." This determination to

keep continually improving is a central theme in TQManagement. But how long can it last? Can the will and determination
of American managers and workers continue indefinitely? And
will those who are skeptical of the TQM process ever be per-
suaded to try this new way of thinking about their organization?

When Fred Smith is asked what the Baldrige Award means
to Federal Express (1991, p. 4), he responds, "It's our license to
practice." Then he goes on to talk about the goals of beating
their best 99.7 percent Daily Service record and to keep trying
to "find ways of delivering the highest quality service at increasing lower costs." At Motorola they continue to press for a Six
Sigma standard (3.6 defects per million) and they talk about
departments that have maintained 100 percent error-free production for three and four months at a time, to demonstrate that
perfection is possible. And at Xerox, they still quote David
Kearns's concept of being in a "race without a finish line."

Resource A

Glossary of TQM Terms

Appraisal costs: costs associated with inspecting a product to ensure that it meets specifications.

Benchmarking: measuring your own products, services, and practice against the best in the field. Benchmarks usually include a measure of results and an analysis of the process used to produce those results.

Best of class: an organization, function, product, process, or component that is superior to all other comparable ones.

Brainstorming: technique used to generate ideas. Most commonly used in groups, its object is to gather as many ideas as possible in a specific time frame.

Cause: an established reason for the existence of an event.

Cause-and-effect diagram: a graphic technique describing the cause of a specific outcome (also known as a fishbone diagram or Ishikawa diagram).

Check sheet: a tally sheet used to gather data based on sample observations in order to identify patterns.

Common cause: see Random variation.

Control: the set of activities used to detect and correct deviation in order to maintain a desired condition.

Control chart: graphic way of identifying whether an operation or a process is in or out of control and tracking the performance of that operation or process against predetermined control and warning limits.

Corrective action: implementation of solutions that result in the elimination of identified problems.

Cost of quality: the sum of the cost of prevention, appraisal, and failure. A financial tool that can be used as an indicator of variation, as well as a measure of productivity and efficiency.

Crosby, Philip B.: founder of the Quality College in Winter Park, Florida. Author of *Quality Is Free* and *Quality Without Tears*. Among the first quality professionals to hold a senior management position (vice president of quality for ITT Corporation) and the first of the American quality "gurus" to become well known. Credited with being the creator of zero defects, he developed a fourteen-step Quality Improvement Process that is the basis for many quality-improvement programs. Crosby emphasizes "cost of quality" (see Feigenbaum) and estimates that American companies spend more than twenty cents of every sales dollar on making mistakes, finding them, and fixing them. For service companies the cost of quality can be as high as thirty-five cents of every sales dollar.

Cross-functional teams: teams whose members come from several different work units that interface with one another. Helpful when work units are dependent upon one another for materials, information, and so on.

Culture: the prevailing pattern of beliefs, behaviors, attitudes, and values of an organization.

Customer: the recipient of the outputs of a body of work, or the purchaser of the organization's product or service.

Dantotsu: striving to be the "best of the best."

Data: information or a set of facts presented in descriptive form. Data is either measured (variable data) or counted (attribute data).

Defect: output that fails to meet customer requirements or your own specifications (if they are higher).

Deming, W. Edwards: world's best-known quality expert. Trained as a statistician, he worked for Western Electric in the 1920s and 1930s. During World War II he taught quality-control techniques to companies that produced military goods. He introduced statistical concepts and "quality" concepts to the Japanese beginning in 1950. He told them that it's impossible to "inspect" quality into finished goods, stressing the need to prevent mistakes by using quality-control charts all along the production line. Deming's research with control charts led him to conclude that about 85 percent of the opportunities for improvement come from changing the system, which is management's responsibility. Only about 15 percent of the improvement opportunities are within the individual employee's control. He achieved fame at the age of eighty following the TV documentary *If Japan Can, Why Can't We?* He advocates constancy of purpose and control of variances to achieve quality and believes in releasing worker power by creating joy, pride, and happiness in work. He is most famous for his Fourteen Points for Management.

Deming Prize: medal presented annually to companies demonstrating a high level of quality. The prize was instituted by the Japanese Union of Scientists and Engineers to recognize and stimulate continuous improvement in Japan, and to honor Deming for his contributions toward Total Quality in Japan. (Only one American company—Florida Power and Light—has ever won the Deming Prize.)

Effectiveness: how closely an organization's output meets its goal and/or the customer's requirements.

Efficiency: production of required output at a perceived minimum cost, measured by the ratio of quantity of resources expended to plan.

Error: the result of failing to correctly perform an action.

Feigenbaum, Armand V.: author and lecturer on quality, he was the manager of worldwide manufacturing operations and quality at GE. He coined the term "total quality control" (Feigen-baum, 1956) and is recognized as the inventor of Cost of Quality. He emphasizes a company-wide, systems approach to quality improvement, brought forth the administrative viewpoint, and considers human relations a basic quality issue. Feigenbaum categorizes quality into four jobs: New Design Control, Incoming Material Control, Product Control, and Special Process Studies.

Fishbone diagram: see Cause-and-effect diagram.

Flow chart: graphic way of using symbols to identify the operations involved in a process, their interrelationships, inputs, and outputs. (This is usually the first step in understanding selected processes in an organization.)

Force field analysis: technique for identifying the forces "for" and "against" a certain course of action or condition. Sometimes called the "helping" and "hindering" forces.

Frequency distribution: the count of the number of occurrences of individual values over a given range (discrete variable), or the count of events that lie between certain predetermined limits over the range of values the variable may assume (continuous variable).

Functional administrative control technique: a tool designed to improve performance through a process combining time management and value engineering. The process involves breaking activities down into functions and establishing teams to target and solve problems in each function.

Histogram: a bar graph showing the frequency with which events occur by displaying their distribution. Since random samples of data under statistical control normally follow a "bell-shaped" curve, the shape of a histogram's distribution is especially helpful in understanding variability.

Ishikawa, Kaoru: one of Japan's leading quality experts. Ishi-kawa was a leader of the Japanese Union of Scientists and Engineers (JUSE) and is recognized as the father of quality

circles and employee empowerment. He edited JUSE's handbook, *Quality Control for Foremen,* which is a guide for establishing
and maintaining quality circles. He is most famous for being the
inventor of cause-and-effect analysis. See Cause-and-effect
diagram.

Ishikawa diagram: see Cause-and-effect diagram.

Juran, Joseph M.: codeveloper of the first statistical process
control techniques for manufacturing, while at Bell Laboratories' Hawthorne Works in 1924. His book, the *Quality Control
Handbook,* was published in 1951 and became a quality bible in
the United States and Japan; however, his work was better received in Japan. His work and lectures influenced the Japanese
to expand quality to include an overall concern for the entire
management of an organization. In 1966 Juran predicted that
the Japanese would achieve world leadership in quality and
introduced quality circles to the United States with an article
titled "The Quality Circle Phenomenon." Juran defines quality
as fitness for use and advocates a "project approach" to quality
improvement. He is perhaps best known for teaching the Pareto
principle, which he named after Vilfredo Pareto, a nineteenth-
century Italian economist; a familiar example of the Pareto
principle is the "80-20" rule (as an example, 80 percent of an
organization's business comes from 20 percent of its customers).

Kaizen: Japanese term used to describe continuous improvement in all aspects of an organization's operations at every level.
Usually thought of as a staircase in which each step upward is
followed by a period of stability, followed by another step upward, and so on. Each improvement is usually accomplished at
little or no expense.

Management by fact: management process in which actions
and decisions are based on facts and data, not opinions. Requires (1) asking appropriate questions; (2) correctly interpreting answers to verify the quality of the data and facts; and
(3) verifying the correct use of data, facts, and statistics in the
work process and decision making.

Mean time between failures (MTBF): the average time between successive failures of a given product or process.

Measurement: the process of measuring to compare results to requirements (a quantitative estimate of performance).

Nominal group technique: a tool for idea generation, problem solving, mission, and key result-area definition, performance-measure definition, and goals/objectives definition.

Normative performance measurement technique: technique that incorporates structured group processes so that work groups can design measurement systems suited to their own needs.

Output: the specified end result, as required by a customer.

Pareto diagram: bar graph showing where scarce resources should be applied to reap the greatest gain. (The rule of thumb is that 80 percent of problems arise from 20 percent of potential causes.)

Policy: a statement of principles and beliefs, or a settled course, adopted to guide the overall management of affairs in support of a stated aim or goal.

Policy deployment: the interactive development of strategies, goals, objectives, and plans and the communication, implementation, and process capability assessment of these strategies, goals, objectives, and plans. Benchmarking data is a critical enabler for policy deployment, which is focused primarily on the process and the organizational system.

Prevention: a future-oriented approach to quality management that achieves improvements through corrective action.

Problem: a question or situation proposed for solution, or the effect of not conforming to customer requirements.

Process: a series of operations or activities linked together to provide a result that has increased value.

Process capability: the ability of a process to achieve the desired end result of meeting the customer's requirements.

Process control: the activities employed to detect and remove special causes of variation in order to maintain or restore stability.

Process flow analysis: technique for identifying and analyzing key processes and areas and methods of possible improvement.

Process improvement: activities employed to detect and remove common causes of variation in order to improve process capability.

Productivity: ratio of outputs produced to inputs required (an expected outcome of Total Quality).

Quality: those attributes of a product or service that the customer values. May include surface finish, functionality, timeliness, size, cost, reliability, or other factors.

Quality circles: a group of workers and their supervisor who voluntarily meet to identify and solve job-related problems.

Quality function deployment (QFD): a technique to build customer requirements into a product design or service process to ensure that customer requirements are met. (Sometimes called the House of Quality.)

Quality of work life: the degree to which an organization's culture provides employees with information, knowledge, authority, and rewards to allow them to work safely and effectively, be compensated fairly, and maintain human dignity in their work.

Random variation: variation in a process output that is usually the result of *common* causes that can often only be improved by management (in contrast to *special* causes that the employee using the process may address).

Range: the difference between the maximum and minimum values of data in a sample.

Reliability: the probability that a product entity will perform its specified function under specified conditions, without failure, for a specified period of time.

Requirement: a formal statement of need, and the expectations of how it is to be met (what the customer wants).

Root cause analysis: the process of eliminating myriad effects and causes to reach the bottom line of a problem—the primary reason for the problem or symptom. (Sometimes called first cause analysis.)

Run chart: a graphic that shows the simplest possible display of trends within observation points over a specified period of time. Points are plotted on a graph in the order in which they occur. The purpose is to identify the truly vital changes in a process or system.

Scatter diagram: a diagram consisting of a horizontal axis representing the measurement values of one variable and a vertical axis representing the measurements of a second variable. Events are plotted and used to test for correlations and possible cause-and-effect relationships.

Seven management tools: tools used to solve problems when data is not readily available, must be rearranged, or is taken from subjective descriptions rather than data bases. Typically used to solve management-level problems. Tools are (1) relational diagram, (2) affinity diagram, (3) tree diagram, (4) matrix diagram, (5) matrix data-analysis diagram, (6) PDPC (Process Decision Program Chart), and (7) arrow diagram.

Shewhart, Walter: person credited with the first application of statistical concepts to production and the development of control charts, when he was a statistician with Bell Laboratories in the 1920s. Shewhart authored two books that had a profound effect on Deming—*Economic Control of Quality of Manufactured Product* and *Statistical Method from the Viewpoint of Quality Control*. It was based on Shewhart's teaching that Deming developed his PDCA (Plan-Do-Check-Action) cycle.

Simulation: the technique of observing and manipulating an artificial mechanism (model) that represents a real-world process that for technical or economical reasons is not suitable or available for direct examination.

Six Sigma: statistical measure of variability of near perfection used by Motorola and other TQM companies. Permits only 3.4 deviations (errors) per million, or 99.9997 percent perfect.

Special cause: a source of variation in the process output that is unpredictable, unstable, or intermittent (also called assignable cause).

Standard deviation: a parameter describing the spread of the process output, denoted by the Greek letter sigma. The positive square root of the variance.

Statistic: any parameter that can be determined on the basis of the quantitative characteristics of a sample. There are two kinds of statistic: (1) descriptive — a computed measure of some property of a set of values, making possible a definitive statement about the meaning of the collected data — and (2) inferential — indicating the confidence that can be placed in any statement regarding its expected accuracy, the range of its applicability, and the probability of its being true. Consequently, decisions can be based on inferential statistics.

Statistics: the branch of applied mathematics that describes an analysis of empirical observations for the purpose of predicting certain events in order to make decisions in the face of uncertainty.

Statistical process control (SPC): application of statistical techniques for measuring and analyzing the variation in processes.

Statistical quality control (SQC): application of statistical techniques for measuring and improving the quality of processes. Includes diagnostic tools, SPC, sampling plans, and other statistical measures.

Statistical tools: graphic and/or numerical mathematical methods that assist in analysis of a process or population of things.

The seven most commonly used are (1) check sheets (or tally sheets), (2) cause-and-effect diagrams, (3) histograms, (4) Pareto diagrams, (5) control charts, (6) scatter diagrams, and (7) run charts.

Strategy: a broad course of action, chosen from a number of alternatives, to accomplish a stated goal.

Suppliers: individuals, teams, or organizations that provide inputs to a work group or customer. Suppliers are internal or external.

Taguchi, Genichi: noted for developing an approach to Quality Engineering that uses designed experiments to improve product and process quality. The objective is to achieve a robust design (insensitive to uncontrollable factors such as usage and environment) and to minimize variations around a target parameter. Taguchi also developed the Loss Function concept, which allows a quantitative estimate to be made of the loss due to variability. His methods are taught and used in product development throughout the world.

Ten times improvement ($10\times$ Improvement): reducing the error rate to one-tenth of its existing rate.

Timeliness: the promptness with which quality products and services are delivered, relative to the customer's requirements.

Total Quality Management (TQM): cooperative form of operating an organization in a way that relies on the talents of both labor and management to continually improve quality and productivity using teams and facts in decision making.

Variable: a data term used to identify values within some range that appear with a certain frequency or pattern.

Variance: in quality-management terminology, any nonconformance to requirements. In statistics it is the square of the standard deviation.

Resource B

Directory of TQM Centers and Organizations

Alliance of Organizational Systems Designers
1365 Westgate Center Drive, Suite L-1
Winston-Salem, North Carolina 27103-2934
919/768-7891

American Production and Inventory Control Society
500 West Annandale Road
Falls Church, Virginia 22046
203/237-8344

American Productivity and Quality Center (APQC)
123 North Post Oak Lane
Houston, Texas 77024-7797
713/681-4020
Fax: 713/681-8578

American Quality Foundation
253 W. 73rd Street
New York, New York 10023
213/724-3170

American Society for Quality Control (ASQC)
611 East Wisconsin Avenue
P.O. Box 3005
Milwaukee, Wisconsin 53201-3006
800/248-1946

American Society for Training and Development (ASTD)
1640 King Street
Alexandria, Virginia 22313-9833
703/683-8100
Fax: 703/683-8103

Arkansas Quality Management Task Force
Arkansas Industrial Development Commission
One Capitol Mall
Little Rock, Arkansas 72201
Fax: 501/682-7341

Association for Quality and Participation (AQP)
801-B West 8th Street
Cincinnati, Ohio 45203
513/381-1959
Fax: 513/381-0070

Center for Quality and Productivity
University of Maryland
College Park, Maryland 20742-7215
301/403-4535

Center for Quality and Productivity Improvement
University of Wisconsin–Madison
620 Walnut Street
Madison, Wisconsin 53705
608/263-2520

Center for Productive Use of Technology
George Mason University
Metro Campus
3401 North Fairfax, #322
Arlington, Virginia 22201
703/841-2675

Community Quality Coalition
c/o Transformation of American Industry Project
Jackson Community College
2111 Emmons Road
Jackson, Michigan 49201
517/789-1627

Defense Systems Management College
Fort Belvoir, Virginia 22060-5426
703/805-2612

Federal Quality Institute
440 G Street NW, Suite 333
P.O. Box 99
Washington, D.C. 20044-0099
202/376-3747
Fax: 202/376-3765

Georgia Productivity Center
Georgia Institute of Technology
219 O'Keefe Building
Atlanta, Georgia 30332
404/894-6101

Malcolm Baldrige National Quality Award
National Institute of Standards and Technology
A903 Administration Building
Gaithersburg, Maryland 20899
301/976-2762
Fax: 301/926-1630

Manufacturing Productivity Center
10 West 35th Street
Chicago, Illinois 60616
312/567-4800

National Center on Education and the Economy
39 State Street, Suite 500
Rochester, New York 14614
716/546-7620
Fax: 716/546-3145

Navy Personnel Research and Development Center
Quality Support Center
San Diego, California 92152-6800
619/553-7952

Pennsylvania Technical Assistance Program (PENNTAP)
Pennsylvania State University
University Park, Pennsylvania 16802
814/865-0427

Public Sector Quality Improvement Network
Michael Williamson
University of Wisconsin–Madison
97 Bascom Hall
500 Lincoln Drive
Madison, Wisconsin 53706

Quality and Productivity Management Association (QPMA)
300 Martingale Road, Suite 230
Schaumburg, Illinois 60173
708/619-2909
Fax: 708/619-3383

U.S. Army Management Engineering College
Rock Island, Illinois 61299-7040
309/782-0470

Work in America Institute
700 White Plains Road
Scarsdale, New York 10583
914/472-9600

Baldrige National Quality Award Winners

Cadillac Motor Car Division, General Motors Corporation
Jeffery Clark
2860 Clark Street
P.O. Box 297
Detroit, Michigan 48232-0297
313/556-1965

Federal Express Corporation
John West
2605 Nonconnah Boulevard
Memphis, Tennessee 38132
901/395-4567

Globe Metallurgical, Inc.
Sherry Hennessy
County Road 32
P.O. Box 157
Beverly, Ohio 45715
614/984-2361

IBM Rochester
Roy A. Bauer
Hwy. 52 North and 37th Street NW
Rochester, Minnesota 55901
507/253-9000

Marlow Industries
Joy Janco
10451 Wista Park Road
Dallas, Texas 75238
214/340-4900

Milliken & Company, Inc.
Newt Hardie
P.O. Box 1926-M-181
Spartanburg, South Carolina 29304
803/573-2092

Motorola, Inc.
Paul Noakes
1303 East Algonquin Road
Schaumberg, Illinois 60196
708/576-5000

Solectron Corporation
Ann Louise Shaeffer
2001 Fortune Drive
San Jose, California 95131
408/957-8500

Wallace Company, Inc.
P. D. Birdsong
P.O. Box 2597
Houston, Texas 77252-2597
713/675-2661

Westinghouse Electric Corporation,
Commercial Nuclear Fuel Division
Michele DeWitt
P.O. Box 0355
Pittsburgh, Pennsylvania 15230
412/374-2274

Xerox Corporation
Joe Cahalan
P.O. Box 1600
Stamford, Connecticut 06904
203/329-8700

Zytec Corporation
Doug Tersteeg
1425 East Bridge
Redwood Falls, Minnesota 56283
507/637-2966

Winners of the President's Quality and Productivity Improvement Award

1989
Naval Air Systems Command
Arlington, Virginia
703/692-3853

1990
No award

1991
Air Force Logistics Command
Wright-Patterson AFB, Ohio 45433
513/257-3316

1992
Ogden, Utah, Internal Revenue Service Center
Ogden, Utah 84400
801/625-6366

Resource C

Annotated Bibliography
of TQM Publications

The books below are just a small sample of the excellent literature being produced at an ever increasing rate by leaders, scholars, and writers in the quality movement.

Books

Backaitis, N., and Rosen, H. (eds.). *Readings on Managing Organizational Quality*. San Diego, Calif.: Navy Personnel Research and Development Center, 1990. Presents articles on new management philosophies, emphasizing the role of leadership at various levels of the organization.

Barry, T. J. *Quality Circles: Proceed with Caution*. Milwaukee, Wis.: American Society for Quality Control, 1988. Examines quality circles through twenty-eight years of management experience with IBM.

Block, P. *The Empowered Manager: Positive Political Skills at Work*. San Francisco: Jossey-Bass, 1987. Describes how to put positive political skills to work to maintain personal and organizational vitality.

Bowles, J., and Hammond, J. *Beyond Quality*. New York: Putman, 1991. A history of the quality movement in the United States, including examples from fifty American companies and offering a persuasive argument for focusing on continuous improvement and using the Baldrige Award as an assessment of progress, not an objective.

Camp, R. C. *Benchmarking: The Search for Industry Best Practices That Lead to Superior Performance.* Milwaukee, Wis.: American Society for Quality Control, 1989. Explains the benchmarking process, including how to conduct benchmark studies.

Carlzon, J. *Moments of Truth.* New York: Ballinger, 1987. Tells the story of the turnaround of Scandinavian Airlines Systems and describes how SAS empowered employees to solve customer problems — "the moments of truth."

Carnevale, A. *America and the New Economy.* Arlington, Va.: American Society for Training and Development, 1991. Describes a new economy founded on a new set of competitive standards that are transforming organizations, economic cycles, jobs, and skill requirements.

Collins, F. C., Jr. *Quality: The Ball in Your Court.* Milwaukee, Wis.: American Society for Quality Control, 1987. Examines a course of action to improve quality by reviewing experiences of dozens of foreign and domestic firms.

Crosby, P. *Quality Is Free: The Art of Making Quality Free.* Milwaukee, Wis.: American Society for Quality Control, 1979. Shows how doing things right the first time adds nothing to the cost of a product or service.

Crosby, P. *Quality Without Tears: The Art of Hassle-Free Management.* Milwaukee, Wis.: American Society for Quality Control, 1984. Covers Crosby's fourteen-step plan for fighting the secret enemies of quality, developing a quality culture, and getting all employees to commit to quality.

Crosby, P. *Let's Talk Quality: 96 Questions You Always Wanted to Ask.* Cincinnati, Ohio: Association for Quality and Participation, 1989. Looks at the major issues in quality improvement and management in a question-and-answer format, such as what quality really means, how to get it, what quality standards should be, and how to measure quality.

Davis, S. *Managing Corporate Culture.* New York: Ballinger, 1984. Describes the connection between corporate culture and strategy, the difference between dealing with "guiding beliefs" and "daily beliefs," and how the executive can go about changing the culture of an organization.

Deming, W. E. *Out of the Crisis.* Milwaukee, Wis.: American Society for Quality Control, 1986. Deming's statement of what American managers have been doing wrong and what they must do to correct the problem — features the famous fourteen points.

Dertouzos, M., Lester, R., and Solow, R. *Made in America.* Cambridge, Mass.: MIT Press, 1989. Identifies what is best and worth replicating in American and international industrial practices and sets out five national priorities for regaining the productive edge.

Desatnick, R. L. *Managing to Keep the Customer: How to Achieve and Maintain Superior Customer Service Throughout the Organization.* San Francisco: Jossey-Bass, 1987. Describes how to achieve and maintain superior customer service.

Dobyns, L., and Crawford-Mason, C. *Quality or Else: The Revolution in World Business.* Boston: Houghton Mifflin, 1991. A companion book to the IBM-funded PBS series, *Quality or Else.* Explains the ideas and innovations of the quality-management philosophy. Argues that America must start working toward a quality-based culture or take a back seat in the global economy.

Feigenbaum, A. V. *Total Quality Control.* Cincinnati, Ohio: Association for Quality and Participation, 1983. Tells how to plan a quality program and set up an appropriate organization structure to implement it.

Garvin, D. A. *Managing Quality: The Strategic and Competitive Edge.* Milwaukee, Wis.: American Society of Quality Control, 1988. Describes eight dimensions of quality: performance, features, reliability, conformance, durability, serviceability, aesthetics, and perceived quality.

Gitlow, H., and Gitlow, S. *Deming Guide to Quality and Competitive Position.* Cincinnati, Ohio: Association for Quality and Participation, 1987. A how-to guide to improving quality and productivity in any type of organization. Discusses Deming's fourteen points as well as labor's corollary eleven points that integrate management's and labor's efforts.

Gitlow, H., Gitlow, S., Oppenheim, A., and Oppenheim, R. *Tools and Methods for the Improvement of Quality.* Homewood, Ill.: Irwin, 1989. Introduces statistical tools and quality-improvement processes and ties them to the Deming management philosophy.

Grayson, C. J., and Odell, C. *American Business: A Two-Minute Warning.* New York: Free Press, 1988. Identifies ten major changes American managers must make to revive American productivity growth and bolster the quality of American products and services.

Guaspari, J. *I Know It When I See It: A Modern Fable About Quality.* New York: American Management Association, 1985. Short story intended to guide managers to a new understanding of what quality really is and how to achieve it.

Guaspari, J. *The Customer Connection: Quality for the Rest of Us.* New York: American Management Association, 1987. Explores, with humor, why quality got such a bad name in this country, why it is hard to meet quality objectives, and the customer/supplier relationship.

Harrington, H. J. *The Improvement Process: How America's Leading Companies Improve Quality.* Cincinnati, Ohio: Association for Quality and Participation, 1987. Reviews what has been done in the United States to improve quality. Also explains how to start, evaluate, and improve a quality program.

Harrington, H. J. *Business Process Improvement.* New York: McGraw-Hill, 1991. Presents what has to be done to improve business process by the principles of continuous improvement.

Hart, M. K., and Hart, R. *Quantitative Methods for Quality and Productivity Improvement.* Milwaukee, Wis.: American Society for Quality Control, 1989. Explains the need for continuous improvement, presents the statistical methods for process control, and shows limitations and alternatives.

Hradesky, J. L. *Productivity and Quality Improvement.* New York: McGraw-Hill, 1988. Describes a twelve-step productivity process for quality improvement and statistical process control.

Hunt, V. D. *Quality in America. How to Implement a Competitive Quality Program.* Homewood, Ill.: Business One Irwin, 1992. Analyzes the present state of the practice of quality in America and shows how to successfully implement a competitive quality program based on the Quality First methodology.

Imai, M. *Kaizen: The Key to Japan's Competitive Success.* New York: McGraw-Hill, 1986. Presents sixteen management practices that support *Kaizen* — the gradual, unending improvement to achieve ever higher levels of quality in an organization.

Ishikawa, K. *What Is Total Quality Control? The Japanese Way.* Cincinnati, Ohio: Association for Quality and Participation, 1985. Explains how to produce higher-quality goods at lower costs by applying quality control at every stage of market research, design, production, and sales.

Ishikawa, K. *Guide to Quality Control.* Cincinnati, Ohio: Association for Quality and Participation, 1986. Contains chapters on the basic statistical techniques used by quality circles and discusses several less familiar techniques.

Juran, J. M. *Juran on Planning for Quality.* Milwaukee, Wis.: American Society for Quality Control, 1988. Outlines Juran trilogy-quality planning, quality control, and quality improvement.

Juran, J. M. *Juran on Leadership for Quality: An Executive Handbook.* Milwaukee, Wis.: American Society for Quality Control, 1989. Provides managers with specific methods they need to successfully lead their companies on a quest for quality; discusses how to apply planning, control, and improvement to quality leadership.

Kearns, D., and Nadler, D. *Prophets in the Dark: How Xerox Reinvented Itself and Beat Back the Japanese.* New York: HarperCollins, 1992. Describes the global challenge to Xerox products and markets beginning in the 1970s, the decision to transform the corporation to a Total Quality company, and the company's success in regaining market share from Japanese competitors.

Mann, N. R. *The Keys to Excellence: The Story of the Deming Philosophy.* Los Angeles: Prestwick Books, 1987. Provides guidelines for senior executives and managers to transform their organizations to become more competitive in the global marketplace.

Messina, W. *Statistical Quality Control for Manufacturing Managers.* New York: Wiley, 1987. Provides a practical guide to tools and techniques for improving quality, increasing productivity, and enhancing the competitive position of a manufacturing line.

Mills, C. *The Quality Audit: A Management Evaluation Tool.* Milwaukee, Wis.: American Society for Quality Control, 1989. Examines the quality audit process from the viewpoints of the person requesting an audit, the organization being audited, and the auditor carrying out the audit.

Mizuno, S. *Management for Quality Improvement: The Seven New QC Tools.* Cambridge, Mass.: Productivity Press, 1988. Explains seven new quality tools that promote a higher level of quality-control activity, total coordination of the workplace, and creative planning.

Mizuno, S. *Company-Wide Total Quality Control.* Tokyo: Asian Productivity Organization, 1989. Describes essentials of a company-wide Total Quality control program, including the manager's role, functions of quality assurance, product liability, cross-functional management, and quality-control audits.

Nadler, D. A., Gerstein, M. S., Shaw, R. B., and Associates. *Organizational Architecture: Designs for Changing Organizations.* San Francisco: Jossey-Bass, 1992. Describes strategies and models for

establishing organizational strategies for continuous improvement, learning organizations, and high-performance work
systems.

Ozeki, K., and Asalea, T. *Handbook of Quality Tools: The Japanese
Approach.* Norwalk, Conn.: Productivity Press, 1990. Offers a
discussion of the management aspects of quality and reviews the
seven basic quality-control tools and five new tools.

Peterson, D., and Hillkirk, J. *In a Better Idea: Redefining the Way
Americans Work.* Boston: Houghton Mifflin, 1991. The former
CEO of Ford shows how you can revitalize a company by driving
responsibility down and tapping the creativity in all employees.

Rosander, A. C. *The Quest for Quality in Services.* Milwaukee, Wis.:
American Society for Quality Control, 1989. How to plan and
start a service quality program. Describes the work of five experts and their influence on services, plus the eight kinds of
knowledge needed for improvement of quality, and tells how to
conduct a continuous customer-opinion survey.

Scherkenbach, W. W. *The Deming Route to Quality and Productivity:
Roadmaps and Roadblocks.* Washington, D.C.: Ceepress, 1986.
Written by the man who guided Ford Motor Company's implementation of Deming's philosophy, this book is a readable account of Deming's fourteen points in action.

Senge, P. *The Fifth Discipline: The Art and Practice of the Learning
Organization.* New York: Doubleday, 1991. Discusses five key
component technologies for the excelling organization of the
future.

Scholtes, P. R., and others. *The Team Handbook.* Madison, Wis.:
Joiner and Associates, 1989. A "how-to" book with guidelines for
making project teams more effective in using data-centered
methods to improve processes.

Tichy, N. M., and Devanna, M. A. *The Transformational Leader.* New
York: Wiley, 1990. Presents an integrated set of concepts and
practical technologies for managing strategic reorientations in

products, services, markets, organization structure, and human resource systems.

U.S. General Accounting Office. *Management Practices: U.S. Companies Improve Performance Through Quality Efforts.* Gaithersburg, Md.: U.S. General Accounting Office, 1991. Reports on the impact of TQM practices on the performance of twenty U.S. companies that were among the highest-scoring applicants in 1988 and 1989 for the Malcolm Baldrige National Quality Award.

Vaill, P. B. *Managing as a Performing Art: New Ideas for a World of Chaotic Change.* San Francisco: Jossey-Bass, 1989. Presents new solutions to deal with the unprecedented challenges brought on by changes in technology, increasingly volatile markets, and intensified foreign competition.

Walton, M. *The Deming Management Method.* Cincinnati, Ohio: Association for Quality and Participation, 1986. Explains Deming's fourteen points and examines the results attained by some of America's most innovative firms.

Walton, M. *Deming Management at Work.* New York: Putnam, 1990. Offers practical applications of the Deming management method. Several successful practitioners of the method are profiled.

Wheeler, D. J., and Chambers, D. *Understanding Statistical Process Control.* Knoxville, Tenn.: SPC Press, 1986. Uses case histories and a variety of graphs to explain how SPC techniques work.

Zemke, R., and Schaaf, D. *The Service Edge: 101 Companies That Profit from Customer Care.* New York: NAL Books, 1989. Profiles 101 companies that benefit from superior service and provides analysis of successful service policies and procedures.

Magazines and Newsletters

Commitment-Plus
Pride Publications
P.O. Box 695
Arlington Heights, Illinois 60004

The Letter
American Productivity and Quality Center
123 North Post Oak Lane
Houston, Texas 77024

Quality Progress
American Society for Quality Control (ASQC)
310 West Wisconsin Avenue
Milwaukee, Wisconsin 53203

Journal of Quality Technology
American Society for Quality Control (ASQC)
310 West Wisconsin Avenue
Milwaukee, Wisconsin 53203

The Quality Review
American Society for Quality Control (ASQC)
310 West Wisconsin Avenue
Milwaukee, Wisconsin 53203

Work in America
Buraff Publications
2445 M Street NW, Suite 275
Washington, D.C. 20037

Videotapes

Customer Service, Innovation, and Productivity Through People
AMA Film/Video
9 Galen Street
Watertown, Massachusetts 02172

The Deming Library (16 tapes)
Films, Inc.
5547 Ravenswood Avenue
Chicago, Illinois 60640-1199

I Know It When I See It
American Management Association
135 West 50th Street
New York, New York 10020

Juran on Quality Improvement
Juran Institute
11 River Road
P.O. Box 811
Wilton, Connecticut 06897-0811

Mining Group Gold
CRM Films
14455 Ventura Boulevard
Encino, California 91423

National Quality Forum VI: The Human Side of Quality
American Society for Quality Control
310 West Wisconsin Avenue
Milwaukee, Wisconsin 53203

The Quality Man with Philip Crosby
The Association for Quality and Participation
801-B West 8th Street
Cincinnati, Ohio 45203-1601

Remember Me?
CRM Films
14455 Ventura Boulevard
Encino, California 91423

References

American Quality Foundation and Ernst & Young. *International Quality Study: The Definitive Study of the Best International Quality Management Practices.* Cleveland, Ohio: Ernst & Young, 1991.

Argyris, C. "The Individual and the Organization: Some Problems of Mutual Adjustment." *Administrative Science Quarterly,* 1957, 2(1), 1–24.

"Baldrige-Winner Wallace Achieves Its Impossible Dream." *Commitment-Plus,* Dec. 1991.

Barnard, C. *The Functions of the Executive.* Cambridge, Mass.: Harvard University Press, 1938.

Beckhard, R. *Organization Development: Strategies and Models.* Reading, Mass.: Addison-Wesley, 1969.

Beckhard, R., and Harris, R. *Organizational Transitions.* Reading, Mass.: Addison-Wesley, 1977.

Bennis, W. "Beyond Bureaucracy." *Trans-Action,* July–Aug. 1956, p. 31.

Bennis, W. *The Unconscious Conspiracy: Why Leaders Can't Lead.* New York: AMACOM, 1976.

Bennis, W., and Nanus, B. *Leaders.* New York: HarperCollins, 1985.

Bowles, J., and Hammond, J. *Beyond Quality.* New York: Putnam, 1991.

Bradford, D., and Cohen, A. *Managing for Excellence: The Guide to*

Developing High Performance in Contemporary Organizations. New York: Wiley, 1984.

Burns, J. M. *Leadership.* New York: HarperCollins, 1978.

Cadillac. *Information Book.* Detroit: Cadillac Motor Car Company, 1991.

California Employment Training Panel. "Malcolm Baldrige Award Goes to ETP Contractor." *ETP Newsletter*, Mar. 1992.

Camp, R. *Benchmarking.* Milwaukee, Wis.: ASQC Quality Press, 1989.

Carlzon, J. *Moments of Truth.* New York: Ballinger, 1987.

Carnevale, A. *Train America's Workforce.* Arlington, Va.: American Society for Training and Development, 1990.

Cartright, D., and Zander, A. (eds.). *Group Dynamics.* New York: HarperCollins, 1947.

Chamfort, S.R.N. *Maximes et Penses.*

Coate, L. E. "TQM at Oregon State University." *Journal for Quality and Participation*, Dec. 1990, pp. 90–101.

Collins, F. C. "The Malcolm Baldrige National Quality Award — A Dream Realized." *Quality Digest*, Apr. 1989, pp. 38–49.

Cooper, G. E. "Does the Baldrige Really Work?" *Harvard Business Review*, Jan.–Feb. 1992, pp. 138–139.

Coopers & Lybrand. *Quality in Government: A Survey of Federal Executives.* Arlington, Va.: 1989.

Cox, C. *Perseverance*, 1488.

Crosby, P. *Quality Is Free: The Art of Making Quality Certain.* New York: McGraw-Hill, 1979.

Cummings, T. G., and Huse, E. H. *Organization Development and Change.* (4th ed.) St. Paul, Minn.: West Publishing, 1989.

Cyert, R. M. "Changes Needed in America's System of Higher Education to Keep the United States Competitive." Paper presented at the 2nd Symposium on the Role of Academia in National Competitiveness and Total Quality Management, Los Angeles, July 1991.

Davis, S. *Managing Corporate Culture.* Cambridge, Mass.: Ballinger, 1984.

Delta Consulting Group. *Concepts for the Management of Organizational Change.* New York: Delta Consulting Group, 1988a.

Delta Consulting Group. *Organizational Frame Bending: Principles for Managing Reorientation.* New York: Delta Consulting Group, 1988b.

Delta Consulting Group. *"Designing High Performance Work Systems." The Emerging Architecture of Organizations: Structures and Processes for the 1990's.* New York: Delta Consulting Group, 1990.

Deming, W. E. *Out of Crisis.* Cambridge, Mass.: MIT Center for Advanced Engineering Study, 1986.

Dertouzos, M. L., Lester, R. K., and Solow, R. M. *Made in America.* Cambridge, Mass.: MIT Press, 1989.

D'Israeli, I. *Curiosities of Literature*, 1834.

Dobyns, L., and Crawford-Mason, C. *Quality or Else.* Boston: Houghton Mifflin, 1991.

Dodson, R. L. "Internal Customer Satisfaction: The Key to Total Quality Control." *American Society of Training and Development Journal*, Apr. 1991. Reprint.

Drucker, P. *People and Performance.* New York: HarperCollins, 1977.

Federal Express. *Information Book.* Memphis, Tenn.: Federal Express, 1991.

Federal Total Quality Management Handbook: How to Get Started. U.S. Office of Personnel Management, 1990.

Feigenbaum, A. V. "Total Quality Control." *Harvard Business Review*, Nov. 1956.

Finnigan, J. "Ten Questions That Make Meetings More Productive." Unpublished article, 1991.

Flanigan, J. "Excess Byproduct of Fear." *Los Angeles Times*, Feb. 1992a.

Flanigan, J. "The News About Platitudes Is That GE Puts Them to Work." *Los Angeles Times*, Mar. 1992b.

Gabor, A. *The Man Who Discovered Quality.* New York: Penguin, 1990.

Galagan, P. A. "How Wallace Changed Its Mind." *Training & Development Journal*, June 1991.

Garvin, D. "How the Baldrige Award Really Works." *Harvard Business Review*, Nov.–Dec. 1991, pp. 80–95.

Germain, J. "Customer Satisfaction." Paper presented at the

Malcolm Baldrige National Quality Award Consortium, Washington, D.C., Apr. 1989.

Gilbert, C. E. "Be Bold and Be Right: The Wallace Co., Inc., Wins 1990 Baldrige Award." *American Productivity & Quality Center*, Feb. 1991.

Ginnodo, W. "Abstract of TQM History and Principles." *Tapping the Network Journal*, Quality & Productivity Management Association, Spring/Summer 1991.

Gitlow, H., Gitlow, S., Oppenheim, A., and Oppenheim, R. *Tools and Methods for the Improvement of Quality*. Homewood, Ill.: Irwin, 1989.

Glaser, W. *The Identity Society*. New York: HarperCollins, 1972.

Goethe, J. W. In conversation with Eckerman, Jan. 31, 1830.

Grayson, C. J., and O'Dell, C. *American Business: A Two-Minute Warning*. New York: Free Press, 1988.

Grettenberger, J. Quoted in "In Perspective, 'The Best of Baldrige.'" *American Society of Training and Development Journal*, Apr. 1991.

Guaspari, J. *I Know It When I See It*. New York: AMACOM, 1985.

Harrington, H. J. *Business Process Improvement*. New York: McGraw-Hill, 1991.

Heilpern, J. "Are American Companies 'Hostile' to Quality Improvement?" *The Quality Executive*, Nov. 1989.

Heilpern, J., and Nadler, D. "Building Organizations for Continuous Improvement." In Delta Consulting Group, *The Emerging Architecture of Organizations: Structures and Processes for the 1990s*. New York: Delta Consulting Group, 1990.

Hicks, J. D. *A Short History of American Democracy*. Boston: Houghton Mifflin, 1949.

Hoffer, E. Quoted in O'Toole, J. *Vanguard Management*. New York: Doubleday, 1985, p. 54.

Horton, M. "Wallace Goes for the Baldrige." *Supply House Times*, Oct. 1990.

Houghton, J. "The Old Way of Doing Things Is Gone." *Quality Progress*, Sept. 1986.

Houghton, J. "The Chairman Doesn't Blink." *Quality Progress*, Mar. 1987.

Hunt, V. D. *Quality in America*. Homewood, Ill.: Business One, Irwin, 1992.

IBM Rochester. *The Quality Journey Continues*. Rochester, Minn.: IBM Rochester, 1991.

Japanese Union of Scientists and Engineers (JUSE). *QC Circle Koryo*. Tokyo: Japanese Union of Scientists and Engineers, 1980.

Jazinowsky, J. "Yes, America Makes Quality Products." *Industry Week*, Nov. 18, 1991, p. 35.

Joiner, B. L. "Total Quality Leadership vs. Management by Results." In N. Backaitis and H. H. Rosen (eds.), *Readings on Managing Organizational Quality*. San Diego, Calif.: Navy Personnel Research and Development Center, 1987.

Joiner, B. L. "The Statistician's Role in Quality Management." *Quality Progress*, Jan. 1988.

Juran, J. *Juran on Leadership for Quality*. New York: Free Press, 1989.

Karabatsas, N. "Absolutely, Positively Quality." *Quality Progress*, May 1990.

Katz, D., and Kahn, R. L. *The Social Psychology of Organizations*. New York: Wiley, 1966.

Kayser, T. A. "Team Goodstart." Rochester, N.Y.: Xerox Corporation, 1989.

Kayser, T. A. *Mining Group Gold*. El Segundo, Calif.: Serif, 1990.

Kearns, D. T. "A Corporate Response." *Quality Progress*, Feb. 1988.

Kearns, D. T. *Values and Direction*. Stamford, Conn.: Xerox Corporation, 1991. Brochure.

Kouzes, J. M., and Posner, B. Z. *The Leadership Challenge: How to Get Extraordinary Things Done in Organizations*. San Francisco: Jossey-Bass, 1987.

Kravetz, D. J. *The Human Resources Revolution: Implementing Progressive Management Practices for Bottom-Line Success*. San Francisco: Jossey-Bass, 1988.

Lader, J. "Getting Emotional About Quality." *Quality Review*, Summer 1988.

Lawler, E. *Managing Employee Involvement*. Center for Effective

Organizations Publication G-90(167). Los Angeles: University of Southern California, Feb. 1991.

Laza, R., and Wheaton, P. "Recognizing the Pitfalls of Total Quality Management." *Public Utilities Fortnightly*, Apr. 1990.

Leach, K. E. "The Development of the Globe Metallurgical Quality System." Unpublished case study, n.d.

Lewin, K. *Field Theory in Social Science*. New York: HarperCollins, 1951.

Likert, R. *The Human Organization*. New York: McGraw-Hill, 1967.

Livingston, J. S. "Pygmalion in Management." *Harvard Business Review*, July–Aug. 1969, pp. 81–89.

Lockheed Corporation. *Guidelines and Tools for Continuous Improvement*. Calabasas, Calif.: Lockheed Corporation, 1989.

Lombardi, V. From an interview, 1962.

Lusk, K., Schwinn, C., Schwinn, D., and Tribus, M. *Creating Community Councils: Applying Quality Management Principles in a Political Environment*. Jackson, Mich.: Community Quality Coalition, 1990.

McClelland, D. "That Urge to Achieve." *Think*, 1966, pp. 82–89.

MacFarland, M. "The Concept of Doing It Right the First Time." *Washington Technology*, Mar. 22–Apr. 4, 1990.

McGregor, D. *The Human Side of Enterprise*. New York: McGraw-Hill, 1960.

Machiavelli, N. *Discourse*.

McLagan, P. Quoted in "New or Improved? Total Quality Demands Both." *Total Quality Newsletter*, Feb. 1992.

McLaughlin, T. A. "Six Keys to Quality." *Quality Progress*, Nov. 1985.

Mann, R. W. *Recognition and Reward*. Rochester, N.Y.: Xerox Corporation, 1985.

Maslow, A. "A Theory of Human Motivation." *Psychological Review*, 1943, *50*, 370–396.

Milakovich, M. E. "Total Quality Management in the Public Sector." *National Productivity Review*, Spring 1991.

Milewski, H. Quoted in "The Concept of Doing It Right the First Time." *Washington Technology*, Apr. 1990.

Milliken & Company. *Information Book*. 1990.

Monroe, M. *City of Madison Quality and Productivity Improvement Program.*

Motorola, Inc. *Quality Information Booklet.* Schaumberg, Ill.: Motorola, Inc., 1989.

Murphy, E. *2715 One-Line Quotations.* New York: Crown, 1981.

Nadler, D. "Going for the Gold." *The Quality Review,* Summer 1988.

Nadler, D. Interview in *New York Times,* Jan. 1992.

Nadler, D., and Tushman, M. "A Congruence Model for Diagnosing Organizational Behavior." In D. Kalb, I. Rubin, and J. McIntyre, *Organizational Psychology: A Book of Readings.* (3rd ed.) Englewood Cliffs, N.J.: Prentice-Hall, 1979.

Naisbitt, J., and Aburdene, P. *Re-inventing the Corporation.* New York: Warner, 1985.

Naval, M. "Total Quality Management in the Health Care Industry." Paper prepared for the Office of Management and Budget, 1989.

Norling, J. E. "Information and Analysis." Paper presented at the Malcolm Baldrige National Quality Award Consortium, Washington, D.C., Apr. 1989.

O'Toole, J. *Vanguard Management.* New York: Doubleday, 1985.

Peters, T., and Waterman, R. *In Search of Excellence.* New York: HarperCollins, 1982.

Peterson, D., and Hillkirk, J. *A Better Idea: Redefining the Way Americans Work.* Boston: Houghton Mifflin, 1991.

Pope, A. *An Essay on Man, Epistle II, Line 303.*

Radin, B., and Coffee, J. "A Critique of TQM: Why It May Not Work in Practice." *Public Administration Quarterly,* forthcoming.

Rawson, H., and Miner, M. *The New International Dictionary of Quotations.* New York: Signet, 1986.

Reich, R. Presentation to the 45th National Conference of the American Society for Training and Development, Boston, 1989.

Robinson, J., and others. "An Open Letter: TQM on the Campus." *Harvard Business Review,* Nov.–Dec. 1991, pp. 94–95.

Roethlisberger, F. J. *Management and Morale*. Cambridge, Mass.: Harvard University Press, 1941.

Rummler, G., and Brache, A. *Improving Performance: How to Manage the White Space on the Organization Chart*. San Francisco: Jossey-Bass, 1990.

Ruskin, J. *Seven Lamps of Architecture*.

Schein, E. H. *Organizational Culture and Leadership: A Dynamic View*. San Francisco: Jossey-Bass, 1985.

Schmidt, W. H., and Posner, B. Z. "The Values of American Managers Then and Now." *Management Review*, Feb. 1992, pp. 37–40.

Scholtes, P. R. *An Elaboration on Deming's Teaching on Performance Appraisals*. Madison, Wis.: Joiner Associates, 1987.

Scholtes, P. R. *The Team Handbook*. Madison, Wis.: Joiner Associates Inc., 1988.

Senge, P. *The Fifth Discipline: The Art and Practice of the Learning Organization*. New York: Doubleday, 1991.

Sensenbrenner, J. "Quality Comes to City Hall." *Harvard Business Review*, Mar.–Apr. 1991, pp. 4–10.

Smith, W. "The Motorola Story." Unpublished case study, 1989.

"A Soft New Edge for Neutron Jack." *New York Times*, Mar. 4, 1992.

Stodgill, R. M. *Handbook of Leadership*. New York: Free Press, 1974.

Sweetland, P. "Implementing Total Quality Practices in the Federal Government." Paper presented at the 5th Annual Quality Conference of the American Society of Quality Control, Cape Canaveral, Fla., Mar. 1991.

Taguchi, G., and Clausing, D. "Robust Quality." *Harvard Business Review*, Jan.–Feb. 1990.

Tannenbaum, R., and Schmidt, W. H. "How to Choose a Leadership Pattern." *Harvard Business Review*, May–June 1973, pp. 162–172.

Taylor, F. W. *The Principles of Scientific Management*. New York: HarperCollins, 1911.

Toffler, A. *Powershift*. New York: Bantam, 1990.

Topfer, M. "Strategic Quality Planning." Paper presented at the Malcolm Baldrige National Quality Award Consortium, Washington, D.C., Apr. 1989.

Tragash, H. *Total Quality Control, 1989 Status in Japan.* Xerox Corporation benchmarking report, Feb. 1989.

Tribus, M. "TQM at the Grassroots." Paper presented at the Ohlone College Business Roundtable Quality Conference, May 1991.

Tzu, S. *The Art of War,* (S. B. Griffin, trans.). New York: Oxford University Press, 1963.

"U.S. Competitiveness Stages a Comeback." *Los Angeles Times,* May 1991.

U.S. Department of Commerce. *Malcolm Baldrige National Quality Award, 1992 Award Criteria,* 1991.

U.S. Department of Defense. *Total Quality Management Master Plan,* Aug. 1988.

U.S. Department of Defense. *Total Quality Management Guide.* DOD 5000.51G, Aug. 1, 1989.

U.S. Department of Defense. *Key Features of the DoD Implementation.* Feb. 15, 1990.

U.S. General Accounting Office. *Management Practices: U.S. Companies Improve Performance Through Quality Efforts.* May 1991.

U.S. Naval Hospital, TQM/TQL Briefing Presentation. San Diego, Calif., Feb. 1991.

Vaill, P. *Managing as a Performing Art: New Ideas in a World of Chaotic Change.* San Francisco: Jossey-Bass, 1989.

Wallace Company. *Information Book.* Houston, Tex.: Wallace Company, 1991.

Walton, M. *The Deming Management Method.* New York: Perigree, 1986.

Walton, M. *Deming Management at Work.* New York: Perigree, 1990.

Westinghouse Corporation. *CNFD 1989 Quality Plan: Continuing the Commitment.* 1989a. Brochure.

Westinghouse Corporation. "Performance Leadership Through Total Quality: A Case Study in Quality Improvement." Unpublished case study, 1989b.

Wiggenhorn, A. W. "Human Resource Utilization." Paper presented at the Malcolm Baldrige National Quality Award Consortium, Washington, D.C., Apr. 1989.

The Winds of Change. Animated film produced by Barr Films, Irwindale, Calif.: 1991.

"Xerox Breaks into the Japanese Market." *Los Angeles Times*, Feb. 1992.

Xerox Corporation. "New Year's Resolution for Xerox Managers: We Will Communicate." *Agenda: A Journal for Xerox Managers.* Stamford, Conn.: Xerox Corporate Communications, Feb. 1982.

Xerox Corporation. *Leadership Through Quality—A Total Quality Process for Xerox.* Leesburg, Va.: Xerox Corporation, 1983.

Xerox Corporation. *Information Book,* 1990a.

Xerox Corporation. *Leadership Through Quality.* Stamford, Conn.: Xerox Corporation, 1990b. Brochure describing history of Xerox's Total Quality effort and pursuit of National Quality Award.

Xerox Corporation. *Today in Xerox: Total Quality Management University Challenge Announces Universities Selected to Participate in Program,* Xerox Public Relations press release. Jan. 22, 1992.

Zytec Corporation. *Zytec Application Summary.* Zytec Corporation, 1991.

Index

401